THIRD EDITION
POLICING
URBAN AMERICA

THIRD EDITION
POLICING
URBAN AMERICA

Geoffrey P. Alpert
University of South Carolina

Roger G. Dunham
University of Miami

WAVELAND
PRESS, INC.
Prospect Heights, Illinois

For information about this book, write or call:
Waveland Press, Inc.
P.O. Box 400
Prospect Heights, Illinois 60070
847/634-0081

Credits

Introduction–Laurie Prossnitz; Chapter 2–NMFPT/Science & Society Picture Library; Chapters 3, 5, 8, & 9–courtesy City of Des Plaines, Illinois, Police Department; Chapters 4, 7, & 11– courtesy Lincolnshire, Illinois, Police Department; Chapter 6–AP/Wide World photo by Reed Saxon; Chapter 10–*Tribune* photo by Michael Fryer.

CONTENTS

Preface   ix
Acknowledgements   xi
Chief Dale Bowlin   xiii

Introduction: Police, Policing, and the Community   1

Chief's Corner: Introduction   6
References   8

Chapter

1   Police in the American System of Criminal Justice   9

Police and the Law   11
Police and the Courts   13
Chief's Corner: Police and the Courts   14
Reference   17

Chapter

2   History of the Police   19

British Heritage   21
Experience in Early America   25
Police Work and Communication   29
Police Reform and Professionalism   32
Emerging Issues   34
The Issues Mature into Crises   35
The Research Era   35
The History of the Future   37
References   37

Chapter
3   Police Recruitment, Selection, and Training   39

Qualifications for Police Officers   41
Chief's Corner: Recruitment and Selection   43
Recruiting Police Officers   44
The Selection Process   51
Police Training   57
Chief's Corner: Training   59
Summary   70
References   71
Cases   73

Chapter
4   Police Organization and Administration   75

Police Bureaucracy   77
Police Operations: The Nuts and Bolts of Policing   81
Police Organization   86
Police Bureaucracy in Action   93
Organizational Change   98
Summary   101
References   102
Case   102

Chapter
5   Police Socialization and Police Subculture   103

Socialization and Professionalization   104
Chief's Corner: Police Socialization   106
Subculture   107
Professionalization   113
Unionization of the Police   115
Orientation Toward Action   117
Summary   119
References   120

Chapter
6   Police Deviance: Corruption and Control   123

The Opportunity Structure for Police Deviance   125
Socialization and Peer Group Support for Rule Violations   128

Defining Police Deviance and Corruption   129
Type I: Rotten Apples and Rotten Pockets   131
Type II: Pervasive Unorganized Corruption   132
Type III: Pervasive Organized Corruption   132
Another Typology of Police Corruption   133
Review of Police Deviance and Corruption   136
Chief's Corner: Police Corruption 137
Controlling Police Deviance and Corruption   138
Summary   144
References   145

Chapter
7   **Styles of Policing   149**

Institutional Behavior   150
Individual Styles   152
Chief's Corner: Police Styles and the Community   155
Beyond Typologies   156
Sources of Variation   156
Discretion   164
Police Patrol   165
Evaluating Police Services: A Consumer's Perspective   170
Community-Based Policing   174
Summary   180
References   181
Cases   185

Chapter
8   **Hazards of Police Work   187**

Personal Assault   189
Chief's Corner: Hazards of Police Work   192
Occupational Stress on Police Officers   194
Vulnerability to Stress   196
Family Life and Divorce   198
Consequences of Stress   200
Chief's Corner: Recognizing and Combating Stress   205
Solutions and Programs   207
Summary   209
References   209

Chapter
9   Critical Issues in Policing   213

Minority Hiring and Promoting   215
Women in Police Work   217
The Use of Force   220
Chief's Corner: Police Brutality   221
Chief's Corner: Do We Expect the Impossible?   231
Police Pursuits   233
Lawsuits Against the Police   241
Police and the Community   245
Summary   254
References   254
Cases   258

Chapter
10   The Future of Policing   259

Standardization of Police   261
Social Influences   263
What to Expect   264
Chief's Corner: The Future of Law Enforcement   265
Summary   268
References   269

Chapter
11   Careers in Law Enforcement   271

Trends in Law Enforcement Careers   273
Chief's Corner: Civilianization   274
Selection Criteria   275
Important Concerns in Choosing a Career in Police Work   277
Types of Law Enforcement Careers   279
Employment Outlook   284
Summary   285
References   286

Index   289

PREFACE

The first two editions of *Policing Urban America* were based upon *The Miami Study*, an empirical examination of neighborhood differences in attitudes toward the police and policing practices. Our initial interest in conducting *The Miami Study* was to produce empirical research with general policy implications for community-based policing strategies. Although we discuss some of the policy implications of our findings in the research monograph, we wanted an outlet for discussing more completely the ramifications of these ideas for the various aspects of policing. The purpose of the third edition of *Policing Urban America* is to integrate the policy implications of empirical research into a comprehensive discussion of policing. This comprehensive review and discussion of topics and issues concerning policing in urban America is tied together by the common thread of community-oriented policing. This expanded edition incorporates more topics than the first two editions and integrates the findings from current research.

The beginning chapters provide a background and history of policing and underscore the presence of the community-based philosophy during the early years of urban policing. The chapters discussing the foundation of police organization, administration and socialization highlight this philosophy and are compared with other perspectives that have a different emphasis. In the chapters examining some of the critical issues of urban policing today, such as solving crimes, managing resources and supervising officers, we suggest a return to community-based principles as a method to improve the effectiveness and efficiency of law enforcement efforts. We also acknowledge the potential problems a career in law enforcement can create for an individual.

This book is our statement of policing in America. We have balanced our academic knowledge with our practical views of policing. To ensure a balance between academic and practical experience we have included "The Chief's Corner": the personal comments of a nationally respected police chief on various issues discussed in the book. This combination of academic knowledge and practical experience provides a useful guide for students, criminal justice professionals, and anyone else interested in American police and policing.

ACKNOWLEDGEMENTS

All researchers and authors rely upon the training they receive as students and as young workers gaining experience, as well as the support they receive from colleagues and family members during the research and writing of a project. We owe our debts of thanks to many people, including mentors, colleagues and family members. James F. Short, Jr. taught both of us to think and become sociologists. As a mentor to the senior author, Jim has been a friend, collaborator and counselor. His assistance is always appreciated, and his friendship is valued. The senior author owes a great debt to Deputy Director G.T. Arnold of the Metro-Dade Police Department (Miami, Florida) and Chief, Darrel J. Stephens of the St. Petersburg (Florida) Police Department. The second author is indebted to Armand Mauss for his early sociological training and especially for his patience and struggles in the development of a writer in his own image.

Both authors wish to thank former students for their comments made on earlier drafts of this book. Our families, including our wives, Vicki Dunham and Margaret Alpert, our collective ten children and three dogs were all supportive and understanding when they suffered our long hours and short tempers while we were researching and writing this edition. Our wives, children and animals all became closer friends, a wonderful consequence of long hours and hard labor.

A special feature of this book is the Chief's Corner. We have included comments in many of our chapters from Dale Bowlin, Chief, Metro-Dade (Florida) Police Department. Chief Bowlin's comments illustrate both real-life experiences from the streets and the considerations of policymakers. This added perspective will provide the readers with a balanced view of police and policing.

CHIEF DALE BOWLIN
BIOGRAPHICAL SKETCH

Dale Bowlin was born into a working-class family in Charleston, South Carolina in 1938. The Bowlins moved to Miami, Florida, in 1943, and Dale graduated from Miami Jackson High School in 1956. Dale became interested in police work during high school and went through the police academy training after serving in the military. He became a member of the Dade County Sheriff's Department (Metro-Dade Police Department) in September, 1961. Since that time, Dale has worked his way through the ranks. He has earned a bachelor of science degree and has almost completed his master's degree.

From 1961 through 1965, Dale was a police officer and a detective. His assignments included uniform patrol, motorcycle patrol and criminal investigations. Additionally, he served as a Miami vice investigator—twenty years before *Miami Vice* became popular. In 1965, Dale was promoted.

During his six years as a sergeant, he was assigned supervisory positions in uniform patrol, selective traffic enforcement and the traffic homicide unit. In 1971, he was promoted to lieutenant.

Lieutenant Bowlin served as a platoon commander and Commander of District Detective Operations, Investigation, and Special Enforcement Section. During his tenure as lieutenant, Dale started college and graduated summa cum laude from Nova University in 1979 with a degree in criminal justice. In 1978, he was promoted to captain. As a captain, Bowlin served as Commander of the Homicide Section and supervised the detectives. Captain Bowlin was responsible for all death investigations in Dade County. In addition, he served as Commander of the Operations and Inspections Bureau to insure compliance with departmental policies, regulations, and procedures.

In 1979, Bowlin was promoted to District Commander and was responsible for the management of 1560 employees, including the uniform patrol and detective operations in Central District, a low socioeconomic, high crime area.

In 1980, after the Liberty City riots, Bowlin was promoted to Chief of the Police Division. This executive-level position gave him direct charge of six police districts, as well as other administrative duties. Chief Bowlin returned to school in 1982 and worked toward his master's degree in Management Science at St. Thomas University. After three years as Chief of the Police Division, he was transferred to Chief-Court Services Division and Chief-Special Services Division (Chief of Detectives). In his duties as a chief, Dale was the top administrative officer responsible for uniformed patrol, all court-related activities, and all criminal investigations.

In December, 1986, Dale was promoted to Assistant Director, Metro-Dade Police Department. In this new position, Chief Bowlin is responsible for all facets of the Metro-Dade Police Department.

Chief Bowlin's accomplishments as a police officer are only outlined above, but they are well known to those who have promoted him to the top and to those who have worked under his administration. In addition, he has become known nationally for his work on the measurement of police officer performance (see Alpert and Dunham, 1986; Landy, 1977), his handling of civil disorders and training for civil disturbances (see United States Commission on Civil Rights, 1982).

Chief Bowlin was instrumental in the revision of the ways in which an officer's performance was evaluated. He recognized the problems of empirical measures, as well as the problems created by simple subjective measures of performance. In addition, when Chief Bowlin was in charge of the area in which the 1980 race riot occurred, he kept his officers aware of their primary goal: to protect lives.

Chief Bowlin was responsible for coordinating the efforts of the police and the National Guard during the riot. He recognized that the police officer would have to go back into the area after the riot, while the National Guardsman would not. When asked about the problems he faced coordinating the law enforcement efforts, he said, "The National Guard even talks a different language than we do. . . . They are combat-trained, and they talk in terms of 'the enemy' and in terms of 'missions.' We are trained to look after the rights of citizens of the United States. Right now, they may be in a riotous condition, but they are still citizens" (quoted in Porter and Dunn, 1980:100). This philosophy, and his ability to enforce it, has earned him respect and admiration within the law enforcement community and from the public.

Chief Bowlin's experience and expertise make him an excellent choice as a commentator on our ideas and observations. His image as a motorcycle cop and his civil-rights activism as a police chief make him a tough critic. His ideas may disagree with our observations and conclusions, but we are pleased to see how often we agree. Regardless, he offers us his insights as an experienced police officer and police administrator in "The Chief's Corner."

INTRODUCTION
POLICE, POLICING, AND THE COMMUNITY

The police are a familiar sight in American society. We see them patrolling the streets in marked and unmarked cars, directing traffic, and serving the public in many different ways. We know that a police officer will respond to an emergency call, and we know that one may appear out of nowhere when we are speeding or rolling through a stop sign.

Our image of the police has been created, in part, by the entertainment and news media. Classic novels such as *The Blue Knight* and *The New Centurians*, both authored by Joseph Wambaugh, provide accounts of the working environments of the police and also give us a glimpse into the private world of police officers. The electronic media has filled the screen with cop shows ranging from *Starsky and Hutch* to *Miami Vice*. Recently, *NYPD Blue*, *Homicide* and *Law and Order* have all tried to provide a little bit of everything. There have been movies, such as *Serpico*, that portray some aspects of police and police work accurately, and there have been some less realistic, but more entertaining, movies such as *Police Academy*. Movies that place the good against the forces of evil have illustrated that police need assistance from the public in order to perform their law enforcement function. Even classic tales such as *Batman* and fads such as the Teenage Mutant Ninja Turtles provide that very important message.

The news industry has also influenced our image of the police by providing a significant amount of expensive coverage of police-related issues. Local and national news programs give viewers a snapshot of high-profile police issues at home and around the country. Newspapers also devote a great deal of space to interesting stories about law enforcement. In fact, there have been scholarly reports written about the effect on viewers of both media coverage of the police and the entertainment industry's proliferation of police stories.

The image created by the media may not mirror what it is really like to be a police officer, or what policing truly entails. Unfortunately, the media's image of police and policing is difficult to erase. It is also often incomplete and misleading. Think about your own experience with the police. In most cases, this will be limited to a few contacts for motor vehicle violations. Perhaps some of us have been victimized and have reported these crimes to the police. While we were not pleased to be given a ticket or to have our belongings stolen, we cooperated with the police and watched the officer go about filling out forms and completing the paperwork. It is truly amazing that few television or movie cops have ever had to fill out the forms real officers must complete. Now, what sponsor would pay the money necessary to have these actors portray the work of real police officers, and who would watch such a show?

Our image of the police and our attitudes about them are often based upon these incomplete media portrayals. These portrayals rarely show the reality of the police experience, and it is rare that we witness it firsthand. How many of us have seen an officer dealing with the tragedy of a drowning or shooting victim, or carrying a dead body and placing it in a coroner's sack? We more often see the seemingly macho police officer taking control of a situation without fear or concern. We seldom witness the "average" police officer frightened that a simple domestic confrontation might turn into a violent situation, sickened by a crime scene, or suffering the trauma of having shot someone or having been shot.

It is inappropriate to base our views of police and police work on inaccurate or incomplete information. Our personal experiences are limited, and the images presented by the media are created to sell, not to inform. The purpose of this book is to bridge the gap between the fiction and the fact of police and policing. We will start with the history of police and end with policing in the late 1990s. Our journey is an interesting circle with one constant—the community.

Before we start, we need a clearer picture of the police officer and what he or she does. The only fair portrait includes a multi-trait and multi-purpose description.

To the young child, "officer friendly" is someone from whom to seek assistance. To the middle-class white citizen, the "police officer" gives out traffic tickets or patrols the neighborhood and keeps an eye on the house during vacations. To the drunk, the "cop" is the one who says "move on." To the injured, "the officer" provides needed assistance. To the kid high on crack, "the pig" is the one to look out for and avoid. To the young black in the ghetto, "the Man" is the enemy. To the middle-aged, middle-class black, "they" are too often not available when needed.

Although illustrative, the above statements by no means include all perceptions held by the public or all duties that police officers perform. Duties for the police may depend upon a large number of influences. Throughout this book, we will describe and analyze these factors in the light of how the police function. We will emphasize that there are only limited ways to describe police work in generic terms. Our aim is to study the frameworks in which the police function and to furnish information on how to understand and to improve police and policing.

Local police agencies are diverse in area and population served. Approximately one-half of all police officers work in departments that serve population centers of 100,000 or more. However, almost 90 percent of the police departments in this country serve population areas of less than 25,000 persons. There are more than 3,000 sheriffs' departments usually organized at the county level that provide services to the unincorporated areas and assist small departments. Further, 49 states (all except Hawaii) have state police agencies whose responsibilities vary from traffic enforcement on the highways to broad crime-fighting duties. There also exist special purpose agencies such as transit and university police. In addition, there are approximately 40,000 federal law enforcement officers.

Before we turn to the role of police and the beginnings of policing in America, it is important to remember that there are many techniques of social control, ranging from informal agreements to physically coercive threats and punishments. Our society has become increasingly dependent upon police and the legal system, not only to control deviant behavior but also to provide needed services to members of the community. We have gone from a society where decisions were made at the community level to one where the government has taken over many of these decisions about social control. Perhaps the single most powerful function of the police is the discretional use of coercive force.

The media events of the decade include the videotaped beating of Rodney King by members of the Los Angeles Police Department (LAPD) on March 3, 1991, the 1995 trial of O.J. Simpson, and the tragedy of the bombing in Oklahoma City. It is crystal clear that King was brutally beaten, kicked and shot with a Taser gun by at least three officers while more than twenty others watched. The Los Angeles Police Department prides itself on having some of the best training in the country; there is no doubt that these officers were aware of the wrongfulness of their actions (or inactions) but intentionally chose to beat Mr. King.

The stress created by a suspect fighting an officer or resisting arrest is immense, and a police pursuit causes enormous stress. As a fellow LAPD officer wrote in *Newsweek*, "Any officer pursuing King that night would have felt: How dare this person put innocent lives in jeopardy? What is he going to try when I catch him? When King's pursuers finally caught him, the adrenaline rush must have fueled the extremes of terror and anger. Police officers are human; those officers lost control and the beating resembled a feeding frenzy" (March 25, 1991:34).

After being acquitted of assault charges brought by the state, four officers were indicted by the federal government on civil rights violations charges. Two of the officers were found guilty and sentenced to thirty months in federal prison. In addition, the civil suit that followed cost the insurance company and taxpayers an amount that includes two commas!

This type of incident has occurred in other jurisdictions in previous years. In 1980 Arthur McDuffie, a black insurance salesman, was involved in a high-speed chase and was beaten to death by police officers in Miami. After a cover-up and acquittal of the officers by an all-white jury, the city of Miami experienced one of the worst riots in history (Porter and Dunn, 1984). Since that time, significant changes in police training have occurred in the region. The improvements in the Metro-Dade Police Department, whose officers were involved in the beating death in 1980, can be attributed to strong administrative leadership. Although the killing of Arthur McDuffie and subsequent riots made national news and invoked hearings by the United States Commission on Civil Rights, reform and improvement of the police did not reach beyond southeastern Florida.

The King incident also included a chase and a beating, but the incident was captured on video and played on television for all to see. This one "lucky" difference has turned an incident which might have been downplayed or regionalized into a catalyst for change. The United States Department of Justice and Congress have once again called for numerous studies and investigations. It is unfortunate that the remedies and recommendations made in the 1970s and 1980s have not been followed (see United States Commission on Civil Rights, 1982). Perhaps the violent reality captured on the videotape and witnessed by so many citizens will provide the necessary impetus to incorporate known, workable policies in all jurisdictions. It may be that we have gone too far and need to return to the days when we sought advice and consent from the citizens at the community level, especially when it comes to the role of police in American society.

The media coverage of the O.J. Simpson case included every aspect of law, crime, and criminal justice. The electronic media had a stable of legal experts commenting on every aspect of the trial. The media attention was so intense that even the divorce proceedings of Marcia Clark, the lead prosecutor, became part of the story. In fact, when she changed her hair style, outside experts were called in to comment on the effect this would have on the jury! This coverage put many aspects of police work under a microscope and revealed them publicly for citizens to evaluate. The amount and intensity of the coverage even surpassed that of the trial of William Kennedy Smith, when Roy Black, live on television, expertly weaved a web of innocence around Mr. Smith.

The terrorist bombing of the Alfred P. Murrah Federal Building in Oklahoma City on April 19, 1995, also elicited strong emotional public reaction exacerbated by media coverage. The investigative tactics, strategies and procedures of the FBI and other law enforcement agencies were put under the media microscope during the investigation of alleged terrorists and their families. The immediate and enhanced influence of the media on police work creates another layer of accountability to the public, and one consequence of this oversight should be more complete and careful law enforcement work.

Having sketched a picture of today's world for the police officer, and its interpretive lens provided by media coverage, we begin our journey by looking at the role of police in the American system of criminal justice. Chapter 1 will integrate the work of police into the larger system of justice. Chapter 2 includes a descriptive analysis of the history and roots of police and policing. Here we will examine the beginnings of community influence on the initial enforcers of law. The recruitment, selection and training of the police officer is the subject of chapter 3 and the administration and organization of police will be examined in chapter 4. Chapter 5 will focus upon the socialization process that affects police officers and the police subcultures that emerge. Chapter 6 will concentrate on police deviance and the internal and external controls on the police, including civilian review mechanisms. The different functions and styles of policing will be examined in chapter 7. Here we will compare and contrast the social work and crime fighting approaches to police work. Chapter 8 will highlight the hazards of police work and related stress, a topic that affects law enforcement and the community at all levels. Chapter 9 will examine the critical issues in police and appropriate community involvement. Chapter 10 will look at the future of the police. The final chapter will present the opportunities for law enforcement students and how they can fit into police work in the 1990s and beyond.

Chief Bowlin's first contribution to the book outlines an experienced police officer and administrator's view of police work: its past, present, and future.

CHIEF'S CORNER
CHIEF DALE BOWLIN
Introduction

I grew up in Miami in the 1950s and was from a working-class family. Miami was a rather small Southern city policed primarily by wiry, leather-tough men who all seemed to have strong roots in the South and especially Georgia. My perception of the police was that they were capable of being brutally tough if necessary, yet in many ways kind and understanding of the nuances it took to enforce the law in an area whose philosophy was strongly connected to the deep South. There appeared to be a bond of mutual respect between the police and the citizens, which was probably a result of policing that was carried out in a much more personal manner than it is today. Police officers who had the choice would often avoid taking someone to jail when they could simply transport him to his home if proper assurances were given that appropriate corrective action would be taken by the parents or other family members. It was this type of understanding, the mutual respect between police and the public, that attracted me to law enforcement. I felt that law enforcement offered me the best chance of making a real contribution with my life's work.

Since becoming a police officer in 1961, I have seen this invisible bond between police and the community greatly erode. Of all the complaints I have heard over the years about the police, there seems to be a consistent theme. It is not that the officer was necessarily discourteous but, rather, failed to be courteous. In other words, officers talk in legalistic terms that the layman many times does not understand; they seem anxious and concerned with the amount of time being spent with the citizen; and finally, they fail to show any personal interest in the citizen's problem. It's almost like a doctor with no bedside manner. He or she may be good, but only fills half of the patient's need for both understanding and treatment.

This condition has not grown out of the police being forced into automobiles to carry out their duties, even though this was a contributing factor. This move took the officer from the sidewalk to the street and, in many cases, behind a closed window. In my opinion, it is a result of conditions brought about by several situations, including judicial decisions, which often specify procedural guidelines that the police must follow or have their efforts negated. As a result, police officers have been forced to talk and act in a legalistic manner rather than in the personal, one-on-one style that most citizens desire. Second, many administrators have come to treat law enforcement as a business with such bottom-line factors as response time, handling time, clearance rate, numbers of arrests, etc. It is these bottom-line factors by which the administrators often evaluate the performance of their organization and personnel. The use of such factors, when applied without equal attention to the humanistic concerns, causes a breach of good will between the organization and the members of the community it strives to serve and protect.

On the one hand, we have a police officer driven by the administration which has a concern for bottom-line factors and reflects this concern in his or her performance appraisal. On the other hand, the officer is driven by members of the community who want to be treated in a more personal and understanding manner. While this is frustrating for the community members, it is even more frustrating for most police officers who joined the force to establish a level of mutual respect and good relations with the people they serve.

In the future, the most successful police departments will be those that learn how to provide a personal style of policing which at the same time conforms to the legal restrictions placed on it by the Courts. Meanwhile, the image of the police will continue to be shaped by the entertainment industry and news media which find it much more lucrative to portray the police as crime fighters continually involved in some violent confrontation with an ever-present criminal element.

References

Alpert, Geoffrey P. and Roger Dunham. 1986. "Community Policing." *Journal of Police Science and Administration* 14:212–222.

Kappeler, Victor, R. Sluder, and G. Alpert. 1994. *Forces of Deviance*. Prospect Heights, IL: Waveland Press.

Landy, Frank. 1977. *Performance Appraisal in Police Departments*. Washington, DC: Police Foundation.

Porter, Bruce and Marvin Dunn. 1984. *The Miami Riot of 1980*. Lexington, MA: Lexington Books.

United States Commission on Civil Rights. 1982. *Confronting Racial Isolation in Miami*. Washington, DC: United States Government Printing Office.

Chapter One

POLICE IN THE AMERICAN SYSTEM OF CRIMINAL JUSTICE

Police operate within a system of government. Municipal agencies are headed by chiefs, who are appointed by city managers or mayors, and in most situations, the chief serves at the pleasure of the politicians or the professional municipal manager (who in turn serves at the pleasure of the politicians). State and federal police agencies have directors who are appointed by the politicians as well. County sheriffs are usually elected officials (constitutional officers) and serve the public which elects them. All of these agencies are charged with various responsibilities, including law enforcement and public safety. Almost by default, they are also responsible for order maintenance which includes a variety of services to the public, often designated as either *policing* or *law enforcement* functions.

There is a great deal of confusion regarding the difference between policing and law enforcement. These terms are often used interchangeably, which adds to the confusion. In the common usage, a police officer is a law enforcement officer, but a law enforcement officer is not always a police officer. The important distinction is that many law enforcement officers are not involved in traditional police work, such as patrolling, traffic enforcement, service calls, etc. For example, a private security guard or store detective may spend considerable time trying to detect crimes, but he or she is not a police officer. In the same light, a detective for a police department or an agent of one of many state or federal law enforcement agencies may have police power and authority but does not participate in traditional police work.

Law enforcement, whether practiced by a specialist sitting in front of a computer terminal, a detective investigating a serious crime scene, or by the general practitioner cruising in a car or walking a beat, has an important role to play in American society. It is difficult to separate police work from that of law enforcement, as they overlap in many situations, but it is the work of the local, uniformed officer that represents the major portion of police work and, consequently, the major emphasis of this book.

Police agencies and departments come in all sizes and descriptions. The federal government supports more than fifty law enforcement agencies, including the Federal Bureau of Investigation (FBI), Drug Enforcement Agency (DEA), United States Marshal's Service, United States Secret Service, Bureau of Alcohol, Tobacco, and Firearms (ATF), and the United States Customs Service, among others. There are approximately 40,000 federal personnel who perform law enforcement duties for these agencies. While it may be necessary to refer to the work of these and other agencies, we will focus our attention on the local police in urban America.

There are more than 900,000 sworn police officers and civilians in state and local police agencies. These range from New York, with approximately 30,000 sworn officers and a budget of more than one billion dollars, to numerous rural areas that employ only one officer (who may work part-time). It is interesting to note that more than 90,000 officers and civilians work in the ten largest departments, but there are more than 10,000 police departments with ten or fewer employees. American police officers work for a large number of departments, but these are mostly small departments with approximately five sworn officers. The one binding force that directs all police officers, regardless of department size, is the law.

POLICE AND THE LAW

The police are the gatekeepers of the American system of criminal justice. They are usually the first to make contact with accused offenders and are in a position to make some very important decisions about what will happen to these individuals. Perhaps the most frequent decision that a police officer makes is whether or not to arrest or seize the person and to initiate an alleged offender's journey through the maze of American criminal justice. This is a decision that deprives a citizen of his or her basic freedom.

Our system of criminal justice operates under the laws of our country and of the various states and municipalities. Before we can understand what it is the police enforce and how they are allowed to enforce it, we must understand the laws, both *substantive* and *procedural*. Our system of criminal law includes a body of rules and regulations which has been identified as necessary by the legislative branch of government to control behavior. These substantive and procedural laws may differ slightly among jurisdictions because they are the products of a political process. Substantive criminal law defines what a person may or may not do. Examples include murder, robbery, theft and hundreds of other actions or inactions. The most serious offenses are called *felonies*, which may be punishable by more than a year in prison, while the less serious offenses are called *misdemeanors*, which are punishable by a year or less in jail.

Procedural law defines how the substantive laws are enforced and administered. They, along with agency policies, rules and procedures, apply to the government officials who operate the criminal justice enterprise against crime and criminals. These include, but are not limited to, police, prosecutors, judges and probation officers. Procedural rights pertaining to unlawful arrest, unreasonable searches and seizures, double jeopardy, and the right to a fair and speedy trial by an impartial jury are among the rules that govern crime control agents. In sum, the rule of law applies not only to the substantive issues concerning the legality of different types of behavior, but also to the procedures used by those who enforce the substantive laws.

Although cities and states may differ slightly in their handling of offenders, we will present a general overview of the relationship of police to the criminal justice system generic to urban America.

As we previously mentioned, the police are the gatekeepers. In many situations, they have the ability to *arrest* a suspect, issue a warning, or do nothing at all. This discretion will be discussed in later chapters, but the decision to arrest or to take a suspect into custody is the first of many decisions that is made within our system of criminal justice. An arrest is when the officer takes control over or restrains the liberty of a suspect. An officer may arrest a suspect if the officer observes any crime being committed. If the suspect offers no resistance, no force is necessary; if the suspect resists, the officer may use reasonable force to complete the arrest.

In some cases, an offender can enter the criminal justice system through a *citation* or *summons*. These written orders are sometimes issued in lieu of formal arrest and require the suspect to appear at a given time and place. In recent years, these "traffic-ticket" types of arrests have increased. They are more efficient than formal arrests, and they are just as effective as a formal arrest for those offenders who will appear for a hearing.

Another basis of arrest is on a *warrant* issued to the police by the court. A warrant is an order from the court that directs the police to arrest a specific person for a specific offense. Based upon information included in a complaint, the court (a judge) can decide that there is *probable cause* that a crime has been committed and that it was committed by the person to be arrested. Many arrests are made without prior authorization and are called *warrantless arrests*. As mentioned above, an officer can arrest a suspect whom he or she observes committing a crime. When a victim or a witness reports a crime, a police officer, with probable cause, may make a warrantless arrest if the crime is a felony. If the offense is a misdemeanor and the officer did not see it occur, then he or she must wait until a complaint is made by a victim or witness and an arrest warrant is issued by a court.

In other words, a police officer may make an arrest for a serious offense (felonies and legislatively accepted misdemeanors) based upon a standard of probable cause. In the case of a lesser crime (misdemeanor), the officer must rely upon a higher standard, usually meaning the witnessing of the act. Once the suspect is arrested, he or she will be formally *booked*. This means a law enforcement agency keeps an administrative record of the arrest.

Many of these terms, such as *search and seizure*, *double jeopardy*, *warrant* and *probable cause*, may be confusing at this point, but each term will be defined and described as it is used in its proper context in later chapters.

Up to this point in the process of criminal justice, the police have been the enforcers and the main players. Once an arrest is effected, either by physically removing the suspect or by issuing a citation or summons, the case is turned over to the next set of players for the state, the *prosecuting attorneys*.

POLICE AND THE COURTS

One of the more interesting relationships within our system of criminal justice is the connection between the police and the courts. Although the police should be aware of all the problems faced by the courts, police officers and administrators often blame the court process for their own inadequacies. Our selection from the Chief's Corner addresses this issue from a practitioner's perspective.

The prosecutor is the attorney representing the state who looks at a case after the police have made an arrest and decides what specific charges, if any, should be brought against the defendant. In some large jurisdictions, this task is completed by a new graduate or a paralegal with only limited experience in the interpretation of a police report to determine what charges to file. This decision affects both the police and the prosecutor and is based on information in the police report. It is this report that stands as the backbone of the state's case. The prosecutor must decide the strength of the case by analyzing the evidence gathered by the police and presented in the report. The state's attorney must then decide its strength according to the requirements of the statute under which the offender will be prosecuted. In some jurisdictions, this review process is methodical and screens out all but the strongest cases, while in other areas, the prosecutor is too busy to review all the cases and accepts the merits of the police officer's complaint. In any event, the charge assessed by the police is not necessarily the formal or final charge filed against the defendant. This decision, which is made by the prosecutor, depends upon several factors but is driven by the legal strength of the evidence.

CHIEF'S CORNER
POLICE AND THE COURTS

Law enforcement at best is a stressful, frustrating career. This fact is underscored by the inordinate number of suicides, heart attacks and stress-related illnesses suffered by police officers. While these are serious problems, perhaps the most frustrating of all is the officers' interaction with the Courts. While there should be a natural bond between the police and the Courts, there is, in reality, a less than cooperative atmosphere. The police see the Courts as a very liberal institution which, in most cases, searches for ways to let defendants loose or to mitigate sentences.

Such perceptions generally arise out of the Courts' handling of a case in which the officer has been personally involved. I can remember obtaining a search warrant for Apartment Number Nine in a particular building where a Bolita operation (gambling) was taking place. Upon arriving, I found that the operation had been moved to Apartment Number Seven, where the subjects had broken in and set up shop. Knowing that they had no right to be in the vacant apartment and being able to look through the window and clearly see the criminal operation taking place, I walked in the door and arrested those involved.

When it came to court, the judge threw the case out because my search warrant was for Apartment Nine, not Seven. Even over my objections and those of the prosecutor, who explained that the criminals had no legal standing in Apartment Seven and had, in fact, broken in illegally to set up their gambling operation, the judge remained adamant and set them free, citing our procedural failure.

It was my feeling then, and is now, that the procedural law was never intended to be interpreted in such a manner. From that point on, I was never really comfortable in court. Like most of my fellow officers, I fear that regardless of how much evidence you have presented or how much hard work you have put into the case, some technicality may arise which sets the criminal free again. It seems almost to be a system that ignores common sense and which has developed over a period of years as a result of our overconcern with the protection of a person's rights. Such a system seems to fly in the face of the rights of the general public, whose protection from the criminal is ignored. Indeed, this escapes the common-sense purposes of laws on which our system of justice was based.

After the suspect has been arrested and taken into custody, he or she must be taken before a judge without unnecessary or undue delay. This initial court appearance usually takes place within twenty-four hours, but can stretch to seventy-two hours. Some major cities hold night and weekend court and will see defendants as soon as they are processed or booked. Those arrested in small towns on the weekend or when a judge is not immediately available may have to wait in the local jail for several days for a judge.

The *preliminary hearing* or *arraignment* has several purposes. First, it provides defendants with formal notice of the charges against them; they are advised of their rights to counsel and their right to remain silent. They are required to plead guilty or not guilty. If the defendant pleads guilty, then he or she is returned to jail or released to await sentencing. If the defendant pleads not guilty, it is the second purpose of this hearing to set *bail* or to *release* the defendant on *personal recognizance*. Depending on the jurisdiction, either *ROR* (release on one's own recognizance) or bail is the most common mechanism of release. In either case, the accused is released from custody and permitted to resume normal activities (and to prepare the defense) until the case is decided by a plea or trial. Remember, in the American system of criminal justice, you are presumed innocent until proven guilty by a court of law. The difference between ROR and bail is the posting of a financial security. If the court decides that an individual owns property, has family in the community or is otherwise responsible and likely to show up for trial, the defendant will probably be released on recognizance without having to post a financial security.

Although the police do not make formal decisions beyond the one to arrest, they are often involved in the various decision-making processes. For example, the prosecuting attorney may call the arresting or investigating officer to ask for an opinion about the witnesses, the offender or the offense. This information may be used to determine either a formal charge or an alternative to charging an offender. The police officer's attitude toward the offense or offender can influence the prosecutor to be tough or lenient. The prosecuting attorney has a variety of charges and alternatives to prosecution from which to choose. If the offender and the community would benefit from some action other than a formal criminal charge, such a choice could be made at this time with the help of information provided by the police. An officer may also provide an opinion to the court concerning the probability of an offender showing up for a court date, and this opinion could influence the decision to release the defendant or the amount of bail to set. In each case, the officer's opinion is a tool valued by the court segment of the criminal justice system.

If the defendant is not released from the system or given an alternative to prosecution that may result in charges being dropped, he or she is given a trial date. The police can certainly assist the prosecutor who is preparing the case for trial and can provide information that can lead to a *plea bargain*. In either case, the input of information by the police is valuable. A plea negotiation (often called a plea bargain) is a deal agreed upon by the defendant, the prosecutor and the court. Usually, the plea negotiation includes the state's reduction of a charge or sentence in return for a guilty plea. The police officer can provide information about the specific offense and offender that can help the prosecutor structure that plea negotiation. Similarly, if the case moves toward trial, the officers involved can be invaluable to the prosecutor in terms of sorting and evaluating the witnesses and other evidence. Unfortunately, many prosecuting attorneys do not realize the full potential of the police officer and seek advice only sporadically.

Once the case proceeds to trial, each of the police officers involved may be called to testify. In this situation, the officer can be considered and treated as a witness with specific information, and defense attorneys can question the officer regarding his or her actions and behavior. Each officer may testify about a specific part of the case, whether it concerns the physical evidence or the arrest.

One of the most controversial issues concerns the *exclusion of evidence* because of an improper *search* and *seizure* (exclusionary rule). An improper search and seizure violates an individual's rights protected by the Fourth Amendment. As Victor Kappeler noted (1993:75–76):

A search is an invasion of a person's privacy for purposes of collecting evidence for a criminal proceeding. . .

All searches and seizures . . . are subject to the provisions of the Fourth Amendment of the United States Constitution . . .

The Fourth Amendment requires the existence of probable cause, or in limited circumstances reasonable suspicion, before a search can be conducted. Normally, this determination must be made by a judge who reviews the evidence and determines whether issuance of a search warrant would be reasonable . . . under any set of circumstances. . . . [T]he courts have recognized many situations that are exceptions to the warrant requirement. These exceptions allow police officers to conduct limited searches without . . . a warrant, but require that these searches . . . be based on probable cause or reasonable suspicion that a crime has been or is being committed.

In other words, if a police officer conducting an inappropriate search seizes evidence, that evidence may be excluded from the trial and may not be used against the suspect. Whether it is a murder weapon, drugs, stolen property or evidence that links an individual to a crime scene, it may be excluded because of some improper or sloppy police work. Although this issue affects only a small number of cases, it is important for two reasons: (1) the possibility that a suspect could be released based on a technicality, and (2) the message it sends to the public.

If the offender is convicted and sent to jail or prison, the officer may participate with the victim in a release decision, such as parole. If the offender is released back into the community, whether acquitted or convicted, the police officer should be made aware of the offender's status and location. Unfortunately, this notification does not always occur and police officers are sometimes surprised to see the individual on the street.

All too often, police officers are not used in the manner presented above. Coordinating and improving police-prosecutor relations is a goal worth achieving. Good police-prosecutor relations can result in a smooth-running system of criminal justice with open channels of communication. The consequences of poor police-prosecutor relations can be inter-agency squabbles, turf fights and a system of criminal justice that lacks efficiency and effectiveness.

The relationships among police and other agencies of criminal justice have been strained since the beginning of law enforcement. To understand the current role of police and criminal justice in society, it is necessary to look at the history of police and trace its progress into the twentieth century. Our next chapter will outline the course of police and policing from British roots to American heritage.

Reference

Kappeler, Victor. 1993. *Critical Issues in Police Civil Liability*. Prospect Heights, IL: Waveland Press.

Chapter Two

HISTORY OF THE POLICE

Police and policing are, at first glance, simple concepts that have been used in recent years to convey and express certain ideas and values. Over time and among different cultural groups, the meaning of these concepts changes. From these changes, we have learned that the terms police and policing are not simple concepts, and the actions taken by the police have serious implications for the preservation of our civil liberties and the social fabric of our democratic society. It has been noted that, by the very nature of their work, police can be viewed as anomalies in a free society (Goldstein, 1977). In other words, police exist to protect our rights and our freedom, but often perform this duty through the use of coercion and physical force.

Since we depend upon the police and their policing to preserve our democracy, we need to understand their historical roots and development. In this chapter, we will look back to the origins of police work and to the evolution of modern American law enforcement systems.

Several years ago Samuel Walker (1983:2) wrote:

> To a great extent, the police are prisoners of the past. Day-to-day practices are influenced by deeply ingrained traditions, citizen attitudes toward the police, and relations between police and community. . . . The study of police history can serve as a guide to the present and heighten our awareness of the complex interaction between past problems, reforms and change.

His suggestion that a review of history is necessary to understand more fully the present and future has not influenced students of police to the extent it should. It is the purpose of this chapter to provide a brief history of social control, to demonstrate how certain ideas and practices led to the invention of the police function, and to trace the movement of policing from its English heritage to its American application. In order to set the scene for the first organized police force, let us first discuss its historical antecedents.

As we have noted, policing is basically the government's entry into the business of social control. Throughout history, there have been controls on behavior, usually based upon survival of the fittest. For example, in the classic scene from Robin Hood, Little John and Robin are on a log over a river and each want to cross to the other side. Although Robin is more crafty and skilled than Little John, the size of the big fellow along with his overpowering strength determines who passes and who falls into the river. The lesson here is one of survival. In the pre-industrial and pre-police era, individuals, groups and societies protected themselves, their ideas and their culture. The only rule was that there were no rules, and the only law was that of survival.

As life became more complicated, so did survival. Groups banded together for protection and organized themselves to maximize their efforts. One of the earliest attempts at collective survival is related to the vigilante movement in which individuals formed groups to assure that a particular way of life was preserved. The vigilante movement in the United States was a response to the typical problem of nonexistent or insufficient law enforcement. It was a case of civilians taking charge of their own destiny. Richard Brown has studied the history of violence in America and has noted:

> Fundamentally, the pioneers took the law into their own hands for the purpose of establishing order and stability in newly settled areas. . . . A vigilante roundup of ne'er-do-wells and outlaws followed by the flogging, expulsion, or killing of them not only solved the problem of disorder but had crucial symbolic value as well. (1969:121)

The distinction between organized movements and more or less disorganized collective actions is often difficult to make. For the purpose of this discussion, the distinction is not nearly as important as the fact that the citizens felt it necessary to take action to protect themselves and their way of life. Although the vigilante movement exemplifies the role citizens have taken in the enforcement of norms and traditions, it also demonstrates the problems encountered when citizens pick and choose the laws they want to obey and disobey.

After a time, the enforcement of laws and the maintenance of order become crucial for daily existence. The traditions of an organized movement that was founded in London were incorporated into American life. In other words, American policing is a direct product of policing in England. The colonists brought to their new country the customs and practices of their old country, including the established patterns of law enforcement.

BRITISH HERITAGE

Much of America's common-law tradition can be linked directly to its British roots. The origins of our modern police are no exception. Policing in the community, crime prevention, and elected sheriffs were all developed from English law enforcement.

The history of police in England includes a variety of stories and colorful scenes that range from a radically conservative interpretation of control to an extremely liberal view of government intervention (Reith, 1938; Calquhoun,

1806). There are many reported observations that are agreed upon, but there are just as many names, places, incidents and ideas that are reported differently by different researchers. Fortunately, our sketch of British influence on the American system of policing does not require such a detailed analysis.

It must be remembered that, initially, all security was an individual matter. Everyone who could afford it lived in a sturdy dwelling that was guarded by servants who served as bodyguards. The rest of the citizens hoped that their neighbors and those chosen as watchmen would deter crime. Citizens protected their homes and families as well as they could. In the country, and in many cities, the increase in crime brought about the need for the enforcement of laws (Clarkson and Hall, 1889). After the Norman Conquest of 1066, a model of community policing called frankpledge was established. In this model an agreement required citizens to act as the eyes and ears of the police and to deliver to the court any member of the group who committed a crime. Craig Uchida (1989:15) has explained the frankpledge system in detail.

> The frankpledge police system required that every male above the age of twelve form a group with nine of his neighbors called a tything. Each tything was sworn to apprehend and deliver to court any of its members who committed a crime. Each person was pledged to help protect fellow citizens and, in turn, would be protected. This system was "obligatory" in nature, in that tythingmen were not paid salaries for their work but were required by law to carry out certain duties.

The consequence of this arrangement was a pledge to protect others and the security of being protected by one's neighbors. Due to inattention by the King, his appointees and the supervisors, by the thirteenth century the frankpledge had fallen into disarray. As the frankpledge system became ineffective, the parish constable system emerged as its replacement.

The British legal system was based upon *four* enforcers of the law. The official of the manor or county parish was known as the *constable*, and it was his job to enforce the laws and keep the peace. The constables were adult males who served one-year terms rotated among the worthy residents (Webb and Webb, 1906). The constable was given the duty of law enforcement, but had only scarce resources to administer justice. The Statute of Winchester in 1285 added a few teeth to the jaws of justice as it required several watch-related duties of all adult male residents. The *night watchman*, then, was the second enforcer. It was his duty to remain at watch boxes (Reith, 1956) during the night to guard against fires, crimes and suspicious persons. These citizens were also required to pursue known fugitives and to keep weapons in their homes for use against intruders and crimes against others (Miller, 1975; Critchley, 1972). In addition, each parish had a *beadle*, who was given minor administrative tasks to assist the constable. By the fourteenth century, an unpaid *justice of the peace*, assisted by volunteers, was added to support the administration of justice or, more accurately, to keep the King's peace. As historian Phillip Smith has noted (1985:17):

> The legal system admirably served the purposes of the ruling classes in the pre-industrial age, and was far from being a hindrance to the cause of social order, given the ambiguities, obscurities, and absurdities in the law.

The English system of criminal justice during the fourteenth century was administered by the constable, the sheriff (originally Shire Reeve) who was basically the tax enforcer and collector, and the magistrate. This system continued to function until the eighteenth century when the city of London had grown into a metropolitan area that required a more organized method of policing.

During the mid-1700s, Henry Fielding (author of *Tom Jones*) and his brother, Sir John Fielding, were responsible for leading an effort to improve policing in London and throughout England. The Fieldings initiated what is now known as community watch or neighborhood crime watch. In several publications, including the *Covent Garden Journal* and *The Weekly Pursuit*, the brothers educated the public on issues surrounding crime and the apprehension of criminals. In a manner similar to what we see in today's post offices, and in many media representations, the Fieldings published descriptions of known crimes and criminals. In this way, some of the responsibility of fighting crime was placed in the hands of the members of the community (Lee, 1901).

In 1748, Henry Fielding became magistrate of London and, as one of his first acts, organized a group of "thief-takers" all of whom had prior experience as constables. This organized force would schedule times to roam the streets to search for offenders, attempt to break up criminal gangs and arrest anyone who was in violation of the law. This was the first time that the constables patrolled the streets instead of remaining at their watch boxes. In fact, Fielding also initiated a mounted patrol to guard the highways (Smith, 1985). The news spread about successes of the Bow Street Amateur Volunteer Force (known as the Bow Street Runners), and Fielding was able to have the members recognized and salaried by the local government (Stead, 1985; Armitage, 1910). It was hoped that this idea of organized patrols would spread to other sections of London. Unfortunately, Henry Fielding died in 1754, and his brother John was unable to maintain the status and integrity of the group. As there was no one who could control the men, the overall effectiveness of the group declined. In fact, there were charges against them of brutality, corruption and mob-like activities (Smith, 1985; Critchley, 1972).

A decade after Fielding's death, several events took place that furthered the establishment of an organized police force. In London, within a relatively short period of time, the Lord Mayor was robbed at gunpoint and the Duke of York and the Prince of Wales were mugged as they walked during daylight hours. In the same period, the Great Seal of England was stolen from the house of the Lord Chancellor and melted down for the silver (Rubenstein, 1973). There was a growing demand for protection, and the private "thief-takers," as well as the societies for law enforcement, prospered. Life in London was changing, and the constables and watchmen were no longer able to preserve order or control the citizens. All too frequently, the magistrates had to read the Riot Act and call out the military to keep the King's peace. The violent tactics of the soldiers encouraged the idea of a civilian police force. The Gordon riots of 1780 produced the most intense mob violence and military response in the history of London. This incident also led to the organization of civilians to control other citizens. There were detractors as well as supporters of organized civilian policing. As Rubenstein (1973:9) notes:

> The wealthy citizens who controlled the constables in their wards did not want to relinquish their perquisites to a central authority who might abuse this extension of power to alter the traditional character of English gov-ernment.

Approximately fifty years after the Gordon riots, civilian police were assigned to the streets of London. The Police of the Metropolis, the official name of the London police force (Smith, 1985), were organized for crime prevention. It is generally accepted that for the first time, in 1829, the entire city was patrolled by men assigned specific territories or beats (Smith, 1985; Reith, 1956). It was Sir Robert Peel, the British Home Secretary, who organized the first police force in London. He structured the 3,000-man force to be commanded by two magistrates, later commissioners, who in turn reported back to him. Peel guided through Parliament the "Act for Improving the Police in and Near the Metropolis." Peel's knowledge and political savvy, which helped to protect the autonomy of already established police forces, aided the timely approval of the Act (Smith, 1985).

The engineers of the London police force, led by Peel, had learned from the Watch and Ward that the men needed a central administration, strict discipline and close supervision. They eventually decided to implement a military-like organization and service in what had been a strictly civilian force. Sir Robert Peel and his bobbies were so successful that requests for help from outside areas were received and assistance was sent. Parliament acknowledged the success of the New Police force and provided the authority for justices of the peace to establish local police forces. By 1856, every parish in England was required to form its own police force based on the model developed for London by Sir Robert Peel.

Several important concepts were implemented by the London police based upon the experiences of the police in other parts of England. First, it was believed that a central administrative structure was preferable to a decentralized arrangement. Second, it was realized that the recruitment of police officers required more than merely locating willing, warm bodies. Third, once those individuals were organized into a police force, it would take a strict military-like organization to control them.

EXPERIENCE IN EARLY AMERICA

There were significant difficulties with the London police, including serious disciplinary and personnel problems. In fact, one suggestion concerning the recruitment of officers was to take them directly from the ranks of the cavalry, the elite of the military. Nonetheless, the New Police, along with its military organization, attracted rave reviews from abroad and, especially, from young, developing American cities (Reith, 1956). The combination of the dissatisfaction with existing law enforcement in America and the admiration of British institutions produced a rapid introduction of the New Police ideals into America and its cities.

Between 1830 and the Civil War, territories adopted the sheriff as the chief law enforcement agent, and cities looked toward the New Police concept. In the territories, the sheriff not only responded to citizen complaints and investigated crimes, but also collected taxes, watched for fires and supervised elections, among many other duties (Rubenstein, 1973). In several of the major cities, local watch committees were abolished and replaced with a police force that was based, in part, upon the ideas and practices imported from London.

FROM LONDON TO NEW YORK

Boston, in 1838, was the first major city in America to sponsor a police force. Prompted by several riots in the early 1830s, nine officers were hired to protect and serve the community. By 1846, this number grew to thirty. Police protection continued as more of an idea than a reality. It was New York City that developed the first large police department in America. We will use it as a model for discussion. The riots in the streets of New York in 1834 and the spectacular murder of Mary Cecilia Rogers prompted the creation of the New York City Police.

Unlike the London police department, which was a highly centralized agency of the national government, the New York police force was decentralized and administered at the neighborhood and ward levels. While the London police officials were highly professional in that they were chosen for their ability to manage a police force, the New York police were administered by amateurs with little police experience. In addition, the political pressures at all levels of the force guaranteed that policing in America would develop along lines quite different from the London police force (Miller, 1975). As the American government was based on principles of democracy, police departments should have been more responsive to the public than their British brethren. As often happens in a new democracy, local control of the police was available to anyone who could control a large number of votes.

In other words, the price of democracy includes the possibility that someone who is ill-prepared or without experience may be elected to a position of power. This notion became all too real in the New York police force. Samuel Walker informs us that "the quality of American police service in the nineteenth century could hardly have been worse. The police were completely unprofessional and police work was dominated by corruption and inefficiency. The source of these problems was politics" (1983:7). The real power in city police rested with the city councilmen and political leaders, as well as with the police captains in each neighborhood. Politics influenced every aspect of policing, including personnel selection, enforcement strategies and discretion, corruption and reforms (Rubenstein, 1977).

Although New York was a major city, it was not the seat of national government or the center of culture or commerce in America. However, New York was a center of immigration and certainly experienced its own local disorganization, including ethnic and class conflicts, poverty and serious crime problems.

One of the major issues of the times was the antagonism among the workers. For example, the native-born workers were concerned that some Irishmen were willing to work longer hours for lower wages. This rivalry was encouraged by employers who were interested only in productivity and profit. Rowdy Irishmen who threatened to disrupt the accepted institutions were in conflict with those who belonged to the organized labor movements. This led to numerous potential conflicts in the streets.

Police officials wisely created a force whose officers conformed to pre-existing, widely accepted patterns of democracy. These officers were recruited from their own neighborhoods, and they won the respect of citizens through individual contact and personal knowledge. Although this helped quell some potential disturbances, the familiarity led to the establishment of political bases from which corrupt practices could grow. Although clubs were the only weapons allowed for enforcement and protection, the police were successful in showing their power. There were complaints against the unnecessary use of force by police, but little was done to control this discretion. New York police officers were supposed to keep the peace; many believed that order should be maintained at any price. At that time in our history, policemen needed to be resourceful, eager and somewhat aggressive.

The New York police became a force in the streets. They were known only by that power and authority until their distinct blue uniforms were first worn in 1853. By 1856, New York had one policeman for every 812 citizens. In 1857, the police were removed from the control of local officials and placed under the control of the state government. Along with that administrative change and related hostility to the new Metropolitan Police force, some violence occurred.

Shortly after the switch from local to state control, many policemen were encouraged to carry revolvers for protection and the enforcement of laws (Miller, 1975). By 1860, since many citizens were armed, revolvers became standard equipment for the police, although they were never formally authorized (MacCabe, 1868). As soon as police armed themselves, complaints surfaced against the unnecessary use of deadly force and the ability of a policeman not only to be the arresting officer but also judge, jury, and executioner.

Theodore Roosevelt, who served as police commissioner of New York between 1895 and 1897, attempted to reform the police by raising standards for recruiting. He hoped to eliminate corrupt cops by regulating who was qualified to serve on the force. His effort failed, in part, because of the strength of the political machinery which governed the city.

BEYOND NEW YORK

After 1860, many American cities formed police departments as part of their natural growth and as a move to provide or improve public services (Monkkonen, 1981). Although the structure of these departments varied somewhat, the consequences of police work had similar effects on officers. Policemen were often isolated from citizens and frequently from each other. It was natural that they would band together for both companionship and for protection. The isolation of police work was both physical and emotional.

Alone or with a partner, police officers walked a beat in all types of weather for several hours each day. When on the streets, their only way of summoning assistance was by swinging the large rattles that made enough noise to attract the attention of other policemen or good samaritans. Patrols and established beats prompted the beginnings of what has become known as the police subculture. While on patrol, the officers were supervised poorly, if at all, and were left to make their own deals and decisions. Unfortunately, this self-reliance and solidarity with other policemen created a distance between the rank and file officers and their superiors. When not on patrol, the remaining hours of their shifts were spent at the station house waiting to be called to assist fellow officers. At the station, officers formed close relationships with other officers. It is interesting to note that these same issues exist today, despite more than 130 years of progress.

In addition to physical isolation, policemen also found themselves emotionally isolated, as the majority of contacts they had with citizens involved the enforcement of laws and the maintenance of order. They slowly developed their own set of attitudes and accepted behaviors which were often different from those of the public. This difference was perpetuated and strengthened by the recruitment and selection process for new officers. Recruits were selected by political contacts and the individual's potential to fit into the perceived mold of a "police personality." No training was provided to new recruits; they were simply handed a badge, a baton, a manual outlining departmental rules and regulations and were sent out into the streets. The new officers relied very heavily upon the advice and consent of the older, more established policemen.

Walker (1983) tells us that there was no textbook written for police until 1906 and that a police officer's pay was almost twice that of the average blue-collar worker. Attractive working conditions helped influence the decision to seek a job as a policeman through political means. Corruption, inefficiency, and ineffectiveness was thus widespread.

The composition of the police force changed drastically as newly elected councilmen, through their appointed police officials, could fire an officer at any time. Policemen began to realize that they needed protection from the whims of the political bosses. Through intense lobbying, civil service protections were instituted at the end of the nineteenth century.

An appointment to the police force was an important step up the social ladder for members of many immigrant groups. Many new policemen realized that their claim to social status within their community was their new uniform and their representation of the law. This new status served to increase further the emotional isolation of police officers from the rest of society.

POLICE WORK AND COMMUNICATION

The invention of the telegraph, two-way radio and patrol car greatly changed police and police work. When the police force was first established, only face-to-face communication was available and foot and horse patrol were the most efficient modes of transportation.

The concept of what we now know as "roll call" was developed to communicate information from the administrators to the supervisors and, finally, to the officers. Supervisors would have early morning meetings to discuss the issues of the day with the commissioner before proceeding to their various districts. This was the only real opportunity the supervisors had to discuss specific events, to coordinate policy, and to receive orders from the administrators. If troops had to be deployed in a manner differently than what had been planned, messengers were sent to the various districts to alert the supervisors. Thus, many districts maintained a reserve force of policemen who lived at district station house barracks and who were available for calls of assistance.

After the morning messages were communicated and assignments made at a group meeting (roll call), it was virtually impossible for supervisors to control what the men did on their daily beats. Many departments had "rounds-men," the equivalent of today's sergeant, who had prearranged meetings with his men and who made rounds to observe the policemen in action. Once in a while, a roundsman would accompany a policeman on patrol, but this would be at the neglect of his other duties. More often, the roundsman would make observations from time-to-time and question the people living in the area about the policeman's activities and behavior. This crude form of supervision was the first attempt at an evaluation of police work.

During the late 1850s, telegraph networks linked police headquarters directly with the districts, alleviating the need for the morning meetings between the supervisors and the commissioner. Soon, locked call boxes, which had been introduced in Boston as fire alarm boxes, were used in New York by policemen to signal the home base. As it was impractical to teach everyone morse code, the box was rigged with a lever that sent a signal to indicate to a supervisor that the policeman was at his assigned post. As communication technology improved, a bell system was developed to relay simple signals. Finally, the telephone introduced in 1880 provided an effective form of two-way communication that greatly improved the ability of policemen to call for assistance and for supervisors to know what their men were doing at any given time (Leonard 1938; McCague, 1968).

The developing technology that improved communication had a beneficial impact on many aspects of police administration and organization. As telephones were placed in the numerous call boxes, two-way communication allowed the quick deployment of troops and greatly reduced any waiting for assistance. This change made it possible to abolish the reserve platoons, the dormitories, the laundries and the kitchens. The police stations of the 1900s were significantly smaller and less elaborate than those built before the implementation of the telephone.

One aspect of policing that remained unchanged by the telephone was the supervisor's "game" of locating his men. There were several strategies used by sergeants to supervise and control their officers. Jonathan Rubenstein (1973:18-19) explains some of the more interesting ways:

> The patrolman's absence could be observed by standing in the middle of the street and looking its length . . . [this] would deter men from seeking out their "holes," favored places used for hiding and resting. . . . Sergeants develop methods for discovering unacknowledged hiding places and for surprising their men to discourage unauthorized loafing. In winter . . . some supervisors would . . . touch [a policeman's] tin badge, whose temperature would reveal immediately whether the man had been walking his beat or had just come outside. Some men wore two badges. . . .

Some policemen would seek refuge in friendly places such as barber shops and restaurants. The shop owners, who enjoyed the added protection, encouraged the officers by providing free food and services. Although times and methods have changed, this "unauthorized loafing" and acceptance of free goods and services remains a serious concern to police administrators.

Policemen seeking refuge from the streets for any reason required control and supervision. Although conditions had improved drastically over the years, the streets were still not as safe as they could be. While communication had improved, lengthy response time still left the policeman in possible danger.

Improved two-way communication advanced the policing function, and call boxes specifically improved the policeman's ability to seek back-up assistance. Unfortunately, the call-box system offered little help to the public. Numerous experiments were tried with open call boxes, but they were abandoned quickly when the number of crank calls overwhelmed the operators and when destruction to the machinery became too great for the administrators to justify. The introduction of the wireless radio and the patrol car were attempts to resolve communication problems between the police and the public (Smith, 1960).

The patrol car was seen as the miracle to end all police problems. It allowed safe and dependable transportation and permitted the policeman to cover a large area in a short period of time. This change increased the protection of the public and the safety of the policemen. The introduction of the wireless radio in the patrol car in 1929 meant that policemen could be informed immediately of any problem and could respond safely and quickly. The radio cruiser also afforded the sergeants and supervisors the ability to seek out their officers and have them tracked at all times. The radio cruiser replaced most foot patrols. The patrol car offered the policeman protection from the elements (but increased his isolation) and improved his sense of security. In fact, one of the leading police reformers, August Vollmer, once suggested:

> . . . with the advent of the radio equipped car a new era has come. . . . Districts of many square miles . . . are now covered by the roving patrol car, fast, efficient, stealthy, having no regular beat to patrol, just as liable to be within feet as 3 miles of the crook plying his trade—the very enigma of this specialized fellow who is coming to realize now that a few moments may bring them down about him like a swarm of bees—this lightening swift "angel of death." (National Commission on Law Observance and Enforcement, 1930:90–98)

A consequence of two-way communication was that the control of routine police work became a function of citizen calls for service. That is, citizen calls to the police department required officers to respond by driving from one location to another. As citizens became comfortable with their ability and opportunity to call the police, a backlog of calls-for-service built up, which required officers to move directly from one call to another. This new method of policing did not permit officers to maintain their relationships with those who owned or operated businesses or with other members of the community. While the automobile created a mobile police force, it took away the officers' opportunity to deal with the public face to face. Thus, officers were unable to spend sufficient time developing relationships and cultivating friendships with individuals who might provide information about crimes, perpetrators, and the general climate of the neighborhood.

POLICE REFORM AND PROFESSIONALISM

Police reform and the concept of a professionalized police force were direct results of years of unrest concerning who would control the police and their methods of policing. Little effort had been given to the selection, training, or management of personnel. Police reformers usually represented the middle-class and native-born citizens who wished to remove the power of the police from the working-class, immigrant political machines. These reformers wanted to create a more professional force controlled by specialists trained in law enforcement. This would prove to be a difficult chore, given the strength and power of the political machines.

The struggle for control of the police force resulted in various experiments in government. New York, in 1853, was the first to attempt to control the police by instituting a commission whose members were appointed by the mayor. The commission was reorganized after four years, and the power to appoint the commissioners was shifted from local control to the state legislature. Other cities tried numerous methods of controlling the police. Every political group conceived some formula by which it could gain some power and control over the police. This struggle for power certainly increased the influence of politics over the police and policing (Fosdick, 1972).

It would be negligent to discuss the history of police reform and professionalism without emphasizing the works of a number of individuals. While it took many to develop, change and reform policing, we have selected the contributions of three, including former chief officers Richard Sylvester, August Vollmer and O. W. Wilson. Each represents a specific movement in policing history. Collectively, they represent a trend of professionalism and reform.

Richard Sylvester was superintendent of the District of Columbia Police Department from 1898 to 1915, and president of the International Association of Chiefs of Police (IACP) from 1901 to 1915. In these influential positions, he encouraged strong professional development among his own police officers. He transformed the IACP into the leading voice for his ideas of professionalism and into a moving force for police reform. Sylvester began a long process of improvements for the police that continues today.

August Vollmer, although better known than Sylvester, relied heavily upon many of Sylvester's ideas. Vollmer served as police chief of Berkeley, California from 1905 to 1932. Vollmer's major contribution was the integration of education into police work. He hired college graduates as police officers and organized the first college-level, police-related courses in 1916 at the University of California (Douthit, 1975). He also worked very closely with his university colleagues in developing the most effective and efficient methods of policing. For example, Vollmer was the first police chief to have a totally mobile force. His officers rode bicycles, as well as patrolled in automobiles. Berkeley, in 1921 under Vollmer's direction, was the first city to have a radio-equipped patrol car. Vollmer's police force represents one manifestation of the greater proclivity for professionalism in the west coast departments. The philosophy of policing found in many departments on the east coast followed the old New York model. On the east coast, police focused on personal relationships with people in the community rather than on the advancement of professionalism.

One of Vollmer's former "college cops" was Orlando W. Wilson. O. W. Wilson moved to Wichita, Kansas to head that city's police department, where he became involved in the study of the deployment of officers for efficiency and effectiveness. He applied all available knowledge to the field of policing and developed innovative methods that were used as models for many years. He served as chief from 1928 to 1939. After his tenure, he returned to the University of California as Dean of the School of Criminology through the 1950s. In 1960, he was appointed as superintendent of the Chicago Police Department. O. W. Wilson introduced scientific principles of policing, including analyses of calls for service and establishment of schedules based upon need, into police work. Along with the technical advancements discussed earlier, Wilson expanded and advanced the police profession.

These three twentieth-century pioneers provide examples of the dedication and innovation that moved American policing from its early roots to its current status. Many individuals along with Sylvester, Vollmer and Wilson are responsible for the rise of professionalism in American policing. The International Association of Chiefs of Police (IACP) and the California Peace Officers' Association were the professional organizations that helped the police gain a respectable reputation. Through education, scientific principles, technical advancements, strict control and supervision, police managers were able to begin the transformation of many departments into efficient and effective units of government.

One further innovation that directed police professionalism was the collection and compilation of crime statistics. The Federal Bureau of Investigation, under J. Edgar Hoover, administered these Uniform Crime Statistics. Although these compilations had many weaknesses, they offered the first national system of crime statistics. The Uniform Crime Reports (UCR) made the FBI the unofficial voice of American policing, since local agencies would send their information to a central location. Additionally, these reports identified the most important crimes upon which police should focus. Police were developing their identity and their mission based upon professionalism as it was being implemented.

This identity was sharpened by the critics of the police and those who believed the police had "gone too far." There were complaints about unjustified use of force and corrupt, incompetent management. It was this public concern that prompted President Herbert Hoover, in 1929, to appoint the National Commission on Law Observance and Enforcement to study the criminal justice system (Wickersham Commission). This report and other forms of public pressure forced many police departments to take critical steps to improve their image and performance. It was acknowledged at this time that one of the most influential aspects of policing was the relationship of the police with the community.

EMERGING ISSUES

Several issues concerning the police and the community were emerging that would eventually explode into major crises in the 1960s. These included police-community relations and police unionism.

Relations between the police and the public they served ranged from positive to physically coercive, depending upon which public you asked. The majority of middle-class citizens approved of police practices, while many members of lower-class minority groups felt oppressed by the same actions. Most problems appeared to be race-related and often turned into skirmishes or violent rioting. Some problems began to develop around 1915 and 1919 and, again, in the early 1940s. What is known as the police-community relations movement developed in the wake of the 1943 riots in Detroit and Los Angeles. As a result, some police departments instituted training and educational programs in race relations, hoping to avert possible violence. The programs focused on what the community wanted from the police. Fortunately, the riots ended while the sensitivity to the problems continued.

The second major problem for the police involved the frontline officers and their efforts to unionize. As we mentioned earlier, police officers were at the mercy of the politicians. As the concept of police professionalism matured, more officers thought in terms of an organized effort to develop and protect their own interests. Fraternal associations and various police unions were an inevitable consequence of police professionalism (Spero, 1972). As a result, many police departments today function as closed shops.

As discussed earlier, policemen have been isolated from the rest of society. They often worked and socialized only with other policemen. Social clubs resulting from these bonds formed the beginnings of police unions, fraternal organizations, benevolent associations and the policemen's Bill of Rights. It appeared that the police subcultures, with their feelings of social isolation, were growing stronger.

THE ISSUES MATURE INTO CRISES

It is difficult to pinpoint the time and place that problems grow into crises, but the sixties was certainly a decade in which problematic issues converged in a volatile manner. By then, police had become better trained, better educated and more professional than they had been in the past. Along with these improvements came more social responsibilities and increased expectations by members of the community.

During the 1960s people expressed their dissatisfaction with a number of issues, including racial discrimination, the United States' involvement in Vietnam and the rapid increase in the rates of violent crime. Perhaps these issues, and the public's response and protests, set the scene. A riot broke out in New York after an off-duty policeman shot and killed a black youth in 1964. Other race riots occurred that year. The Watts riot in Los Angeles broke out in 1965. Rioting continued in 1966 and 1967. There appeared to be a trend of summertime urban disorders. In fact, it was thought that the hotter the temperature, the more likely it was that a riot would occur. Perhaps the worst riot took place in Detroit in 1967 after police raided an after-hours bar. The common factors in all of these disturbances were race and police; members of the community focused their anger on the police.

THE RESEARCH ERA

The turbulent times of the 1960s and the riots that took place on the streets of many of our major cities focused national attention on the police and their relation to the communities they served. Three major studies were commissioned to examine the police in detail and to update the 1931 Presidential Commission. These included the 1967 President's Commission on Law Enforcement and Administration of Justice, The National Advisory Commission on Civil Disorders (1967) and the National Advisory Commission on Criminal Justice Standards and Goals (1973). Each represented a major effort by a large number of scholars and practitioners focusing upon police and criminal justice. However, a surprisingly small amount of new information was reported, and no solutions to policing problems were determined. The recurring themes in these reports revolved around styles of policing, police and minority relations, and community support of police, including the hiring and promotion of minority officers and administrators. These issues were apparent to Sir Robert Peel so many years ago and remain apparent today; unfortunately, the answers continue to escape us. More will be said about these reports, their findings, and recommendations in subsequent chapters.

The most important outcome of these reports includes the research that was commissioned directly for the reports and the research revolution that was generated by the interest and publicity of the reports. In addition, the federal government established the Law Enforcement Assistance Administration (L.E.A.A.) to be responsible for the guidance and administration of research, training, and program funds directed toward the overall improvement of justice in the United States (Cronin et al., 1981). L.E.A.A. was able to fund a great deal of research on police and to integrate the research findings into policy recommendations and guidelines. Although L.E.A.A. ultimately failed in its mission to control crime or even to bring the fragments of a so-called criminal justice system together, it was successful, to a degree, in the funding of new programs and innovative research.

It was this research revolution fostered by L.E.A.A. funds and organization that brought us to our position today. Our current knowledge is the result of a combination of trial and error, and empirical research. In many of our major city police departments, training and procedures are state of the art, and the officers and administrators have attained a high degree of professionalism (see Petersilia, 1989). The tradition of small-town and local administration, however, prevails, and the responsibility for policing remains divided among more than 20,000 agencies. Many of the larger, more progressive departments have been willing to analyze research findings and change their policies for the improvement of law enforcement and the public. Unfortunately, many smaller and less progressive departments are more concerned about the status quo, politics or history, and are unwilling to change. They remain no more effective than their predecessors.

THE HISTORY OF THE FUTURE

Four dilemmas are apparent for police in the 1990s, and each has its roots in history. First is the *fiscal crisis* that has hit almost every one of the approximately 20,000 law enforcement agencies. Inflation, poor management at several levels of government, and the tax revolt, balanced against higher prices, increased salary demands and higher crime rates, have placed police administrators in an awkward situation. Second, results from the *research revolution* have provided us with a great deal of knowledge about the difficulties of policing and what does not work, but have provided only a few suggestions as to how to make improvements. For example, it was thought that education alone or the use of technical innovations would improve the quality of policing, but this has not always been the result. Third, the problems of *police corruption*, both individual and systemic, have been made public and analyzed but still exist. Discovering the reasons for corruption, and what is being done to end it are important aspects of policing. Finally, the general problems and conflicts between police and the community may have changed over time, but remain as the area of policing that requires the most attention. These issues and many more will resurface as we discuss the various aspects of police and policing in the remaining chapters.

References

Armitage, Gilbert. 1910. *The History of the Bow Street Runners, 1729–1829*. London: Wishart.

Brown, Douglas. 1956. *The Rise of Scotland Yard: A History of the Metropolitan Police*. London: Harrap.

Brown, Richard. 1969. "Vigilante Policing." In Hugh D. Graham and Ted. R Gurr (eds.) *Violence in America: Historical and Comparative Perspectives,* Vol. 1, pp. 121–69. Washington, DC: United States Government Printing Office.

Calquhoun, Patrick. 1806. *A Treatise on the Police of the Metropolis*. London: Mawman, Cadell and Davies.

Clarkson, Charles and J. Hall Richardson. 1889. *Police*. London: The Leadenhall Press.

Critchley, Thomas. 1972. *A History of Police in England and Wales*. Montclair, NJ: Patterson-Smith.

Cronin, Thomas, Tania Cronin, and Michael Milakovich. 1981. *U.S. v. Crime in the Streets*. Bloomington: Indiana University Press.

Douthit, Nathan. 1975. "August Vollmer, Berkeley's First Chief of Police, and the Emergence of Police Professionalism." *California Historical Quarterly* 54 (Spring): 101–24.

Fosdick, Raymond. 1972. *American Police Systems*. Montclair, NJ: Patterson-Smith.

Goldstein, Herman. 1977. *Policing in a Free Society*. Cambridge: Ballinger.

Lee, William. 1901, *A History of Police in England*. London: Methuen.

Leonard, V. A. 1938. *Police Communications Systems*. Berkeley: University of California Press.

MacCabe, James. 1868. *The Secrets of the Great City*. Philadelphia: n.p.

McCague, James. 1968. *The Second Rebellion: The New York City Draft Riots of 1863*. New York: Dial Press.

Miller, Wilbur. 1975. "Cops and Bobbies, 1830–1870." *Journal of Social History* (Winter): 81–101.

Monkkonen, Eric. 1981. *Police in Urban America, 1860–1920*. Cambridge: Cambridge University Press.

National Advisory Commission on Civil Disorders. 1967. *Report*. Washington, DC: United States Government Printing Office.

National Advisory Commission on Criminal Justice Standards and Goals. 1973. *Police*. Washington, DC: United States Government Printing Office.

National Commission on Law Observance and Enforcement. 1931. *The Police*. Washington, DC: United States Government Printing Office.

President's Commission on Law Enforcement and Administration of Justice. 1967. *Challenge of Crime in a Free Society*. Washington, DC: United States Government Printing Office.

Petersilia, Joan. 1993. "The Influence of Research on Policing." In Roger Dunham and Geoffrey Alpert (eds.) *Critical Issues in Policing: Contemporary Readings*, 2nd ed., pp. 220–36. Prospect Heights, IL: Waveland Press.

Reith, Charles. 1956. *A New Study of Police History*. London: Oliver and Boyd.

———. 1938. *The Police Idea: Its History and Evolution in England in the Eighteenth Century and Beyond*. London: Oliver.

Rubenstein, Jonathan. 1973. *City Police*. New York: Farrer, Straus and Giroux.

Smith, Phillip. 1985. *Policing Victorian London*. London: Greenwood Press.

Spero, Sterling. 1972. *Government as Employer*. Carbondale: Southern Illinois University Press.

Stead, Philip. 1985. *The Police of Britain*. London: Macmillan.

Uchida, Craig. 1993. "The Development of the American Police: An Historical Overview." In Roger Dunham and Geoffrey Alpert (eds.) *Critical Issues in Policing: Contemporary Readings*, 2nd ed., pp. 16–32. Prospect Heights, IL: Waveland Press.

Walker, Samuel. 1983. *The Police in America*. New York: McGraw-Hill.

Webb, Sidney and Beatrice Webb. 1906. *English Local Government from the Revolution to the Municipal Corporations Act: The Parish and the County*. London: Longmans, Green and Co.

Chapter Three

POLICE RECRUITMENT, SELECTION, AND TRAINING

It is difficult to emphasize sufficiently the importance of recruitment, selection and training. After all, a police agency is no better than those who perform the day-to-day tasks. Police work is a labor-intensive service industry in which roughly 85 percent of the agencies' budgets are devoted to these personnel costs. The review of these figures reveals that the most significant investment police departments make is the recruiting, selection and training of their personnel. Unfortunately, many of those selected leave after only a short tenure and require the agency to go out and recruit, select and train others. Millions of dollars per year could be saved by selecting the most appropriate individuals to be police officers. Recruiting, selecting and retaining these applicants raises several issues. First, many persons think they want to be police officers but after a short time realize that they are not suited for the work. Second, the organization may learn that there are individuals who are not able to perform the tasks. Third, there are family pressures which influence good officers to leave the profession. Fourth, some officers burn out quickly and leave, and finally, some officers leave for better paying professions. Of course, many officers jump from one agency to another because of pay differentials or benefits.

The hiring of a police officer involves two decisions: an individual's choice to become a police officer and a law enforcement agency's decision to hire that person. Individual career choices will be discussed in chapter 11. This chapter will analyze the decision-making processes of the municipality and the police department interested in hiring a particular applicant. We will first look at the process in general and then analyze more thoroughly each segment of the process.

As we just discovered, early American police departments had no requirements for new recruits, except that they have the right political connections and the right attitude. Police positions were often given to those new immigrants who provided the greatest political support and number of votes. Planning a career in policing was difficult, as jobs were neither secure nor based on competence. Recruiting was little more than the rounding-up of warm bodies.

In the late 1800s, a reform movement for the selection of police personnel and other government workers was initiated. The Pendleton Act, which was passed in 1883, sought to ban political patronage as the sole criterion for personnel selection for a majority of federal positions. The intent of the Act was to have the most qualified person hired for the job. In addition, this act incorporated a competitive system by which employees would be selected and retained based upon experience and ability. This included protection against arbitrary discharge or discrimination. Several states, including New York, enacted similar laws that year. In 1886, a disgruntled office seeker assassinated President Garfield, and public attention was focused upon the problems of the spoils system. The passage of Pendleton-type legislation and its enforcement became a reality during the 1900s. Unfortunately, problems with political machines still exist and political interference in American policing has not disappeared.

QUALIFICATIONS FOR POLICE OFFICERS

Prior to discussing the specific qualifications for police recruits, it is important to emphasize that several states still have no formal requirements. Many states elect county sheriffs as constitutional officers and require little or no education or formal training. As constitutional officers, the sheriffs are permitted to hire deputies without any selection process or testing. Only a statutory prohibition would prevent the hiring of a felon! Municipal government officials who have the authority to appoint chiefs are usually controlled by state law and administrative regulations, including some civil service requirements. It would be instructive to review your state laws concerning the mandated criteria for law enforcement officers and to determine if some departments have additional standards. In 1861, the police in Washington D.C. were required to meet only the following criteria (Alfers, 1975:201):

1. read and write English;
2. hold United States citizenship;
3. have no criminal record;
4. be between 25 and 45 years old;
5. be in good health;
6. be at least 5'6"; and
7. have a good moral character.

Hiring practices have gone through a slow and painful transformation during the past decades. New requirements include that a person's vision must be good or correctable and that he or she possess a driver's license or voter's registration card. The majority of the criteria have not changed drastically, but how the selection criteria are measured has been clarified. In most states, the criterion to read and write English has been changed to the requirement of a high school education or its equivalent. In many departments, specific height and weight restrictions have been replaced by a reasonable proportion of weight to height. One must still be a United States citizen to be a police officer. Having a good moral character is still a requirement for becoming a police officer, but how a good moral character is defined and measured is often left to the discretion of the individual agency.

The selection and promotion of police officers has changed from a system of political spoils to a complex, psychometric and behavioral assessment process. Various tests measure a candidate's physical agility and personality. States can still enforce age restrictions and, in addition, check the moral character of the candidate by extensive background investigations. Reasons for in-depth analysis of potential police officers include the desire to increase the professional nature of policing as well as to reduce exposure to litigation concerning negligent hiring, negligent retention and negligent entrustment (Smith, 1995; Kappeler, 1993; Alpert, 1991; and Gaines, Costello and Crabtree, 1989). In other words, what has changed the most over the past 140 years is the way in which police departments screen potential recruits.

The first screening method used to predict success in police work was that of determining intelligence. It was initially suggested that a minimum intelligence quotient of 80 was required for employment as a police officer (Terman, 1917). Today, the ability to think in both abstract and well-defined ways has proven to be a necessary skill for police work. This ability is important, but it is not the only indicator by which candidates should be selected to become police officers and supervisors.

Applicants are now tested to assess other qualifications for police work. The goal is to make an appropriate evaluation of the candidate and his or her decision-making abilities or psychological traits. If this is not accomplished, there will be insufficient information known about the candidate. He or she may be hired but may not have the traits or predisposition to become a good officer. It is lack of information that causes the potential problems.

The process by which a person moves from applicant to police officer should be straightforward. First, one applies for the position. Upon receipt of an application, assuming there is an opening, the department or a civil service agency conducts several background investigations. These include inquiries into the applicant's education, work history, financial background and criminal history, as well as personal references. In addition, the applicant's psychological profile, based upon tests and a clinical evaluation is assessed. Finally, physical tests are conducted to determine health, strength, and height-weight proportion. If the applicant fits the criteria of one who is likely to be successful as a police officer or does not demonstrate any characteristics or attributes of one not likely to perform adequately as a police officer and meets all other departmental requirements, he or she may be advanced to the police academy for training. Before we discuss the issues surrounding ways in which police departments recruit, select and train their officers, a quick look at one police chief's experiences will illustrate the complexities of choosing and training police officers.

CHIEF'S CORNER
RECRUITMENT AND SELECTION

Over the past several years, it has been interesting to find that each generation of police officers claims that the academy just doesn't turn out quality cadets "like they did when I went through." I first noticed this complaint when increased numbers of minorities were being employed. The Anglo officers were certain that such employment practices, in response to affirmative action, were going to be the ruin of modern law enforcement.

Strangely enough, the complaints did not subside when large numbers of minorities were inducted into the mainstream of the organization. For they, too, began to perceive a lowering of quality and an easing of the military regimen required by the academy. It's apparent to me that no one feels that those coming after them ever had it as hard as they did.

The truth of the matter is that there are higher quality recruits turned out now in our department than there were ten, fifteen, and, especially, twenty-five years ago. Of the thirty-one recruits who were in my academy class in 1961, one was fired before graduation, one went to prison for bank robbery, one went to prison for smuggling narcotics, two were forced to resign in lieu of prosecution when it was suspected they were shaking down gamblers, and one was shot and killed by a prisoner whom he was allegedly physically abusing at the time. Strangely enough, members of my academy class were considered to be high-quality recruits when we graduated. We probably were, for I remember subsequent classes having a similar number of personnel problems.

It is very difficult to determine at the time of selection how people will react to the stresses and temptation that police work puts on them. However, my observation is that modern research has identified several indicators of success, such as personality traits, that go hand-in-hand with those who react in a more positive manner and who are able to withstand the stress to a greater degree. Because of such research, we have begun to see a distinct increase in the quality of police officers that are hired.

RECRUITING POLICE OFFICERS

Many citizens are interested in police work for the same reasons they enter other professions: status, rewards, the educational requirements, and the conditions of service. The general consensus among police officers is that job security, material benefits and the nature of police work influenced their decision to enter the profession (Walker, 1992). Unfortunately, many potential applicants learn about policing from television shows and movies and are shocked to learn what the job really requires. Consequently, recruitment information must be focused toward the potentially successful candidate and must also dispel some of the misconceptions held by the public. The recruiting of potential applicants does not usually receive the attention it deserves. In the late 1990s, recruitment efforts will be focused on several specialized groups, including women, minorities, college students, and experienced police officers.

The major problems in recruiting involve the number of available positions in relation to the number of available applicants. As in any profession, police departments must seek recruits who are likely to be successful candidates for the job openings. Attributes that are generally perceived as highly desirable include positive personality characteristics such as honesty, integrity, reliability, good communication skills, initiative, and intelligence. Basic human relations skills and motivation are also important. These traits are not necessarily distributed evenly among community members and, as a result, finding a pool of good applicants can be demanding. As Jennie Farley points out, "Where employers look for their applicants may well determine who they find" (1979:44). In addition, *how* recruiters look for their applicants can also influence who applies. The purpose of recruiting applicants was to locate the best persons for the job.

Currently, an important consideration for the recruitment of officers is the changing role of police in the community. Departments may no longer discriminate against women and minority group members. In fact, some departments are mandated to recruit women and minorities actively so the police force will reflect the demographic composition of the community. This requirement certainly affects where departments seek and how they recruit their applicants.

In the past, deliberate policies of discrimination and fixed selection criteria excluded many members of minority groups from police work. In 1972, Congress amended Title VII of the 1964 Civil Rights Act to include local and state governmental agencies. This meant that, officially, neither ethnicity nor gender could be used as selection criteria. Title VII was the most important legislative action taken to prohibit discrimination in employment. A series of Supreme Court decisions interpreting Title VII resulted in structured requirements for those involved in hiring (and promoting) police officers. Police agencies were required to demonstrate that their hiring procedures did not discriminate or show that any discrimination was a Bona Fide Occupational Qualification (BFOQ). That is, hiring or promoting decisions had to be non-discriminatory or based upon required job tasks. As a response to the law, pressure from minority groups, and a desire to have agencies mirror the community, self-imposed or court-imposed quotas were used for minorities. These regulations were established to force employers to select the best qualified applicants without discriminating against women and minorities (Gaines, Costello and Crabtree, 1989). The need to have an agency mirror the ethnic and gender of the community has required affirmative action. One unintended consequence of this action is that agencies often hire the best qualified persons—"on a representative basis" (Whisenhand, 1995:509).

In addition to these safeguards, required tests in an application process could not be discriminatory and must be job-related. In spite of these changes, many of those interested in careers in law enforcement believed that they were victims of discrimination. As a result, some of these disgruntled applicants sued the municipalities on the basis of under-representation. This meant that the courts, not the administrative unit or police department, often had to decide the ratio of male to female officers and the ratio of minority to nonminority group membership (Alpert, 1984). Population comparisons were frequently used to determine the impact of hiring and promoting practices. When challenged, few departments were able to deny allegations of discrimination, as demonstrating the non-discriminatory practices required a substantial amount of research (Alpert, 1991). Because of the increasing involvement of the judiciary, many major cities have come under court order to hire and/or promote minority group members. This development has drastically changed the way police departments recruit potential officers (see *Guardian Association of the New York Police Department v. Civil Service Commission of the City of New York*).

For many years, police agencies relied solely on advertising in the major media outlets and public-service commercials for recruitment. Now, however, many municipalities must hire a diverse group of candidates. Police recruiters seek candidates in various settings and programs, including high schools, colleges, shopping centers, parks, county fairs and community centers, among other locations. A police department is limited in its ability to seek potential candidates only by the imagination of its recruiting officers and by budget restrictions. These decisions, as Farley (1979) noted, certainly have an impact on who becomes a police recruit.

WOMEN

Recruiting female candidates is not substantially different from recruiting male candidates. As with any group, recruiting strategies among women must include a special effort to locate potential candidates. In some cases, females may be found in many of the same places potential male candidates are found, such as schools and community centers. A special emphasis may be placed on youth groups that cater to young women, including the YWCA, Camp Fire Girls, Girl Scouts and women's colleges. The recruiter must be prepared to answer questions about the role of females in what is considered a male-dominated profession. This line of questioning must be handled truthfully and carefully, as many potential officers can be mistakenly attracted or turned off to police work at this stage. Female police officers have made important contributions to policing, and their successes and potential for advancement should be emphasized. One of the major problems has been recruiting women to apply for police jobs. To be effective, a recruiting strategy should mirror the new opportunities which must be made available for women in policing (Martin, 1993). Although the numbers in the general populace do not reflect minority status, police departments classify women as minorities.

MINORITIES

The recruitment of minority applicants has become a very important part of policing in the 1990s. As police agencies create methods to screen applicants, they are tested either in the courts or by the Equal Employment Opportunity Commission (EEOC). Only those requirements or standards that are found to be clearly and fairly relevant to police work have been allowed to stand (Alpert, 1984). Since discriminatory practices have been in existence for so long and many ethnic groups are under-represented, a positive effort to rectify the situation has been undertaken. This positive effort is usually expressed in the form of an *affirmative action* plan or some method to remedy unfair practices, which occurred in the past, regarding hiring and promoting minority group members. As we mentioned earlier, if an agency has failed to implement a plan and is taken to court because of alleged discrimination, the court may require a plan to be submitted or may create a plan for the agency.

An excellent example of this type of action and relief comes from a Miami, Florida case. In this case, the city was sued for discriminatory practices (*United States v. City of Miami*), and the parties (the city and the federal government) agreed upon a settlement in the form of a consent decree. This agreement assured fairness and nondiscrimination in the selection and promotion of police officers. It required the Miami Police Department to operate in a manner consistent with the following testimony to the Miami Overtown Blue Ribbon Committee (1984:174-175):

> The [City] Commission added to the Police Department's budget . . . approximately 300 positions; 186 positions last year and 100 positions the year before. That's 286 positions, plus 50 positions to be added the first of April this year. Recognizing this statistically, we have found that only 20 percent of those people that apply actually become police officers; we knew we had to recruit over 1250 people to apply for these positions. The consent decree . . . states that we must actively try to make the police department reflect the makeup of the community, which indicates that we must target our recruitment effort. The [City] Commission, through formal action, adopted a policy that we must recruit 80 percent minorities and women, which meant that we were given some very strict parameters on how to do our recruiting.

The example cited above helps us understand the kinds of assistance the courts can provide to minority group members to counter past practices of discrimination. Specifically, Miami police officials agreed to recruit actively and to hire minority group applicants at a very high ratio to non-minority applicants. Another important issue in this case was the requirement to hire first those applicants who lived within the city of Miami.

Sometimes the court-ordered requirements placed on municipalities can be harsh and have negative ramifications, as well as positive influences. What happened in Miami helped to balance the police department ethnically, but the implementation of the decision has also led to lawsuits based upon reverse discrimination. That is, white males have suggested that they were not hired and were the target of discrimination simply because they were not members of a minority group. In addition, it has been claimed that the hiring requirements and practices decreed for the city of Miami created or aggravated many of the problems the department had faced during the past several years (Overtown Blue Ribbon Committee, 1984). We will discuss more of these problems and their possible relationship to affirmative action in our chapter on police corruption.

Recruiting minorities requires a focused effort similar to that required to recruit women. First, the recruiting message must be brought to the minority population, and the message must be communicated in a language and style the people understand. For example, a police recruiter who speaks Spanish is more likely to be influential with Hispanic young people than a recruiter who does not speak the language. Even more important than fluency in another language is a recruiter's understanding of the culture, social environment, attitudes and values of the minority community. Black, Hispanic, Native American or Asian youths do not necessarily possess the same attitudes toward society in general, or toward law enforcement specifically, as white, middle-class youths. Recruiters who do not share the same cultural background as the potential recruits must at least be trained to understand it (Farley, 1979). Finally, the message given to members of minority communities must be fair and honest and relate the opportunities, challenges and problems which will be experienced in police work.

COLLEGE STUDENTS

Recruiting college students for police work is difficult but should be a major part of an overall recruiting effort (see Reppetto, 1980). Whether or not police recruits should possess a college education is a controversial question for which there is no clear answer. On one hand, it is believed that a college-educated officer will be less cynical, less prejudiced, less authoritarian, less hostile and less likely to use force than a noncollege-educated officer. On the other hand, a college education may encourage dissatisfaction with the job, high rates of turnover and hostility toward noncollege-educated officers.

There is little doubt that a good, general education is helpful in any profession, but in terms of specific job preparation, there is no consensus. There is agreement, however, that a college education is helpful for promotions and preferential duty assignments. When recruiting college students, the emphasis should be on career advancement and the potential effect a college graduate can have on police and policing.

The most comprehensive study on higher education and the police is the Sherman Report (Sherman et al., 1978). This report concluded that significant changes in police and criminal-justice-related education were necessary to reach the goal of a college-educated police force. The report identified areas which required upgrading and improvement, including curriculum, faculty development and emphasis on general education rather than on specific vocational training. While this report generated active debate among law enforcement officials and academics, once again, no clear consensus was reached. The issues discussed in the Sherman Report relate to the general improvement in the quality of education. The specific conclusions were controversial for the police profession, but they are generally accepted as important stepping stones in higher education.

In 1989, Carter, Sapp and Stephens published *The State of Police Education*. On one hand, police administrators reported that college-educated officers are more likely than their less-educated counterparts to question orders, to request reassignments, to have lower morale and to exhibit more absenteeism. Further, this study noted that college-educated officers are more likely than others to become easily frustrated with bureaucratic procedures. On the other hand, the administrators reported that college-educated officers have a wider range of skills and are more effective than noncollege-trained officers. These educated officers are more likely to see the big picture, adapt more easily to change, have superior written and verbal skills, and maintain more relationships with those outside police work than officers with less formal education.

Requiring or providing more education for the officer is viewed as a necessary approach for the police administrator. The more educated an officer, the more likely that he or she will be an effective and efficient officer. The advantages of encouraging college-educated individuals to enter police work or requiring those in the field to increase their level of education far outweigh potential disadvantages. Any disadvantage of educating the police can be diminished by proper administration and management. The success of a police department depends upon its brightest stars. In the 1990s, there appears to be a trend whereby police departments will hire a recruit with some college course work over a candidate with none.

AMERICANS WITH DISABILITIES ACT

One of the most important anti-discrimination measures was signed into law on July 26, 1990. The Americans with Disabilities Act of 1990 (ADA) extends the basic protections of the Rehabilitation Act of 1973 to government and private industry (Rubin, 1994). Discrimination on the basis of disability will be prohibited by all governmental entities and all but the smallest private employers (Smith and Alpert, 1993). As it relates to hiring new officers and promoting old ones, the ADA prohibits discrimination of disabled persons who can perform the essential functions of the job in spite of their disability. Further, it establishes an affirmative duty to reasonably accommodate qualified disabled persons unless doing so would create an undue hardship. The screening procedures will have to accommodate disabled individuals, and testing will have to be performed in places available to disabled applicants. The substantive areas covered by ADA include physical agility tests, psychological examinations and drug testing. As insufficient time has passed for these issues to be interpreted by the law enforcement agencies and the courts, we can only speculate what "reasonably accommodate," and "undue hardship," will mean or how psychological testing will be affected by the ban on pre-employment medical examinations. The ADA will have a significant influence on the recruitment and selection of police officers in the late 1990s. It will also be an area that will require litigation to define its terms. In any case, police agencies will be receiving more applications from individuals who would have been routinely rejected in the past.

LATERAL ENTRY

One of the most difficult tasks in hiring potential police officers is the recruitment of officers with experience. Law enforcement is one of only a few professions that discourages the transfer of employees from one jurisdiction to another. Many agencies have policies against *lateral entry* and will not credit the training, experience, or time one has spent in another department. Most agencies that prohibit lateral movement cite that there are problems involved in the transfer of pensions and other personnel benefits or blame civil service regulations or state laws.

Another commonly heard explanation is that the few promotional opportunities that exist are guarded for those already in the department and that the different administrative policies, individual styles of policing, and the social environment are so different among jurisdictions that an officer with experience from one jurisdiction may have to be totally retrained to be competent in another jurisdiction.

It is true that each state has specific training requirements to become a licensed police officer, but there is a great deal of overlap among the various state requirements. Also, there are many common threads that exist among the experiences of policing, regardless of the specific police department. Common sense tells us that these experiences will transfer to a new social and legal environment with the help of training. Unfortunately, common sense does not always prevail over politics, and seldom do departments permit lateral transfers. Some major cities whose police departments have not kept up with urban growth, or whose force is very young, encourage lateral entry for a period of time to attract police officers with experience. These departments usually institute a shortened training session for officers with more than a year of police experience in other departments.*

Although recruiters and police administrators have little control over who applies for a job in their police department, they can seek out applications from certain groups of people and individuals. In addition, recruiters can familiarize youths interested in police work through a police cadet corps and through programs that permit observers to ride along with police officers or volunteer their time. As we noted from the Miami example, police administrators calculate that it may take twenty applicants to find one acceptable recruit; therefore, it is important to set a wide net to attract a large number of potential candidates.

The path from initial application to the police academy is a long one, and many serious decisions about applicants must be made. Although an individual who appears unsuited for police work may be discouraged from submitting an application, he or she may still apply. Similarly, it is not always obvious that an individual is unsuited. An applicant's suitability must be decided by some preliminary process of evaluation known as *selection*.

THE SELECTION PROCESS

After an application has been filed, the next step in the process includes selecting candidates to move ahead to lengthy and expensive training. The basic steps the law enforcement agency will follow include making sure that the applicant fits the profile established by the civil service board or individual police department. This is accomplished by a review of the application, a series of background investigations, a lie-detector test, a physical, and an oral interview. The bottom line is a series of hurdles one must get through or over.

CLEARING THE HURDLES

The traditional method of selecting recruits to be trained from a group of applicants involves the use of several, or a series of, tests. Stone and DeLuca describe the multiple-hurdle procedure as follows:

*It is interesting to note that many chiefs and administrators are hired from other departments. Lateral entry is discouraged for those at the lower and middle stages of their careers.

The tests used vary from one agency to the next, and the order in which the tests are applied also varies. However, a typical sequence might begin with a written test that the applicant must pass with a specified minimum score. Those who fail the written test are immediately dismissed; those who pass the written test are then given a thorough physical examination; those who pass it are required to complete a physical agility test. After that, some agencies either use a written psychological test or applicants are interviewed by a clinical psychologist or psychiatrist. Each test or "hurdle" produces a clear pass-or-fail decision; those who fail any one test are not allowed to continue. (Stone and DeLuca, 1985:296)

Each department may vary its tests or hurdles and the sequential order of evaluative items somewhat. Assuming that the first hurdle is a written application, it will be obvious if an applicant fits a number of the initial criteria. A quick review of the form can determine if the applicant's characteristics are appropriate and fit the selection profile. If the characteristics correspond, the candidate moves to the next step.

Whether or not some applicants meet other criteria is not so easy to determine. For example, a good moral character is a vague concept but must somehow be determined. One of the issues currently being debated is an applicant's history of drug use. If an applicant has experimented with marijuana and tells the truth, is that not a sign of a good moral character? If an applicant has smoked marijuana only once, but has lied about it on the application, is that a sign of a good or faulty character? This list of possible scenarios could be expanded, and each would end with a big question mark. Excessive drug use, along with other serious criminal activity, will prevent an individual from being selected to attend training. Once the applicant passes over this hurdle and meets this set of requirements, he or she is given a series of paper-and-pencil tests to help the agency predict if the applicant can become a competent police officer.

METHODS OF SCREENING

Psychological screening for entry-level recruits has been an established goal for police agencies for quite some time. In 1967, the President's Commission on Law Enforcement and Administration of Justice (110) suggested that all police recruits should be tested to help determine their emotional fitness and stability. By 1973, the need for psychological testing had increased to the point that the National Advisory Commission on Criminal Justice Standards and Goals suggested that (338):

Police officers are subject to great emotional stress, and they are placed in
positions of trust. For these reasons, they should be very carefully screened
to preclude the employment of those who are emotionally unstable, brutal,
or who suffer from any form of emotional illness. A growing number of
police agencies have turned to psychological screening to eliminate those
who are emotionally or otherwise unfit for the police service.

The paper-and-pencil test used to screen candidates is related to the duties
a police officer will perform. The respondent's answers are used to predict
whether or not he or she will become a competent police officer. The goals of
the screening process are twofold. First, these procedures should identify
characteristics which can predict good police officers. This goal, known as
"selecting-in," identifies those individuals best suited for police work. The
purpose of this screening and testing is to provide, without discrimination, the
best candidates for entry level and promotions. Second, the test must eliminate
or "screen out" those applicants who are unfit for police work. This must be
accomplished despite the fact that there is no accepted definition of a competent
police officer. Further, there is no written rule regarding what qualities are
necessary to increase competence (Burbeck and Furnham, 1985).

It was not until 1980 and *Guardian Association of the New York Police
Department, Inc. v. Civil Service Commission of the City of New York* (1980)
that a court interpreted and analyzed the creation and implementation of a
psychological test used to screen police officers. The court commented in detail
on the need to conduct task analyses and to avert any adverse impact on
protected groups from testing. In other words, no test is acceptable if it
discriminates against a minority group. The court laid the foundation for others
to follow in the creation, validation, implementation and interpretation of
psychological tests.

Three types of validity issues are recognized as important to fulfill this
goal. They include content, criterion and construct validity (Carmines and
Zeller, 1979; Maxfield and Babbie, 1995). Content validity implies the test
elements represent the tasks required of the position. A test with criterion-re-
lated validity predicts future on-the-job behavior (predictive validity) and
requires a comparison of scores with job performance. A test with construct
validity establishes the purity and consistency of measures.

Unfortunately, one of the unintended consequences of this form of testing
is that methods of employee selection tend to rely more on disparate theory or
the notion of adverse impact than the hiring and promoting of the best candidates (Alpert, 1991). Therefore, two related problems must be addressed: the
definition of a competent police officer and the validity of the tests that are used

to determine that competence. What makes a good, stable or suitable police officer depends on who is asking the question and for what purpose. Allen Brenner (1989:77) has offered the following answer:

> The answer to "who or what is a good, stable, or suitable police officer" is . . . situational. An officer who needs to get information about a crime from the denizens of skid row acts differently from the officer who is trying to elicit information from a distraught mother whose three-year-old child is lost. Similarly, an officer who is called to break up a barroom brawl acts differently than the officer called to deal with a juvenile delinquency problem. Finally, the officer who takes a crime report from a family needs to act differently when stopping the same family in their vehicle for a violation. The dynamics of the situation and perspectives of those involved determine their assessment of whether the officer they encountered was "good, stable or suitable."
> An individual officer may be called upon to perform in each of these situations. The likelihood that he or she will "measure up" to the public's expectations in all cases is very unlikely.

One author has summed up the problems of identifying the prospects of a good police officer as follows (Fyfe, 1994:114):

> The requirements for entry into an occupation . . . should be those that best predict satisfactory job performance. But the absence of clearly articulated standards for assessing police effectiveness means that police entry requirements can be no more than guesses about which candidates are likely to be abusive, to beget scandals, or . . . create legal liability . . . Some police candidates are screened out on the basis of bizarre personal histories or criminal records. Others, however, survive this screening and demonstrate their lack of suitability for policing only after they have been locked into it by civil service tenure.

Going back to an earlier point, it is easier to be specific about what is not wanted in an officer. A "bad," "unstable," or "unsuitable" officer is more easily recognized than a good one.

In what appears to be the most exhaustive review of the literature on police officer selection and the individual psychological tests used for selection, Burbeck and Furnham (1985:64-65) report that:

> . . . no test has been found that discriminates consistently and clearly between people who will make good police officers and those who will not . . . even when psychological testing is used to screen out, rather than screen in, the results are not reliable or particularly predictive of future performance as a police officer.

Because of the many questions raised by the research that has been conducted on the psychological tests and their interpretations, many law enforcement agencies have modified their hurdles. For example, an investigation into the recruiting and selection processes of the Miami Police Department concluded that ". . . the psychological tests used by the Department of Human Resources to select police officers may be providing scores which mean something other than their current interpretations, or scores which mean nothing at all. It is imperative that the City of Miami Police Department not be forced to hire or be precluded from hiring someone based on the faulty interpretation of a test" (Overtown Blue Ribbon Committee, 1984:178). Police departments are always looking for a more predictive test and a better way of selecting police officers. Many departments will not eliminate an applicant who has scored poorly on one test but well on another. These departments often provide remedial assistance for these applicants. It is hoped that with this extra help, the applicant will increase the needed skills and perform adequately when tested a second time. This provides another chance for those who do not take tests well, but also opens the door for advancing an applicant to police training who is not adequately suited.

The Independent Commission on the Los Angeles Police Department (1991) (Christopher Commission), which reviewed the events surrounding the beating of Rodney King, determined that psychological evaluation is an inexact predictor of an applicant's behavior. The Commission raised concerns about psychological screening which takes place only prior to becoming a police officer. Their point was that emotional and psychological problems may or may not exist before one becomes a police officer. A test at this point is designed to screen out applicants with serious problems. One suggestion made by the Commission which will be discussed in chapter 6, is that police work may create or bring out manifestations of emotional or psychological problems (which could not be detected by earlier tests). Therefore, the Commission urged regular re-testing of officers for fitness-for-duty. Recently, Grant and Grant (1995) reviewed officer selection issues and tests. They concluded:

> . . . we cannot be sure that the tests we use to describe mental health give us an accurate picture of the individual's psychological condition. A further problem is that responses to test items may change over time. We cannot answer questions such as: How permanent are the "personality" responses of the officer following recruitment? How much do these measures reflect permanent personality traits and how much do they reflect changing situations and attitudes? (1995:154–155, citations omitted)

One approach that has gotten away from relying on these controversial tests is the use of an *assessment center*. This technique of assessing job-related behavior characteristics was first used in a military environment and adopted by law enforcement in the 1970s (see O'Leary, 1995). Departments using this method bring groups of applicants to a central location and put them through a series of assessments, including intelligence and other paper-and-pencil tests. Those who fit the desired profile based on the first-level tests, progress to the next three stages of assessment which include: observation, scoring, and discussion. First, a recruit participates in simulated activities and role-playing. These activities are created scenarios that are designed to get a person to respond, and are discussed below. Second, a group of assessors individually take notes and score the recruit's actions and activities. The assessors have specific categories on which to evaluate the applicant's ability to perform police-related tasks. Third, the assessors (usually there are three to five from different backgrounds and a police administrator) are brought together to discuss the recruit's performance. This process, which includes performance in several different situations, provides the applicant with a wide opportunity to demonstrate his or her potential to be a good police officer and gives the assessors a way to provide the agency with the most accurate description of the applicant's skill and potential. One specific example comes from the Ft. Collins and Colorado State University assessment center:

> . . . the applicant [was] brought to the testing room and given a gun belt to wear. He or she was then briefly instructed in handcuffing and frisk procedure and was handed a card on which minimal instructions were typed. An example would be, "You are driving on patrol in the downtown area when you notice a young man (approximately 25 years of age) prying at a parking meter with a screwdriver. It is 4:45 P.M. Do your duty."

> When the applicant had read and understood the card, he or she entered the room in which an irate citizen was kicking and prying at the parking meter. The "theme" that the confederate followed in this situation was that he had been looking for a parking place for 15 minutes and that, when he finally found one, his nickel jammed in the meter. . . . (Filer, 1979:224)

Other common examples of exercises used in assessment centers include the domestic fight, a routine traffic stop and a barroom disturbance. Individual assessment centers have drawn on real-life experiences of local police officers which can bring reality to the evaluation. Further, not all scenarios require a tough, macho response. One example is a situation in which a police officer responds to a call at a home where an elderly woman wants to report a home burglary. While she is unharmed, she is visibly upset. It is the officer's responsibility to help her, but the officer must also answer the other calls on his radio. Each time the officer attempts to leave, she begs him to stay, offers him coffee and may even begin to cry. In this scenario, the assessors grade the recruit on how he or she handles the situation, balancing a humanitarian concern for the woman's fear with the need to return to answer other calls.

The assessment center method can provide new opportunities to assess the actual responses of applicants to stressful scenarios. During the past few years, research has been initiated on the success rate of this technique. Although no definitive results have been reported in the literature, the assessment center method appears to be an important tool for police recruiters, trainers and evaluators. Assessment centers can also be used to assist with promotions and the identification of common deficiencies among officers of all ranks.

Regardless of the method used, many applicants will not make it past the initial screening process. Some will receive remedial assistance and still not make it to the academy. The successful applicants will be selected for formal police training. For these individuals, it may appear that they have "made it." However, as we will see, they too may be disqualified.

POLICE TRAINING

The selection of appropriate candidates for training is the first step in the making of good police officers. *Initial training* at the academy is the second step, and the various forms of *in-service training* are also necessary as a third step in the development of good police officers. Training, in its many forms, is the one tool that is necessary for creating and maintaining the effectiveness of police performance, both individual and organizational. As Richard Holden puts it, "One cannot expect adequate policing from untrained officers regardless of their dedication" (Holden, 1986:231).

In 1965, The International Association of Chiefs of Police (IACP) discovered that only approximately 15 percent of all police agencies provided their recruits with any training or required training before an individual was given a badge, a gun, a set of rules and was told to go out on the streets (Kuykendall and Usinger, 1975). Although that has changed in the last thirty-two years, training required for police recruits still varies greatly from one agency to another and from one state to another. The vastly disparate training has discouraged any lateral movement among police officers and has slowed the acceptance of policing as a profession. A brief discussion of these differences is presented below.

Fortunately, the training of police officers in the 1990s has become a top priority. More effort and financial resources are being allocated to training than ever before, but these problems cannot be solved merely by financial means. Training needs to be appropriate and of high quality; untrained or poorly trained officers cannot police adequately. In other words, police training must be ethically bound and legally and morally defensible (Alpert and Smith, 1990).

Sheehan and Cordner (1995:81) have identified several dichotomies concerning the approaches to police training:

> The police training task can be broken down into a number of different approaches: in-class and on-the-job training, physical and mental training, formal and informal, theoretical and practical training, recruit and in-service training, and specific and general training.

These approaches can all be utilized in the training and instruction of the new cadet (and the experienced officer). One of the first tasks of the academy is to orient the individual to law enforcement. As we have noted, many enter police work with pre-conceived notions about police work. The initial orientation, which should provide a realistic impression of the field, sets the scene for other learning and education. Without a good orientation, police training can be viewed by the officers as a mechanism of constraint. This perspective reinforces a defensive posture of training which can only be seen as reactive and outdated when compared to a proactive or interactive training model. Obviously, the proactive approach is most beneficial to officers and citizens alike, as it fosters appropriate preparation and reduces officer anxiety.

The building blocks of a good law enforcement training program are anchored to two common assumptions: First, the programs should incorporate the proper statement of mission and ethical considerations; and second, training should be based on what an officer does on a daily basis (Alpert and Smith, 1990; Bayley and Bittner, 1989).

It is the mission of the police to protect life; all duties and responsibilities must be controlled by this consideration. Police officers must understand that their actions represent governmental interests and must be guided by integrity and values that place the highest priority on life first and property second. The behavior of the police must influence positive support of the public. Some type of job performance study must be conducted and its results integrated into the police training curricula. In other words, until it is known what precisely officers do or are expected to do, it is impossible to train them to do it. There

CHIEF'S CORNER
TRAINING

There are numerous factors which affect the probability that a police department will successfully carry out its mission. Training is by far the most important. I have experienced and observed the evolution of training from where it was generally thought to be a waste of time once you got out of the academy to the current state where it is or should be scheduled on a regular basis through an officer's career.

With the development of training as a prime element of a department's operation, I have seen organizations develop professionally from second-rate to first-rate departments. This has happened in organizations which utilize modern teaching techniques such as video presentations and role-playing. These techniques have become so successful because they both hold the officers' attention, as well as assist them in visualizing what it is that the administration wants them to learn. For example, our department was experiencing a number of complaints of discourtesy concerning the manner in which officers were conducting traffic stops. In response, we developed a training program which utilized the video replay of officers as they simulated traffic stops with other officers and actors. The officers were amazed at how they came across when they viewed themselves in such situations. Instead of looking and acting professional as many thought themselves to be, they realized that, in many instances, they were acting abrupt and brusque. Through such training we were able to reduce our citizen complaints drastically. I think such hands-on training is going to become one of the most important and positive developments law enforcement will experience in the next several years.

Another area that seems vitally important is the total development of the officer throughout his or her career. As officers are promoted upward within the organization, there is a definite trend towards less and less formal training. For example, many departments no longer require their officers to attend formal training and only train or educate through bulletins, memoranda, roll-call, and seminars with other law enforcement officers. As a result, law enforcement managers tend to be inbred in their thinking and are short-changed by not being exposed to state-of-the-art training.

Modern management concepts utilized by the private business sector are another tool from which police managers could benefit. Because law enforcement agencies are becoming more and more of a business, certain decisions must be made due to budgetary constraints. Resource management and discretionary decision making requires that managers take advantage of knowledge and experiences outside the traditional police management training but common to other large-scale organizations.

As you can see, I believe training is vital. Yet no amount of training can overcome the damage inflicted by a poor first-line supervisor or Field Training Officer. In the case of a supervisor who does not respect that position or appreciate the organization, he or she will allow sloppy work or display questionable integrity, which directly affects the performance of those within that command. If the supervisor doesn't believe in the role of the trainer, he or she will not set the parameters of behavior necessary to ensure effective police work, and, eventually, that negative influence will erode the abilities of even those officers who want very badly to do well.

Field Training Officers (FTOs) are also a vital link to successful training. Along with first-line supervisors, they must be carefully selected and indoctrinated with the department's philosophy of service. Time and again, I have seen very poor officer performance which can be traced back to the FTO of that particular officer. In law enforcement, we have talked about this phenomenon many times. Show me an officer who had an FTO who was unmotivated, disruptive, suspicious of management and lacked integrity, and I will more than likely show you an officer who has these same attributes. It seems that new officers are so impressionable at the time that FTOs get them that they quickly develop like patterns of behavior that are very difficult to change even through subsequent training. That is why it is advisable to utilize several FTOs so that the new officer is exposed to a range of behavior from which to choose the most appropriate course of action.

must be an agreement between high-frequency or high-risk activities and intense training. It would be inefficient to provide intensive training for infrequent duties that are not life supporting. For example, if a department rarely serves civil papers, it would be unproductive to devote more than cursory attention to civil process instruction. Time restraints and training costs dictate that priorities be established and receive appropriate attention (Alpert and Smith, 1990). In the 1990s, it is also necessary to prepare police officers to think as well as to respond or act. In other words, it is important to prepare officers for tasks that may not be commonplace today but will be required in the near future. For example, it will be important for all officers to know the elements of problem solving and community-oriented policing. These strategies should be introduced at the academy and made a part of the recruits' culture.

Most police officers receive their training in police academies that are administered through community or junior colleges. Other academies are located in four-year universities or by themselves. Regardless of the structure, there are several related questions dealing with the content of the curriculum that need to be addressed. These include: what are the skills, information and attitudes that one must develop to be a good police officer and what are the most efficient and effective methods to provide the necessary training and education?

THE ACADEMY

These are not new questions; progressive law enforcement officials have been asking them and proposing answers since the need for formal training was acknowledged more than a century ago. It is now generally accepted that the development of any training program should be based upon the current and future needs of the potential officers. Training is not an end in itself, but rather a means of producing good police officers. Police training must be viewed as a dynamic, changing process. What was thought to be an important tool for the police during the 1960s may have become irrelevant or unnecessary in the 1990s. Similarly, as innovative techniques are developed, they must be passed on to new recruits. Many variations on the traditional theme developed originally by the IACP have been created, analyzed, and implemented among the various jurisdictions. Today, there exists such a diverse spectrum of training programs in both quantity and quality that it is possible to discuss police training only in general terms.

In most academies, the formal training is heavily weighted toward the technical aspects of police work. While there are model curricula, major differences exist among the states and within the states. Generally, police recruit training includes the following:

1. orientation to policing;
2. criminal and procedural laws;
3. traffic laws and investigation;
4. vehicle operation and patrol procedures;
5. criminal investigation;
6. techniques of arrest and control;
7. physical training;
8. weapons training;
9. courtroom training; and
10. policies and procedures.

Each category can include a variety of specific issues and responsibilities. Different states and agencies require different levels of training. For example, ethics can be included as a separate category or discussed in the various areas of policing. Vehicle operations can include pursuit driving as well as defensive driving, and weapons training can emphasize decision-making skills as well as target acquisition. Some states require less than 200 hours of training while others mandate almost 1,000 hours of training (Gaines, et al., 1994). Similarly, some agencies require only the state mandated minimum while others have additional requirements. A recent trend in the progressive academies is to include some instruction on the elements of community-oriented policing and problem-solving policing.

Police academies differ in structure as well as style and content. Some academies serve the whole state (South Carolina), while others serve regions of a state (Florida), and others are run by the specific agency (New York City). Of course, some of the differentiation is based on size and demand. However, the structure of the academy also influences its content. Some academies serve states, regions or singular agencies; some have instructors as full-time staff; still others use a variety of instructors who are "on loan" from the police agencies.

Each recruit must pass the requirements of the academy to graduate. Many academies insist that the recruit pass all courses the first time to graduate. Other academies have built-in provisions for remedial training to help marginal students pass. Remedial training has become a controversial issue, as it is claimed that some recruits receive preferential treatment.

As mentioned earlier, states vary considerably in their structure, style and content. For example, Florida requires a minimum of 450 hours of training; across the state line to the north, the state of Alabama requires only 240 hours of academy training (Alabama State Statutes § 36–21–46). In fact, the state of Alabama permits officers to work the streets *without* any training for a period of nine months. The statute (§ 36–21–46 [3]) reads:

> Prior to appointment, the applicant shall have completed at least 240 hours of formal police training in a recognized police training school . . . approved by the commission; provided, that an applicant may be *provisionally appointed without having completed the police training prescribed in this subdivision, subject to the condition that he shall complete such training within nine months after provisional appointment*; and should he fail to complete such training, his appointment shall be null and void (emphasis added).

It is difficult to understand why a state would permit a police officer to work the street, even provisionally, without any formal training. This is reminiscent of the days when officers were given a gun, a badge and a rule book and told to go enforce the laws. Fortunately, this practice is not common, and soon all police officers will be trained before they are permitted to work the streets. There is no justification or defense for this deliberate indifference to training. In any case, it is necessary to check your own state laws to determine the mandatory minimum. Similarly, each agency should inform its recruits of what training it requires. The training received at the academy represents the *minimum* and should be considered only the beginning of a career in law enforcement.

Regardless of the total number of hours and specific content of the training, the police academy is an experience that plays a significant role in shaping the officer's attitudes about policing in general, the specific tasks that will have to be performed, and the role of police in society. Upon entry into the academy, recruits are usually anxious about the training, concerned about performance, and uncertain about what is expected of them. Studies indicate that they are however, confident that their accomplishments to-date are substantial, and success is all but guaranteed. John Van Maanen (1983:390) informs us that this perception is not necessarily reality:

> The individual usually feels upon swearing allegiance to the department, city, state and nation that "he's finally made it." However, the department instantaneously and somewhat rudely informs him that until he has served his probationary period he may be severed from the membership rolls at any time without warning, explanation or appeal. It is perhaps ironic that in a period of a few minutes, a person's position vis-a-vis the organization can be altered so dramatically.

As the education and training begin, the recruits adopt a new identity. This includes uniforms, badges, weapons and, more important, a system of discipline which teaches them to take orders and not to question authority. A successful experience at the academy provides police recruits with certain attitudes about police and policing. Outside the classroom, recruits spend hours discussing the material, the "war stories" they have heard, and their possible interpretations. From the formal classes and informal discussions, collective understandings about policing begin to form and the emotional reality of police work starts to take shape. The recruits gradually develop a common understanding of law enforcement, a common language with which they express themselves, and a common set of interests from which they learn.

THE FACETS OF TRAINING

The rookie officer who emerges from the academy is a product of his or her past experiences and the nature and quality of the training received. Proactive training must include skills but must also emphasize decision making. Peter Manning remarked about twenty years ago that (1977:289): "the striking thing about order-maintenance methods is how little they are taught, how cynically they are viewed, and how irrelevant they are thought to be in most police departments." Unfortunately, there has been little change in this area during the past nineteen years. This lack of change can be attributed to the style of instruction provided at the academies.

Police training must emphasize the need and ability to make decisions. First, it is important to demonstrate to a recruit *why* specific training is required. In most situations, the need for "nuts and bolts" training can be made obvious with good examples and innovative techniques including advanced computer-driven teaching tools. However, the justification for ambiguous and boring aspects of police training are often lost to the recruit. For example, human relations or ethnic diversity training is an area in which many recruits feel confident and few trainers know how to instruct. This combination often results in a confusing and boring curriculum.

One way to attack this problem of lethargy is to send recruits (and trainers) to an area populated by members of other ethnic groups and to have them ask a simple question such as directions to a public telephone or convenience store. In most cases, it will become clear to these young recruits that they can benefit from learning how to talk and deal with members of other ethnic groups. Using examples of cultural diversity, recruits can be shown "why" just as easily as "how." Recruits can benefit in other areas when removed from the classroom and placed in situations, real or created, which make them think. Bayley and Bittner (1989:103) have noted that:

> . . . formal training programs must give more attention to the problematic
> nature of police work. Oddly, police keep talking as if policing were a
> craft, but recruits are instructed as if it were a science. . . . What is needed
> in police training . . . is frank discussion, with case studies of the realities
> of the field decision. Training in academies is too much like introductory
> courses in anatomy in medical schools and not enough like internships.

Academy training must bring the realities of police work into the classroom so that recruits can understand the objectives of their training and proper methods to achieve them. Recruits must be trained to observe and distinguish cues meant to elicit decisions or responses from those that have little meaning.

This can be achieved by discussing written scenarios found in assessment centers. More advanced training could utilize real-life experiences of officers in the department. Video tapes of re-enactments with a discussion led by the involved officers could be a very helpful tool. Simply providing the details of one's experience or telling war stories must be avoided. Further, the recruit must be provided enough information and sufficient experiences as well as a forum to start asking a variety of "what-if" questions.

Only recently has the academy started providing training in values (Kleinig, 1990; Delattre, 1989). As we mentioned earlier, ethics is appropriately finding its way onto the curriculum. Patrick Murphy, a former police commissioner of New York reported, "[I]nsufficient guidance has been available to those who must grapple with the moral implications involved in resolving disputes, confronting violence, making arrests, issuing citations, detaining disturbed persons, separating families, protecting children, aiding the poor, and other confrontations with unpredictable behavior" (Murphy, 1989:xiv). That is, the nature of law enforcement includes interaction with people in crisis situations combined with the authority to use force when necessary. Under these circumstances, the ordinary constraints of morality and conventional values may have little meaning. Thus, officers must be prepared for extraordinary situations.

Training in values must provide the officer with the ability to understand a situation from the perspective of others and to realize the various consequences of their own reactions. As most officers who enter police work have moral convictions, a curriculum should emphasize the importance of morality and the strengthening of one's values. It is important to build integrity and character so the potentially corrupting influences of experience are minimized (Kleinig, 1990). Values in policing are important as they represent beliefs which guide the mission and general perspective of a police department. Kelling et al., (1988:3) provide an interesting example:

> ... [L]oyalty to peers can conflict with the maintenance of high standards of professional practice. When police officers decide to close their eyes to the incompetence or corruption of colleagues and draw the "blue curtain" around them, they choose the value of loyalty to peers over the other values, such as quality service to the community. In many police departments, other values, some explicit and others implicit, can be identified that shape and drive police performance: "stay out of trouble," "we are the finest," "machismo," "serve and protect," and many others.

It is important for recruits to establish early in their careers the appropriate values that will influence their behavior. It is the police academy that serves as the first and most influential point at which these values are introduced.

The academy also leaves the recruit with a new attitude about those people who are not police officers. It is this process of social adjustment that influences the newly formed "police personality" of the recruit. With new attitudes learned while in the academy, the young officer moves to the streets.

TRAINING IN THE FIELD

Field training is a relatively new approach to training police officers. It was not until the 1970s that training was taken to the field! Although recruits should have been exposed to a number of real-life experiences during academy training, these have been created for training or role-play scenarios. In almost all agencies, recruits are sent to the field for additional training. This on-the-job training, or field training, is meant to bridge the gap between the protected environment of the academy and the isolated, open danger of the street. The new officer, or "rookie," is hired for a probationary period ranging from one month to two years. The typical period is six months. As Van Maanen informed us, during a probationary assignment, an officer has few rights. This young officer is under a great deal of pressure to satisfy the expectations of the supervisors.

There exists a long-standing concern in policing that each rookie is told by an experienced officer to forget what was learned at the academy and to just watch and learn how things are done right. The message is that the formal training just received at the academy is irrelevant or unrealistic. A consequence of this advice is the erosion of the confidence the rookies have just developed and the possibility that a rookie, eager to please a superior, will take the advice literally and learn some very bad habits. Different departments handle their new officers in many ways, but there is always some ceremony of initiation. One example of the "ritual" a recruit might encounter is the advice from an older officer on the midnight shift to take turns driving and sleeping. The traditional prank has the new recruit take the first nap while the older officer patrols the beat. After the recruit falls asleep, the officer drives quietly to headquarters, and the rookie awakens to the ridicule of his or her sergeant.

During the 1970s, field training became the most acceptable method of promoting a rookie to officer. Today, most modern departments around the country provide rookie training through a field-training officer (FTO) model.

This model places the young graduate in the hands of an older, more experienced police officer (or series of officers) who teaches the rookie how to survive and, ideally, how to become a good police officer. It is a serious responsibility to mold a new officer into an experienced one. It is important to select FTOs who are good teachers as well as good officers. Police organizations must not allow new officers to be molded into stereotypical macho, tough-guy, images. In other words, field training should be an extension of the formal training learned at the academy. It should help the recruit apply the knowledge he or she has gained from the academy.

Field training programs are often divided into several phases. Although agencies vary the length and scope of their field training, all programs should include introductory, training and evaluation phases (McCampbell, 1989). The introductory phase is structured to teach the rookie officer about the agency's policies, procedures and local laws and ordinances. Departmental customs and practices are also communicated at this time. During the training and evaluation phases, the young officer is gradually introduced to complex tasks which require involved and complicated decisions. The young officer will have to interpret and translate into action what was learned in the academy and the field. He or she will be forced to make decisions on what was absorbed from the classroom instruction as well as what has been observed in the field. Each decision and action will be evaluated by the training officer. Eventually, the rookie officer handles calls without assistance from the field-training officer.

A major issue is the selection and remuneration of the FTO. Not only should this officer be a volunteer, a good teacher and an officer with experience, but he or she should be well trained in the evaluation techniques accepted by the department. The two major roles of the FTO include training and evaluation. This is why a young officer should be exposed to several FTOs on several different assignments. One Commission report noted that:

> . . . to become FTOs, officers should be required to pass written and oral tests designed to measure communication skills, teaching aptitude, and knowledge of departmental policies . . . Officers with an aptitude for and interest in training junior officers should be encouraged by effective incentives to apply for FTO positions. In addition, the training program for FTOs should be modified to place greater emphasis on communication skills . . . Successful completion of FTO School should be required before an FTO begins teaching probationers. (The Independent Commission on the Los Angeles Police Department, 1991:xvii–xviii)

The evaluation of a rookie should be from several individuals looking at different experiences. These independent evaluations can be combined to determine the suitability of the young officer and what the first assignment should be. After an officer has passed the probationary period, he or she may think training is over. Many departments do not end their training here, but require refresher courses, training on new issues and other sorts of in-service training.

IN-SERVICE TRAINING

Many states have now mandated in-service training for police in the same way lawyers and teachers must continue their education. In-service training is designed to provide officers with new skills and changes in laws, policies or procedures. Also, since many skills learned at the academy or while in field training are perishable, in-service training can refresh an officer's skills. Some agencies send officers to lengthy management schools or specialized training. It is hard to believe that some agencies do not train veteran officers aggressively. Police work is constantly changing, and remaining a good police officer is different from becoming one.

There are several methods to provide in-service training to officers. First, large agencies can create and maintain their own in-service academies. For example, the Metro-Dade Police Department in Dade County, Florida, has established a full-service academy and requires each sworn officer to attend at least one training session four times each year. This quarterly training includes changes in rules, procedures or tactics. Additionally, the training bureau selects special topics for training. In the past few years, these topics have included the use of force, pursuit driving skills, and police-citizen encounters, among others. It is the purpose of these sessions to update the officers and standardize the responses of the more than 2,700 sworn personnel.

Agencies which are not able to build or maintain an in-service academy have other options. Agencies can bring in trainers to train the officers or can designate a training officer(s) to attend selected seminars and conferences and present the material to his or her officers. Changes in the laws, policies or other rules can be disseminated by short presentations, hand-outs or other printed documents. Some departments use video presentations to update officers on a variety of issues. Agencies can use short radio training sessions which takes advantage of down time to broadcast information over the radio. Many agencies rely on roll calls, printed documents, and word-of-mouth to inform the officers of any changes in the department's operating procedures. In the late 1980s, a cable network was created exclusively for the training of police officers. Based upon an idea developed by the FBI, Law Enforcement Television Network (LETN) has filled a void in small departments which cannot afford to send their officers to conferences or seminars. LETN has produced and presented programs about training in police tactics and current methods. The programs are available on a rotating basis during the day and night.

Another use of in-service training is to remedy deficiencies noted in officer evaluations. Experienced officers may be lacking in one or more skills or attributes. Whether an officer is overweight or out-of-shape, a poor shot, uses poor judgment, or is too socialized into the police subculture to provide good community policing, in-service training can be used to restore skills or to improve attitude. Data compiled from assessment centers or from the collective evaluations of officers can be used to address common issues in quarterly training or other in-service training.

If conducted properly, in-service training can provide a critical component to the agency's training scheme. There must be training for supervisors and managers, communication specialists and investigators. In other words, patrol officers need certain skills and those on specialized assignments need others. Some skills, such as those used in the control of persons, emergency vehicle operations and other high-risk activities, need more frequent and in-depth training than more routine tasks (Alpert and Smith, 1991). Officers must not only be provided with proper information but they must be given the opportunity to ask "what if" questions of the instructor. Further, officers must pass an examination before it can be assumed that he or she knows the information and is competent to practice it.

Many police departments have integrated computers, e-mail, and distance education into their training programs. Computer-based learning has become part of many academies, and most rely on some type of computer-driven decision training. As agencies begin to accept reports from laptop computers, officers are being trained in their efficient use and analytical capabilities. Software programs are being developed and improved that allow agencies to do important functions that range from instant crime analysis and typing to voice recognition reporting.

The Internet has provided a new forum for training police officers. First, many departments are creating home pages which provide information about the agency and the community served. There are also many "chat rooms" which allow individuals to share information and have "discussions" about many topics and issues. Innovative trainers can take advantage of these technological advancements for the improvement of their officers' knowledge and experience.

The expense of training is one of the real issues many departments must consider. Not only is it costly to evaluate needs, to plan and to provide for training, but it is very expensive to remove officers from the streets to be trained. In the short term, the expenses are great, but, in the long term, the training and its related costs are beneficial.

SUMMARY

The process of recruiting, selecting and training police officers is complex and confusing. Many decisions must be made that are dependent upon issues outside the police department. For example, recruitment from target populations requires strategies different from those used for recruitment from the general population. The selection of applicants based on results from paper-and-pencil tests can lead to recruits who may be inappropriate for police work. In many cases, these decisions are made by municipal employees who are not involved directly with the police department and who may not be aware of the specific qualities desired by police administrators. Training police officers requires hundreds of hours of intense classroom work and fieldwork in many areas. After successful completion of an academy program, however, many recruits are still not prepared to be on the streets with a badge and a gun (see Carter et al., 1989). In fact, a recent study by the International Association of Chiefs of Police (1989:53) noted:

> There is no guarantee that an individual of good character, hired by a police department, will remain honest. There are a variety of factors, different for each individual, which can erode an officer's commitment to integrity. Many officers face temptation every day. Fortunately, most do not succumb. . . . Management has the capacity and control to reinforce high integrity, detect corruption, and limit the opportunity for wrongdoing.

Department administrators must plan for these and other concerns and try to meet them before problems are created. This chapter has focused only upon the beginning stages of police work; the career development stages will be discussed in subsequent chapters. As in any bureaucratic organization, both responsibilities and rewards for police tend to flow upwards, so we turn next to how police departments are organized and administered. As we will see, the social environment within which the police operate can affect their organizational form, administrative style, and the police officers' responsibilities and rewards.

References

Alfers, Kenneth. 1975. "The Washington Police: A History, 1800–1866." Unpublished Dissertation, George Washington University.

Alpert, Geoffrey P. 1984. "The Needs of the Judiciary and Misapplications of Social Research." *Criminology* 22:441–56.

———. 1991. "Hiring and Promoting Police Officers in Small Departments." Criminal Law Bulletin 27:261–69.

Alpert, Geoffrey and William Smith. 1990. "Defensibility of Law Enforcement Training." *Criminal Law Bulletin* 26: 452–58.

———. 1991. "Developing Police Policy: An Evaluation of the Control Principle." *American Journal of Police* 13, no. 2: 1–20.

Bayley, David and Egon Bittner. 1993. "Learning the Skills of Policing." In Roger Dunham and Geoffrey Alpert (eds.) *Critical Issues in Policing: Contemporary Readings*, 2nd ed., pp. 106–29. Prospect Heights, IL: Waveland Press.

Brenner, Alan. 1989. "Psychological Screening of Police Applicants." In Roger Dunham and Geoffrey Alpert (eds.) *Critical Issues in Policing: Contemporary Readings*, pp. 72–86. Prospect Heights, IL: Waveland Press.

Burbeck, Elizabeth and Adrian Furnham. 1985. "Police Officer Selection: A Critical Review of the Literature." *Journal of Police Science and Administration* 13:58–69.

Burke, Michael and Patricia Burton. 1989. "Defining the Contours of Municipal Liability Under 42 U.S.C. Section 1983: *Monnell* through *City of Canton v. Harris*." *Stetson Law Review* 18: 511–47.

Carmines, Edward and Richard Zeller. 1979. *Reliability and Validity Assessment*. Beverly Hills, CA: Sage Publications.

Carter, David, Allen Sapp and Darrel Stephens. 1989. *The State of Police Education Policy Directions for the 21st Century.* Washington, DC: Police Executive Research Forum.

Cascio, Wayne and Leslie Real. 1979. "The Civil Service Exam Has Been Passed: Now What?" In Charles Spielberger (ed.) *Police Selection and Evaluation*, pp. 115–41. Washington, DC: Hemisphere.

Dalattre, Edwin. 1989. *Character and Cops.* Washington, DC: American Enterprise Institute for Public Policy Research.

Farley, Jennie. 1979. *Affirmative Action and the Woman Worker.* New York: American Management Association.

Filer, Robert. 1979. "The Assessment Center Method in the Selection of Law Enforcement Officers." In Charles Spielberger (ed.) *Police Selection and Evaluation*, pp. 211–29. Washington, DC: Hemisphere.

Fyfe, James. 1994. "Good Policing." In S. Stojkovic, J. Klofas and D. Kalinich (eds.) *The Administration and Management of Criminal Justice Organizations*, 2nd ed., pp. 104–24. Prospect Heights, IL: Waveland Press.

Gaines, Larry, Patrick Costello, and Annis Crabtree. 1989. "Police Selection Testing: Balancing Legal Requirements and Employer Needs." *American Journal of Police* 8: 137–52.

Grant, J. Douglas and Joan Grant. 1995. "Officer Selection and the Prevention of Abuse of Force." In William Geller and Hans Toch (eds.) *And Justice for All*, pp. 151–62. Washington, DC: Police Executive Research Forum.

Harris, Richard. 1973. *Police Academy: An Insider's View*. New York: John Wiley and Sons.

Holden, Richard. 1986. *Modern Police Management*. Englewood Cliffs, NJ: Prentice-Hall.

Independent Commission on the Los Angeles Police Department (Christopher Commission). 1991. *Report of the Independent Commission on the Los Angeles Police Department*. Los Angeles: Independent Commission on the Los Angeles Police Department.

International Association of Chiefs of Police. 1989. *Building Integrity and Reducing Drug Corruption in Police Departments*. Arlington: International Association of Chiefs of Police.

Kappeler, Victor. 1993. *Critical Issues in Police Civil Liability*. Prospect Heights, IL: Waveland Press.

Kleinig, John. 1990. "Teaching and Learning Police Ethics: Competing and Complementary Approaches." *Journal of Criminal Justice* 18: 1–18.

Kuykendall, Jack and Peter Usinger. 1975. *Community Police Administration*. Chicago: Nelson-Hall.

McCambell, Michael. 1993. "Field Training for Police Officers: State of the Art." In Roger Dunham and Geoffrey Alpert (eds.) *Critical Issues in Policing: Contemporary Readings*, 2nd ed., pp. 130–39. Prospect Heights, IL: Waveland Press.

Manning, Peter. 1977. *Police Work*. Cambridge, MA: MIT Press.

Martin, Susan. 1993. "Female Officers on the Move? A Status Report on Women in Policing." In R. Dunham and G. Alpert (eds.) *Critical Issues in Policing: Contemporary Readings*, 2nd ed., pp. 327–47 . Prospect Heights, IL: Waveland Press.

Maxfield, Michael and Earl Babbie. 1995. *Research Methods for Criminal Justice and Criminology*. Belmont: Wadsworth Publishing Co.

Murphy, Patrick. 1989. Foreword to Delattre, Edwin, *Character and Cops*. Washington, DC: American Enterprise Institute for Public Policy Research.

National Advisory Commission on Criminal Justice Standards and Goals. 1973. *Report on Police*. Washington, DC: United States Government Printing Office.

Overtown Blue Ribbon Committee. 1984. *Final Report*. Miami: City of Miami.

President's Commission on Law Enforcement and Administration of Justice. 1967. *Challenge of Crime in a Free Society*. Washington, DC: United States Government Printing Office.

Reinke, Roger. 1977. *Selection Through Assessment Centers*. Washington, DC: Police Foundation.

Reppetto, Thomas. 1980. "Higher Education for Police Officers." *FBI Law Bulletin* (January): 19–24.

Rubin, Paula. 1994. *The Americans with Disabilities Act and Criminal Justice: Hiring New Employees*. Washington, DC: National Institute of Justice.

Sherman, Lawrence, et al. 1978. *The Quality of Police Education*. San Francisco: Jossey-Bass.

Smith, Michael. 1995. "Law Enforcement Liability Under Section 1983." *Criminal Law Bulletin* 31:128–50.

Smith, Michael and Geoffrey Alpert. 1993. "The Police and the Americans with Disabilities Act—Who is Being Discriminated Against?" *Criminal Law Bulletin* 29:516–28.

Spielberger, Charles, ed. 1979. *Police Selection and Evaluation*. Washington, DC: Hemisphere.

Stone, Alfred and Stuart DeLuca. 1985. *Police Administration*. New York: John Wiley and Sons.

Terman, Leonard. 1917. "A Trial of Mental and Pedological Tests in a Civil Service Examination for Policemen and Firemen." *Journal of Applied Psychology* 1:17–29.

Van Maanen, John. 1983, "On the Making of Policemen." In Carl Klockars (ed.) *Thinking About Police*, pp. 388–400. New York: McGraw-Hill.

Walker, Samuel. 1983. *The Police in America*. New York: McGraw-Hill.

Weisenhand, Paul. 1995. "Personnel Selection." In W. Bailey (ed.) *The Encyclopedia of Police Science*, pp. 508–15. New York: Garland Publishing, Inc.

Cases

Guardian Association of the New York Police Department, Inc. v. Civil Service Commission of the City of New York, 630 F2d 79 (1980).

United States v. City of Miami 664 F.2d 435 (5th Cir 1981).

Chapter Four

POLICE ORGANIZATION AND ADMINISTRATION

Once a recruit graduates from the academy and becomes a police officer, he or she enters a working environment that is unique to law enforcement. To understand and to appreciate better the organization and administration of police work, we must be alert to the functions of the police in modern society and the environment in which the police operate. The purpose of policing, beyond protecting life, is to control crime and to maintain order. As a result, there is an organization of institutionalized violence which has been given the capacity to use force to conduct its business. Unlike the military, which uses force to control outsiders, the focus of police force is on its own citizens, although police often view criminals as "outsiders."

Given the unique character of the police, it is little wonder that police organization and administration is different from most other types of social organization with which we are familiar. Police organization and administration revolve around the control and standardization of the use of force.

In many respects, police work is a "tainted occupation" (Bittner, 1970:8). The police nearly always represent the interests of one group over other social groups in a conflict situation. This often results in the police being viewed in a negative light by at least one of the groups. Further, the police are rarely able to resolve a conflict by satisfying all of the demands of one side or the other. Some type of compromise is usually necessary, even if it is in the form of protecting the rights of an alleged offender. It is perhaps because of this role as arbitrator that the police have come to be viewed with distrust and suspicion.

Historically, some have viewed the police as being just a little above the evil they are charged with controlling:

> Because they are posted on the perimeters of order and justice in the hope that their presence will deter the forces of darkness and chaos, because they are meant to spare the rest of the people direct confrontations with the dreadful, perverse, lurid, and dangerous; police officers are perceived to have powers and secrets no one else shares. Their interest in and competence to deal with the untoward surrounds their activities with mystery and distrust. One needs only to consider the thoughts that come to mind at the sight of policemen moving into action: here they go to do something the rest of us have no stomach for! (Bittner, 1970:7)

This contempt for the police comes from many sources: from the fact that many believe that it takes a brutal bully to control other bullies or from the history of police corruption, which will be discussed later. As a result, and in reaction to this contempt displayed by the outside world, the police view themselves as "insiders" who need to band together against a hostile world of "outsiders." The police organization and its administration are molded specifically to protect the police from this perceived hostile world and the potential liability of involvement in a conflict situation with the lawful ability to use force. Controlling illegal behavior predominantly through force and the "tainted occupation" label do more to shape police organization and administration than perhaps anything else.

This chapter discusses police organization and administration in light of their mandate and functions. The examination of police bureaucracy and its various unusual characteristics, such as the chain of command and code of secrecy, will be followed by a discussion of the bureaucracy in action. This analysis will look at the influence of politics, administrative styles, and leadership on policing. Like recruitment and training, police organization and administration varies greatly among police departments. An attempt is made in this chapter to generalize so that the information will apply to many different police departments.

POLICE BUREAUCRACY

Some of the earliest bureaucratic organizations were established for military purposes. In fact, as indicated in chapter 1, the first police force in London was partially formed from military troops used to control crime. The bureaucratic form of social organization appears to be the most efficient method of using force to protect one's homeland or to attack another country. This form of organization is especially effective in convincing people to do tasks that they might not want to do or to act rationally in emotionally charged situations, such as war. A bureaucracy is a type of social organization that has clearly defined goals and rules, highly specialized roles, explicit social control, and clear lines of authority linking the various levels within the organization. Since police organizations are paramilitary by nature, it is little wonder that they take the form of rigid bureaucracies.

Police departments are organized in a style similar to the military, using ranks to designate authority (captain, lieutenant, sergeant, and so on). True to the bureaucratic form of organization, police departments are divided into special divisions and units with lines of authority leading from the chief to the line officers. Police department hierarchies of authority vary in respect to how tasks are divided and which divisions report to which supervisors.

The traditional hierarchy is represented by a pyramid-type structure with a minimum of four elements or divisions. On the top, to set and enforce policies and to provide overall leadership is the chief. The other divisions include internal affairs, communication, and patrol. Small departments may combine the elements, but all agencies must perform the duties.

Internal affairs personnel investigate all allegations of police misconduct. These concerns can be initiated by civilian complaints or by fellow police officers. This division or section is of paramount importance to the operations of any law enforcement agency and must receive support from the chief administrators. Many internal affairs divisions report directly to the chief of police to avoid any question of prominence or importance. Tasks performed in the inspections bureau are closely related to those of internal affairs. In the larger departments, this function is separate from internal affairs. However, in the smaller departments, the tasks are sometimes combined and may be performed by the chief. The Inspections Bureau examines the organization's adherence to policies, procedures, rules, and regulations. Whether an independent division or a part of a larger section, all police agencies have these responsibilities.

One of the most critical elements of police work is its system of communication. It is this "heart line" that receives calls for service and forwards information to officers in the field. The communication division forms the link between the community and the police. The information provided to officers is the basis on which they prepare and respond. In other words, if officers are told about a particular situation, they must recognize how many officers are needed, how quickly they need to respond and where they need to be. As mentioned later (in chapter 7), this emphasis on responding to calls for service forces the law enforcement agency to react and can impede strategic planning for service delivery or efforts at crime suppression.

Just as communication is the heart of the police network, the patrol division has been the backbone of traditional policing. The conventional role of the patrol division has been to respond to calls for service from the dispatcher in the communications division. In addition, patrol officers could keep an eye on changes in the communities or areas they patrol and reduce response time to emergency calls. Recently, police critics have questioned the response-time model of policing and research has confirmed that responding more rapidly to calls for service does not result in more criminals being caught (Reiss, 1992). This has led to questions concerning the central role patrol has played in police strategies of the past. In fact, some claim that motorized patrol has insulated the police from the public and resulted in lowered confidence in the ability of the police to handle their problems (Reiss, 1992). Many departments have focused on community-based policing and problem solving to integrate the police back into the communities.

Many small departments maintain only this skeletal framework, but the larger departments specialize their structure beyond these elements. It is important to understand the significance of matching the structure of the department to the stated goals of management. In other words, there are a variety of structures and alternatives, but the structure must be designed to achieve goals which can blend with the management style. A police administrator must design the organizational structure to emphasize its strengths and overcome its weaknesses. For example, if a chief wanted to emphasize a community-policing orientation, then these functions should be structured as an *overlay* of the organizational structure rather than as an add-on. That is, the aspect of police work to be emphasized should be integrated into other functions and activities. The result of any administrative plan is that you get what you design! What is featured by design is what the organization, its personnel, and its constituents determine to be important. Five important issues must be stressed in the design of any organization:

1. maintenance of *stability* in internal management;
2. identification and analysis of *organizational assets*;
3. realization of the benefits of *participatory management*;
4. understanding problems of those individuals whose role or function is affected by *change*; and
5. management of issues associated with *external forces*.

The degree of centralization in the organization is one of the most critical decisions an administrator must make. A centralized structure, with a dominant boss, will have strong controls and may be cost effective. A decentralized structure will have flexibility and will be cost efficient as it emphasizes team building as a mode of problem solving. As each structure has positive and negative characteristics, the goals of the organization, with input from the community, should serve to design the structure. Certainly, large departments can centralize administrative and certain investigative functions while they decentralize patrol and other activities. The trend has been to decentralize many police functions and to be more responsive to the unique characteristics of communities.

The structure of a department that fits this traditional model by dividing its tasks into divisions and defining its direct lines of authority is presented in figure 1. This model represents a large metropolitan police department and reveals its divisions and lines of authority.

Figure 1

Organizational Structure of a Metropolitan Police Department

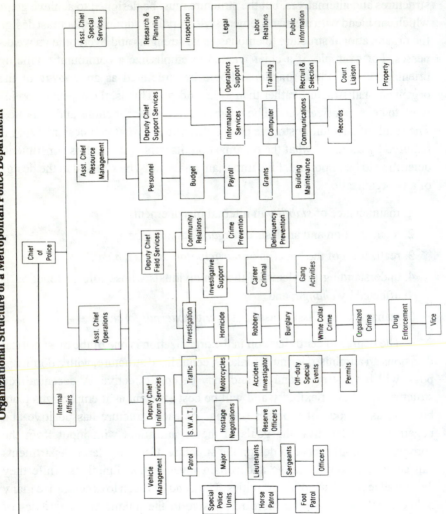

The titles of the various divisions in figure 1 indicate that fighting crime is only one of the many responsibilities given to the police. This organization chart also shows the extremely complex nature of large police departments. Although the size of a department somewhat dictates how tasks will be divided into units or divisions, most departments follow a fairly consistent pattern of dividing responsibilities.

Typically, the three major organizational divisions are operations, administration and technical services. The administrative services division (under the resource management division in figure 1) is designed to increase the chief's capacity to fulfill administrative functions. Management tasks such as budgeting, payroll, personnel and building maintenance are enhanced by a specialized unit working full-time on the task. Conversely, technical services enhance the line functions. Tasks such as record keeping, communications and computer services are accomplished by this unit. An operations unit is found in all agencies and comprises the necessary and direct functions for which the agency exists. Operations is critical to the mission of the agency and usually includes the following subunits: patrol, criminal investigations, traffic and special services such as tactical or SWAT. In figure 1, special services has its own division and reports directly to the chief of police, instead of being a part of operations; however, the SWAT unit is under operations. Since the operations division is the most critical of all the divisions and contains the essentials of police work, we will discuss some of its subunits in more detail.

POLICE OPERATIONS: THE NUTS AND BOLTS OF POLICING

PATROL

Traditionally patrol has been thought of as the most important function of the police organization because it enables the initial response to almost every call for service and provides the presence for deterring criminal behavior. All other units function to support the patrol function. The purpose of patrol is to place officers in plain view of citizens to deter crime, to maintain order, to enforce laws, and to serve the community. The patrol division has the responsibility to provide twenty-four-hour protection and surveillance of its entire jurisdiction. This requires tremendous resources. For example, in order to maintain twenty patrol officers for three shifts, the division must employ eighty officers. This figure allows for two days off per week and for vacation time. Other units simply concentrate on covering an eight-hour block of time for five days per week.

An important issue concerning the patrol function is the deployment of patrol officers. Strategies are devised to provide the greatest deterrence through high visibility, quick response to calls, and saturation of high crime areas. In chapter 7, "Styles of Policing," these strategies will be discussed in considerable detail. In the more progressive departments, the patrol officers are critical to the identification and solution of problems. This proactive, problem-solving method may take some officers off the street, but it allows the officers to operate more efficiently and effectively when done correctly than if they merely react to calls.

As already mentioned, recent research has pointed to some deficiencies in the traditional patrol models. While it appeared to be very efficient to have police patrol from their police cars with the ability to call into headquarters and to receive calls for service quickly, this method actually had some important drawbacks. It contributed to poor police-community relations, because the public had very little contact with the police except when being questioned or arrested. Further, the police tend to be isolated from the communities they serve and have very little knowledge about the community and citizen concerns. In some extreme situations, this form of detached patrol led to citizens viewing police as hostile outsiders or an occupation force that cared little about the community.

Maybe even more troublesome is the fact that traditional patrol models focus mostly on reacting to crime, rather than being proactive by focusing on prevention and problem solving. Problem solving and community-based policing emphasize the larger picture. Rather that just responding to crime through enforcement, officers should try to understand the relationships between crime incidents and the conditions that cause them. Then the police should try to eliminate the conditions, or at least to reduce the conditions that are the major cause of the crime. This requires an intimate knowledge of the community and its citizens that is learned only by contact and interaction. Thus, rather than using traditional patrol procedures, officers need to be more closely integrated into the communities they serve. Foot patrols, community forums, and crime prevention activities are some of the structural ways for officers to become part of the community.

TRAFFIC

An obvious function of the police department is to control and manage traffic. As a result, many major departments have a specialized traffic detail or unit. It is true that there is a financial incentive for this detail, as considerable revenue for the government is produced through traffic citations; however, there are other reasons for the formation of this specialized unit. There are more citizen deaths each year due to traffic accidents than as a result of crime. One major purpose of this unit is to reduce the number of traffic-related deaths by enforcing traffic laws and providing a highly visible deterrent. In spite of the importance of this function, traffic problems and the resulting enforcement activities consume an inordinate amount of the patrol officer's time, which otherwise could be focused on controlling crime. A specialized traffic unit can remove a great deal of this burden from the patrol officer.

Another important function of the traffic unit is uncovering more serious criminal activity. The standard traffic stop results in numerous arrests for more serious crimes. The standard practice of stopping a driver for a traffic citation and running his or her ID card through the computers can reveal information concerning stolen autos, outstanding warrants, and criminal records. In addition, the officer can spot suspicious objects in the stopped car. A surprising number of arrests for serious criminal activities have been initiated by standard traffic stops. In fact, specialized traffic patrol may have a greater effect on controlling crime than an increase of manpower in general patrol. Although the police can not enforce all traffic violations, a method of selective enforcement, as discussed below, can fulfill the needs of traffic as well as crime fighting functions.

Two general patterns of traffic enforcement have evolved. *Random enforcement* is the first which includes the routine driving of officers on patrol and taking action on any violation observed. This type of enforcement works well in departments that have patrol divisions with officers who routinely patrol within their jurisdiction. Unfortunately, this strategy has only a limited effect on the rate of accidents, but when it works properly, it provides the patrol officer with an excuse to investigate suspicious persons or situations. To make it work properly, some departments have had to establish strong supervisory techniques, including citation quotas for their officers (Lundman, 1980). Second, *selective enforcement* relies upon the identification of problem areas and the assignment of a disproportionate share of citizen contacts at those areas. Further, the strict enforcement of traffic laws does reduce the number of accidents, injuries, and deaths.

INVESTIGATION

Next to patrol, the investigation division is probably the most prominent division in most departments. Note in figure 1 that investigation is located central to the overall organization and is divided into seven units: homicide, robbery, burglary, white-collar crime, organized crime, drug enforcement, and vice. Investigators are usually called to a crime scene in an attempt to identify the offender. In other situations, an investigator will be mobilized when a crime scene requires a thorough analysis. Often, investigators are requested to do undercover work, or to work on vice, stolen property, drug enforcement or other specific types of criminal activity. Other times, detectives will be called upon to provide help on a case because of their knowledge of the street environment and their relationship to informants. It is interesting that officers who work in *investigative* divisions are often called detectives. In spite of the title, a detective seldom *detects* crime. He or she spends more time investigating crimes that already have been detected.

In a nationwide study of the criminal investigation process, Chaiken et al. (1983) discovered that detectives spend about 7 percent of their time on activities that lead to solving crimes. They report:

> Our data reveal that most of an investigator's casework time is consumed in reviewing reports, documenting files, and attempting to locate and interview victims. For cases that are solved (a suspect is identified), an investigator spends more time in post-clearance processing than in identifying the perpetrator. (Chaiken et al., 1983:172)

As we can conclude from the above discussion, investigation divisions are a specialized function formed to assist the patrol force when it becomes too overloaded to complete follow-up investigations adequately. This division is usually the first to be created when a small department expands. As a result of its function being interwoven with the function of the patrol division, close communication and cooperation between the two are essential to a properly functioning department. In fact, the success or failure of the police department in fulfilling its overall mission rests with operations, and no divisions are more important than patrol and investigation.

DRUG ENFORCEMENT

Drug enforcement is one of the fastest growing concerns of police and the public. Law-abiding citizens must rely on the tactics of the police to rid their neighborhoods of drug dealers, drug users, and the crimes they commit. It is no longer acceptable for the police merely to investigate drug crimes *after* they are committed and attempt to arrest and prosecute the offenders. Police must create strategies and tactics to tackle the drug problem in American cities and communities proactively (Police Executive Research Forum, 1990; Chaiken, 1988).

SWAT

A controversial law enforcement tool is the tactical squad or SWAT (Special Weapons and Tactics) team. August 1, 1966, was the day that Charles Whitman climbed the tower at The University of Texas and shot forty-five people, killing fifteen. That incident had a profound impact on policing as administrators from all over the country began to realize that they possessed no plan or method to deal with such a disaster. The massacre in Austin marked the beginning of SWAT.

These squads are an elite group of police that are trained in aggressive and overtly militaristic approaches to dealing with exceptionally dangerous situations. The SWAT officers are carefully chosen and receive the special training in tactics and weapons needed to respond to the holding of hostages, airplane hijackings, prison riots, and so on. After negotiations fail, or immediate threats to life are realized, SWAT teams are called upon to use their training and experience.

The function of these units is to step in and respond to situations for which the average officer is not trained. With an increase in these unusually dangerous situations during the 1960s and 1970s, SWAT teams were created to support the patrol units. This was much more efficient than trying to provide the entire force with expensive training and equipment necessary for these relatively few instances.

COORDINATING SPECIALIZED UNITS

Within the operations division of most large police departments, there are a number of specialized units. One can readily imagine the problems inherent in attempting to coordinate these various units when their cases overlap. The problem becomes even more difficult when multiple jurisdictions or multiple agencies within the criminal justice system become involved in the same case.

Recently, innovative methods have been developed to coordinate these various units and jurisdictions. Special teams such as homicide, rape, burglary, drug enforcement, and gang activities have been created that include investigators from the various units or jurisdictions. These teams provide a structure for sharing information and coordinating operations. This innovation seems to have increased the overall efficiency of the police, in addition to saving money.

One example is the Tactical Narcotics Team of the Metro-Dade Police Department in Miami. This unit is structured to promote public cooperation and to support programs that identify drug users and to refer them for treatment or other appropriate care. The objectives are to force recovery choices on drug abusers, to pursue enhanced penalties for sellers, and to produce maximum punishment for traffickers. This effort is coordinated by the police with direct input and assistance from social service agencies and the prosecutor's office.

Visible street sales and high volume drug sales are relentlessly targeted with both covert and visible sustained enforcement programs. Citizen cooperation is promoted to maximize the effective targeting of both offenders and locations offering the greatest drug and crime threats to the communities. The goal is to improve the conditions that contribute to neighborhood decline and criminal behavior. Included targets are unsafe and abandoned structures, abandoned vehicles, dark and dangerous alleys, overgrown properties, and unauthorized dump sites. In order to improve the quality of life in affected areas, police authorities, government agencies, concerned organizations, and citizens must work together to reduce levels of crime, drug use, drug sales, and drug trafficking.

POLICE ORGANIZATION

Police officers are responsible for following the procedural rules and regulations set forth by the United States Constitution, the relevant state constitution, state statutes, court decisions, state administrative rules and departmental regulations. This *formalization* and *specification* of rules and procedures was created, in large part, to control discretion in the controversial aspects of police work, mainly the use of force. Although society confers the right to enforce laws and to use force when necessary, it is concurrently concerned with making sure that this right is not abused.

Over the centuries, police organizations have become more and more bureaucratized in an effort to control this high level of power, authority, and discretion. This increasing level of control and accountability has resulted in considerable progress toward preventing corruption and increasing the rationality associated with the use of force. More than twenty-five years ago Egon Bittner (1970:1) informed us:

> In his assessment of the police, Bruce Smith wrote in 1940 that, in spite of the still rather bleak picture, "the lessons of history lean to the favorable side." He pointed to the fact that the then existing police forces had moved a long way from the past associated with the notorious names of Vidocq and Jonathan Wild, and he suggested that the uninterrupted progress justifies the expectation of further change for the better. It is fair to say that this hope has been vindicated by the events of the past 30 years. American police departments of today differ by a wide margin of improvement from those Smith studied in the late 1930s. The once endemic features of wanton brutality, corruption, and sloth have been reduced to a level of sporadic incidence, and their surviving vestiges have been denounced by even generally uncritical police apologists. Indeed, police reform, once a cause espoused exclusively by spokesmen from outside the law enforcement camp, has become an internal goal, actively sought and implemented by leading police officials.

There are many important aspects of police organization, perhaps too many to include in a chapter of this size. However, we will discuss several of the most important characteristics of police organization, each of which illustrates the extremely bureaucratic nature of police departments.

POLICY: AN INTEGRAL ASPECT OF MANAGEMENT

Law enforcement agencies must have rules, regulations, training, and supervision to guide and control the broad discretionary powers of their officers. In the performance of duty, officers are confronted with a variety of complex situations which require action. Written and enforced policies are necessary for the proper management of all law enforcement functions. These policies must cover all operations and must anticipate potential activities. They are formulated by analyzing stated objectives and declaring those principles or ideas which will best guide the officer in achieving the objectives. A *policy* is not a statement of what must be done in a particular situation; it is a statement of guiding principles which must be followed in activities that fall within either specific organizational objectives or the overall police mission. A *procedure* is the method of performing a task or a manner of proceeding on a course of action. It differs from policy in that it directs action in a particular situation to perform a task within the guidelines of policy.

Policies and procedures must cover general duties and obligations as well as the methods to achieve them. In other words, law enforcement agencies must have regulations, provide training and supervision, and hold officers accountable for their actions. Regardless of the specific situation, departments must have plans for their officers to follow. The Metro-Dade Police Department in Miami, Florida, in its 1995 manual has defined policy as ". . . principles and values which guide the performance of a departmental activity. Policy is not a statement of what must be done in a particular situation; rather, it is a statement of guiding principles which should be followed in activities which are directed toward attainment of objectives."

Standard Operating Procedures (SOP), General Orders (GO) or policies based upon relevant laws, serve to provide guidance from the administrators and command staff to the officers so they can adequately perform their day-to-day operations. As James Auten (1988:1–2) has noted:

> To do otherwise is to simply leave employees "in the dark" in the expectation that they will intuitively divine the proper and expected course of action in the performance of their duties. Discretion must be reasonably exercised within the parameters of the expectations of the community, the courts, the legislature and the organization, itself.

Since a policy is objective rather than situation-oriented, it must be sufficiently broad to encompass most situations. When specific direction is required, policies may include *rule*s. A rule is a specific prohibition or requirement to prevent deviations from policy or procedures. In situations involving activities which are common to the police or can be predicted as likely to occur, departments must promulgate some policy informing its officers of what will be tolerated and what will not be tolerated. Anything less may fall into the abyss that the United States Supreme Court in *City of Canton, Ohio v. Harris* called "Deliberate Indifference."

An example of a practice in need of a policy, which will be explored later in greater detail, is pursuit driving. There are several ways to control this dangerous activity as demonstrated by the following illustrations. The State of Nebraska has an excellent law requiring each law enforcement agency to adopt and implement a written policy regarding police pursuit that must include the consideration of the original offense, the degree of danger created by the pursuit, the likelihood of later apprehension, the number and type of vehicles permitted to pursue, the nature of supervision, the interjurisdictional issues, and an ongoing training program regarding these issues (Section 29–211). However, Nebraska law also states that "[I]n case of death, injury, or property damage to any innocent third party proximately caused by the action of a law enforcement officer . . . damages shall be paid to such third party by the political subdivision employing the officer" (Section 13–911). Obviously, this creates a fiscal responsibility that all but eliminates pursuit from the tactics available to police in Nebraska.

Minnesota law requires the adoption and implementation of a detailed policy similar to that required in Nebraska, but their legislation also requires that each pursuit be evaluated by the policy criteria and that the critique be submitted to a state clearinghouse for analysis (Minnesota Statutes, Section 609.487). Unlike Nebraska, Minnesota law does not financially punish a jurisdiction which conducts a pursuit properly even if it results in an accident or injury to an innocent third party. An obvious example would be the pursuit of a known serial killer, which, although conducted properly but resulting in an injury to an innocent third party, would cost the taxpayers in Nebraska a significant amount of money. If the same pursuit took place in Minnesota, the likelihood of a successful lawsuit would be minimal.

California has taken the most conservative position by implementing a law which provides immunity from liability for civil damages resulting from a collision involving a pursued driver and an innocent third party if the law enforcement agency adheres to an appropriate written policy (California Vehicle Code). Often the laws established by larger bodies of government will dictate the type of policies created by the different police departments.

The three examples above illustrate that individual police departments must tailor their policies to accommodate the laws in their jurisdictions. These examples demonstrate that some agencies may find it necessary to provide detailed policy on what type of behavior is and is not permitted regarding certain situations. Other agencies might adopt a more generalized style of guidance for the same issues. In other words, discretion is available to officers in varying degrees. There exists a policy continuum, ranging from detailed and controlled to general and vague. General policies emphasize officer discretion while detailed policies provide the officer with more structure. There is a strong relationship between the type of policy and the training necessary to support it. That is, the more discretionary power a police officer has, the more he or she needs to be trained in proper decision making. Although policy provides guidelines, officer behavior is controlled by the chain of command.

THE CHAIN OF COMMAND

Because of the detailed division of labor and the delegation of authority and responsibility to the various parts of an organization, a chain of command is required. The chain of command is the route or channel along which authority and responsibility flow. The sensitive nature of police responsibility and authority has led to a very rigid chain of command in police organization. Most police organizations follow what Stone and DeLuca (1985) call the "unity-of-command principle," which maintains that each person in an organization must be accountable to only one higher official. The intent of this principle is to guard against confusion along the line of command that might interfere with the performance of crucial functions. The unity-of-command principle is generally a good one; however, it can create serious problems of inefficiency, especially at those times when emergency action is needed and people are quickly assigned to work with new supervisors. Stone and DeLuca (1985:64–65) cite a good example of one of the problems that can arise as a result of this concept of command:

> . . . in some very large metropolitan police agencies, detectives are assigned to the various precinct headquarters. To whom are the detectives accountable: to the precinct commanders or to the chief of detectives for the whole department? Most agencies following the principle of unity of command, place the precinct detectives under the authority of the departmental chief of detectives. But this puts the detectives in the position of resident aliens in the precinct stations. Since they are not accountable to the precinct commanders and must carry out assignments from the departmental headquarters, they are not available to assist in precinct-level operations and they are not necessarily bound by the precinct commander's rules and policies. On the other hand, making the detectives answerable only to the precinct commander diminishes the role of the chief of detectives to that of a technical adviser and breeds inconsistency in the investigative policies and procedures followed from one precinct to the next.

Nearly everyone has had some experience with the lack of efficiency involved in bureaucracies that require strict adherence to a rigid chain of command. By the time one sifts through all of the red tape required at each level, it either may be too late to solve the original problem or simply not worth the effort. Whether the issue is pursuit driving or some other police activity, each must be regulated by policy and managed by what is known. To obtain the necessary information, one is required to have formal documentation of all important communication.

FORMAL NATURE OF COMMUNICATION

Another feature of police bureaucracy is the formality of communication. Written documents preserved in permanent files are the prevalent means of communication in modern police organizations. One major purpose of establishing formal communication procedures is to mitigate precarious supervision. Officers who are on patrol or out on the streets are extremely difficult to supervise and control. Written documentation helps supervisors keep track of the activities of their officers. Formal communication is more permanent than informal communication. Permanent documentation of communication allows for the reconstruction of activities, orders, and events that may come under question at a later time. Given the extremely controversial and volatile nature of police work, the organization is often confronted with the need to reconstruct specific events for legal purposes, either civil or criminal.

Estimates of the percentage of an officer's time spent filling out reports and logs range from 40 to 80 percent. Only a few potential recruits are aware of this aspect of police work when they apply for a career in law enforcement. Police officers in most departments must keep a patrol log that includes details of when they went on duty, the weather conditions, their assigned radio calls, the pedestrian and traffic stops they initiated, the miles driven during their shift and the times of their lunch breaks. All of this information is used by the supervising sergeants to keep tabs on the individual officer's activities.

In addition to the patrol log, officers must fill out reports on all activities during the course of their shift. For example, when an officer handles a theft, burglary, or traffic accident, he or she must complete the relevant report. If involved in a traffic accident that damages the vehicle, a high-speed pursuit or other chase, the use of force to control an offender or the discharge of a weapon, the officer must complete a special report detailing the circumstances of the incident.

Modern technology is often helpful to police officers when dealing with situations which might occur during the course of their shift. Video cameras have been useful when interviewing and arresting persons suspected of impaired driving. Further, some departments have mounted video cameras in patrol cars. The cameras are activated automatically when the emergency lights are turned on. This keeps an accurate record of what is said and done during a police-citizen encounter. Video records can also be kept of interrogations and other interviews.

Other advanced communication techniques help the supervisory communication process. For example, some patrol cars are equipped with cellular telephones and/or computer terminals. Simple computer-driven information systems can assist with incoming calls for service and the deployment and tracking of personnel.

In addition to the electronic technology, which helps supervisors communicate with the officer on the street, more sophisticated systems have the ability to compare field notes and locations of crimes to determine if any trends exist. Systems which include geographic, environmental and population data assist in crime prevention, crime analysis, and the identification of suspects. A resourceful supervisor who has immediate access to this information will be better equipped to analyze or anticipate various situations. Further, computerized management systems can keep administrators informed of current spending habits and financial resources.

Analyzing the flow of information in a police department requires a review of all channels used to transmit data (see Manning, 1988). Although modern technology is beneficial in assisting with the management of police work, it takes an enormous effort to enter the data. Whether recorded on a hard paper copy or electronically on a disk, all of this written material is available to supervising sergeants, detectives, prosecutors, and others in the justice system.

ESPRIT DE CORPS AND THE CODE OF SECRECY

The special nature of the police bureaucracy, with its unique functions and special tools for carrying out those functions, has led to the development of an important component within the organization. As we learned earlier, the isolation officers often feel leads to an *esprit de corps* among and within police organizations. It is perhaps this isolation, along with the dangers and risks surrounding the occupation, that encourages an unspoken rule: when an officer is in trouble, right or wrong, he or she deserves the help and support of fellow officers. This spirit of close-knit camaraderie is a cherished feature of police work for the officers who face danger daily. The reassurance of unquestioned support helps them overcome the fears of the job. The peril that police officers face, however, is not limited to physical risk. The possibilities of legal and personal liability are a constant threat to officers due to the nature of the job. It is in this area that the *esprit de corps* can have serious, negative consequences.

The *esprit de corps* camaraderie tends to segregate police officers from the rest of society and encourages a code of secrecy. It contributes to a feeling of "them against us" in the police culture, a belief that begins in the police academy. This feeling often extends to relations with any groups outside of the department and can become an obstacle to civilian attempts to make meaningful suggestions for change. It is common for officers to "close ranks" and to present a united front against any outside critics. While this reaction is not unique to police, it is easy to understand in this type of organization. Many groups within the organization can use it as an inside tactic when disagreements or sensitive issues arise. In a police department, for example, one division may close ranks when dealing with other divisions, thus creating obstacles to cooperation.

Subordinates have traditionally been able to close ranks against their superiors, preventing effective supervision. This code of secrecy not only makes performance look better than it really is, but also helps protect officers from the dangerous uncertainties inherent in police work. Partners do not talk about each other in the presence of others; subordinates do not talk about each other in the presence of ranking officers. Most importantly, officers do not talk about police work in the presence of outsiders. The unwritten rule is that you do not tell anyone more than is absolutely necessary. Never volunteer information to anyone. This rule results in a complex network of information denial, mutual dependency, and solidarity within subunits based upon the perception of external risk to the group (Bittner, 1970). This topic of police socialization and the police subculture will be discussed more fully in chapter 5.

POLICE BUREAUCRACY IN ACTION

Although the police bureaucracy has evolved to its present form in an attempt to fulfill most efficiently the major functions of an institution of social control, it is subject to, and continuously shaped by, a multitude of forces at work in our larger society. We must remember that it is not enough to say that the function of the police is to enforce the law. The police must enforce the law so scrupulously that neither public support nor approval is lost. The police bureaucracy does not operate in a vacuum; it is an integral part of a dynamic and ever-changing society. Procedures that met with general public approval ten years ago may cause an uproar of disapproval today. Procedures perfectly consistent with the values of one community may produce serious conflict in another. In sum, the police have to fulfill their very sensitive responsibilities in a potentially volatile environment that is influenced by politics as well as by internal administrative and leadership styles. Each of these influences helps to shape the effect of the police bureaucracy in action and will be discussed in more detail.

POLITICS: INTERNAL AND EXTERNAL INFLUENCES

Politics are integral to any police operation and involve the exercise of influence and power. As such, political influences on the police organization take two major forms. *Personal politics* involve the exercise of influence and power for personal gain. For example, a police chief may promote one officer over another because of loyalty to the chief or to a set of values they hold in common. Also, there may be subgroups that are positioning their members for more influence in a department. Another form of politics comes from outside of the department, yet can exert as much or more influence over police operations than can personal politics. *Community politics* involve democratic control over the policing function. A fundamental value of our society is that policing should be subject to and under some control of the public. As various community agencies and organizations compete for influence and power over the policing function, external politics become interwoven with internal politics to produce a complex network of influences and power. Even though many police chiefs have vowed to keep politics out of their police departments, it is nearly impossible. As we have seen, politics have always been a part of policing.

ADMINISTRATION: AN INTERNAL INFLUENCE

The administration of the police organization has much in common with the management of other organizations. Generally, "administration is a process in which a group of individuals is organized and directed toward the achievement of the group's objective" (Holden, 1986:2). Of course, the exact nature of the administrative task varies considerably among the different types and sizes of law enforcement agencies; however, the general principles used and the form of administration are similar. For example, *administration* involves a focus on the overall organization, its mission, and its relationship with other organizations and groups external to it. *Management*, which is a part of administration, is more involved in the day-to-day operations of the various units within the organization. It is management that directs the subunits to be consistent with their goals, and staffs the unit with qualified personnel. *Supervision* involves the individual direction of staff members in their day-to-day activities. Often, all three of these tasks are required of one administrator; however, each level focuses more or less on one of these tasks. A police chief may be involved somewhat in management and supervision; yet, his or her main task is administration. A captain in charge of a division may get involved with administration and spend some time supervising staff; however, most of his or her time will be involved with management. Police sergeants spend most of their time supervising police officers involved in their day-to-day activities. Strategies for accomplishing these three separate, yet related, responsibilities have been conceptualized into two general theories.

ADMINISTRATIVE THEORIES

There are two major organizational theories that are often discussed as providing alternative types of police administration (see Swanson et al., 1993). Each suggests a different way of organizing work and work processes. The first is *traditional organization theory*. Traditional theory is associated with organizations that are mechanistic, have closed systems, and are bureaucratic. The second is *open-systems theory*. Organizations that are flexible, adaptive, and organic are associated with open-systems theory.

The type of police administration suggested by traditional organization theory involves large patrol units of 100 to 250 officers with quasi-militaristic supervision. The shift responsibility includes eight- or ten-hour shifts, with only unit commanders having responsibility for around-the-clock operations. Assignment is on the basis of the first available car to respond to a call for police service, with a priority system to serve emergency calls. Officers are routinely rotated to new divisions or assignments. Special police units (tactical, detective, etc.) operate in local neighborhoods without informing local patrol officers. Under the traditional administrative approach, community relations are viewed as "image building." Special units exist especially for dealing directly with community relations. Police officers respond to calls and use aggressive policing, such as stopping and frisking suspicious-looking people. Planning is centralized around the police chief and his or her staff, so innovations come from the top down.

The open-systems administration is often referred to as neighborhood team policing. This administrative style is most effective when there are only twenty to thirty officers to a unit or team. Supervision follows a professional model. There is considerable consultation between supervisors and officers regarding the setting of objectives, as well as an emphasis on in-service training programs. Officers are encouraged to make suggestions and are permitted to exercise considerable discretion in their work. A team leader is responsible to the commander or the chief for all aspects of police service within a given area. The team provides all police services for its neighborhood, except in emergencies. Officers are not rotated routinely; rather, they are given extended assignments to a specific neighborhood. Special police units discuss team goals and, whenever possible, consult in advance with the local team leader. Community relations are seen as an integral and essential patrol function (not just image building) and are planned by the team and its commander. They consist of good police service, positive demeanor, and input from the various community groups. The open-system administrative style uses decentralized planning.

Functions such as crime analysis, use of plain clothes or special tactics, preventive programs, referral programs and service activities are all responsibilities of the neighborhood team rather than direct responsibilities of the centralized administration of the police chief. In other words, this style creates a proactive, problem-solving approach.

Until the 1990s, the administration of most police organizations has been based upon traditional organizational theory. Since nontraditional approaches usually reduce specialization and the number of levels in the organization, they negate the importance of the mid-level managers. A closer inspection of these failures reveals poorly conducted organizational change, rather than a failure of the concept itself. Even though there has been renewed interest in neighborhood policing (Alpert and Dunham, 1986), the traditional approach remains dominant in many police departments.

Large police departments require a certain amount of specialization to handle diverse tasks efficiently. Duties such as homicide investigation, vice, and narcotics require specialized training and supervision. In addition, there is a natural tendency toward centralization in large organizations. Often inroads made by the open-systems approach are limited to the periphery of the police organization, while the core will continue to be dominated by traditional principles. Perhaps the challenge of police administrators today is to rely on the traditional approach as the basis of police administration and to retain its best features, while tempering them with doses of new approaches, including many facets of the open-systems approach.

LEADERSHIP: AN INTERNAL INFLUENCE

Another important aspect of the police bureaucracy is leadership. The ability to lead is the most important managerial skill for an administrator to possess. In many respects, leadership in a police organization is no different from leadership in any other social organization. The real test of a good leader is the ability to obtain the respect of subordinates and to develop a rapport with them. The leader of a police organization is faced with the challenge of gaining the respect of subordinates in all of the diverse units and specialties which fall under the designation, *police operations*.

Leadership is a difficult term to define, in part because there are so many aspects of it. Many definitions have focused upon the character traits of the leader, such as courage, intelligence, integrity and empathy. Others have focused upon leadership style, for instance autocratic versus democratic. In regard to police departments, a generally accepted explanation is that leadership is the influence on subordinates which organizes and guides their energies to achieve the mission, goals and objectives of the police department (Swanson et al., 1993).

Good leadership requires a blend of several different, yet related, skills. Human relations skills, conceptual skills and technical skills are three major requirements for good leadership. Each leader has some degree of each of these skills, but the balance of each varies considerably among them. One leader might possess a very high degree of technical skill, thereby gaining the respect of subordinates; however, this same leader might possess only minimal human relations and conceptual skills. *Human relations skills* involve the capacity to interrelate successfully with others at all levels of the police organization. These skills include the ability to motivate subordinates, to resolve conflicts among officers and between units, and to communicate effectively. *Conceptual skills* involve the ability to understand and to transmit various types of information up and down the chain-of-command, as well as horizontally across the various units. Communication is best accomplished by developing a view of the whole organization rather than focusing on specific functions. The formulation and communication of policies and procedures may be involved in this process. *Technical skills* involve the knowledge of how to do specific tasks and how to carry out responsibilities that are necessarily a part of the specialized police organization. Technical skill might involve the identification, collection and preservation of physical evidence or the knowledge of the law and the procedures specified for carrying out certain responsibilities.

Leadership positions at different levels of the police bureaucracy require different blends of each of these skills. As one advances up the hierarchy of a police department (first-line supervisors or sergeants, middle-managers or lieutenants and captains, and top managers or majors and chiefs), the relative importance of each of these skills changes. Because sergeants usually supervise directly the greatest number of people and spend more of their time in this role, human relations skills become more crucial as we move down the hierarchy of leadership roles. To the contrary, conceptual skills become more crucial as one moves up the levels of leadership. As one progresses upward toward the middle- and top-management positions, the range of technical skills narrows as the conceptual skills tend to dominate.

All leaders must be sensitive to three main responsibilities: (1) contributing to the fulfillment of the department's mission, (2) ensuring that the effort of subordinates is productive and that they are achieving success, and (3) making an impact on their areas of responsibility (Swanson et al., 1993). Meeting these key objectives effectively is a great challenge and requires the leader to possess the many outstanding characteristics mentioned above. He or she must practice sound leadership principles such as time management, positive thinking and dedication to one's work. It is important that the supervisor is not merely an officer with stripes and that he or she receives sufficient training. Walsh and Donovan (1990:13) have noted:

> Supervision of police personnel is the critical factor in achieving departmental performance objectives and officer compliance with procedures, policy, and the law. The supervisor is the basic link in the police organizational structure between management and the operational level. It is his/her responsibility to see that the day-to-day tasks of policing are performed according to law and departmental procedures. The supervisor is required to possess a knowledge of police operations, law, organizational procedures, and policy including an understanding of the managerial skills needed to achieve performance results.
>
> The world of the supervisor is one of conflicting role expectations. Both management and subordinates place specific role demands upon the supervisor that often conflict. Understanding these expectations, as well as being aware that supervision is a unique activity requiring a distinct set of knowledge, skills and abilities, are important factors in supervisory development. The knowledge, skills and ability required in the supervisor's role are directly related to the basic managerial functions of planning, organizing, coordinating, motivating, and controlling the work of others to achieve effective performance.

To be a truly successful leader, one must master each type of skill as subordinates will quickly learn one's weaknesses. In addition to these challenges from within the organization, the leader will be confronted with challenges external to the organization. One of these challenges is the constant need to change.

ORGANIZATIONAL CHANGE

Police departments and organizations are processes rather than static entities. In the dynamic society surrounding law enforcement today, there are many influences acting upon the police bureaucracy. Community leaders and agencies positioning themselves for influence and power over the police organization, new demands from minority groups, the constantly changing nature of crime and criminals, and changes in the law and our criminal justice system are among a few of the important factors creating a dynamic social environment to which police organizations must adapt. Within the police organization, there are changes in the background, training, and expectations of police officers themselves. This also creates a need for change. All of these factors, both external and internal to the police organization, have created a decade of change.

It is no longer a question of whether change is necessary or not. Within today's fast-paced world, the issue is how best to cope with the barrage of changes that confront police executives daily. Although change is a fact of life, police executives cannot be content to let change occur as it will. They must develop strategies to plan, direct, and control change.

There are two major ways of implementing change: reactive and planned. Change is called *reactive* when problems occur first and then adjustments in organization follow. It may be a change in the state or federal regulations that necessitates a reaction on the part of police procedures. It may be a public outcry concerning excessive use of force that requires increased training of officers and a new policy. In each of these situations, the change in departmental policies or organization is the result of solving a problem defined by someone outside of the police department. In contrast, *planned* change involves active efforts on the part of the police department to change the status quo. Skilled police executives have the foresight to identify changes in the social environment and to adjust their organization and policies ahead of time through planned change. They do not wait for the problems to occur before dealing with them. They foresee potential problems and orchestrate planned change to prevent these problems. They monitor changes in the social environment, anticipate potential problems for law enforcement and develop appropriate coping mechanisms to avert the impact of the problems for their organizations. This cannot always be accomplished successfully, but it is much better than simply waiting for the problems to occur, accepting the damage, and then reacting to minimize the disruption.

Change seems to revolve around three aspects of an organization: structure, technology, and personnel. Structural change is the most difficult to stimulate and involves revisions of the organization, policies, or procedures. For example, decentralization of authority is an organizational change. Through decentralization, each division will have more autonomy to make decisions. Changes in technology are constantly occurring and create an atmosphere in which a department is constantly trying to keep up with the "state of the art." Technological changes involve new work methods, new tools or equipment or other changes resulting from new information. Chapter 1 discussed how the introduction of technology into police work, such as the automobile and two-way radio, resulted in drastic changes in the organization of law enforcement agencies. Similarly, the types of communication discussed earlier or a vehicle tracking system (VTS) that electronically or mechanically monitors the patrol vehicle's activities, including speed, stopping and starting, can lead to changes in supervisory practices. When this technology is applied to police work, fewer sergeants are needed to supervise the officers directly, and the supervisors' time can be spent more effectively and efficiently. Personnel changes involve new demands made of personnel, as well as the need for new skills, modified attitudes and increased motivation. The human resource is the most valuable resource in any organization. Changes in the nature of police work have led to the need for an increasing amount of education and training of police officers, and thus a change in the nature of police personnel.

One example of planned change is the accreditation process. Accreditation has a rich history in many areas but is relatively new to criminal justice and law enforcement. The process of accreditation includes the institutional establishment of minimum standards. Currently, the Commission on Accreditation for Law Enforcement Agencies accredits police departments with the voluntary approval of the major professional groups in law enforcement, including the International Association of Chiefs of Police (IACP), the National Organization of Black Law Enforcement Executives (NOBLE), the National Sheriffs' Association and the Police Executive Research Forum (PERF).

Representatives of these groups, along with other professionals, establish standards for most areas of law enforcement which reflect the most current practices in management, administration, operations, and support services. These standards are well known and vary slightly by size of department. As accreditation is a peer-review process, a team of experienced professionals, armed with the guidelines and standards, will visit a department to determine if it is in compliance with the standards. The short-term costs of accreditation are high, but it is argued that the costs of not achieving certain standards of excellence will be higher in the long term. Change always generates concern in organizations, but planned change is certainly more desirable than change brought about as a reaction to some crisis.

Any change may be resisted by those within and without the organization. An important element that accounts for much of this resistance is the concern held by members of the organization that change will adversely affect their position, income, or status. In the unusual event that a particular change will not affect anyone adversely, the unfounded fear of loss can incite members of the organization to obstruct change. In addition, the burden of change, which involves learning new procedures, studying new manuals and developing new relationships and contacts, can create resistance to organizational change.

In spite of this fear of change, there are three focal points of the police mandate that are in constant need of assessment and revision, namely officer morale, public trust and crime focus. Attending to these three responsibilities in a turbulent social environment requires constant vigilance in adapting to change. In other words, the police must preserve life and control crime, yet, at the same time, keep all elements of the public happy and maintain a high level of job satisfaction among officers. It is the organizational structure that oversees and manages these responsibilities.

SUMMARY

The organization and administration of police agencies have been based on a military model. These agencies have utilized the traditional pyramid-type hierarchy with a strict chain of command. Although agencies may differ in their emphasis, certain characteristics of organization and administration are common among most departments.

Departments which choose to modify their organizational characteristics are likely to introduce a system of participatory management which will empower officers at all levels. On the technological side, modern computerized communication techniques with user-friendly language and a concern for human relations will assist in the administration of the agency. One consequence of this high-tech approach will be computerized information for all aspects of the agency, including the identification and tracking of suspects, accountability of officers, and modern methods to manage departmental budgets.

Police agencies are closely linked to the larger political environment and the communities they serve. These outside influences, as well as internal influences, direct many aspects of the police bureaucracy in action. These pressures on the police organization create an atmosphere of potential change. It is the responsibility of police leaders to be sensitive to the various influences and to be prepared to respond with planned changes rather than employing crisis management techniques.

References

Alpert, Geoffrey and Roger Dunham. 1986. "Community Policing." *Journal of Police Science and Administration* 14:212–22.

Auten, James. 1988. "Preparing Written Guidelines." *FBI Law Enforcement Bulletin* 57:1–7.

Bittner, Egon. 1970. *The Functions of the Police in Modern Society*. Washington, DC: United States Government Printing Office.

Black, Donald. 1984. *Toward a General Theory of Social Control*. New York: Academic Press.

California Vehicle Code, 1987 (Chapter 1205), sec. 17004.7.

Chaiken, Jan, Peter Greenwood, and Joan Petersilia. 1983. "The Rand Study of Detectives." In Carl Klockars (ed.) *Thinking About Police*, pp. 167–84. New York: McGraw-Hill.

Chaiken, Marcia (ed.). 1988. *Street-level Drug Enforcement: Examining the Issues*. Washington, DC: National Institute of Justice.

Holden, Richard. 1986. *Modern Police Management*. Englewood Cliffs, NJ: Prentice-Hall.

Lundman, Richard. 1980. "Police Work with Traffic Law Violators." In R. Lundman (ed.) *Police Behavior: A Sociological Perspective*, pp 51–65. New York: Oxford University Press.

Manning, Peter. 1988. *Symbolic Communication*. Cambridge, MA: MIT Press.

Metro-Dade Police Department. 1995. *Metro-Dade Police Departmental Manual—1995*. Miami: Metro-Dade Police Department.

Police Executive Research Forum. 1990. *Tackling Drug Problems in Public Housing: A Guide for Police*. Washington, DC: Police Research Forum.

Reiss, Albert J. Jr. 1992. "Police Organization in the Twentieth Century." In Michael Tonry and Norval Morris (eds.) *Modern Policing*. Chicago: University of Chicago Press.

Stone, Alfred and Stuart DeLuca. 1985. *Police Administration*. New York: John Wiley and Sons.

Swanson, Charles, Leonard Territo, and Robert Taylor. 1993. *Police Administration: Structures, Processes, and Behavior,* 2nd ed. New York: Macmillan Publishers.

Walsch, William and Edwin Donovan. 1990. *The Supervision of Police Personnel: A Performance Based Approach*. Dubuque: Kendall/Hunt.

Case

City of Canton, Ohio v. Harris, 489 U.S. 378 (1989).

Chapter Five

POLICE SOCIALIZATION AND POLICE SUBCULTURE

As we learned in chapter 3, the socialization process for police recruits begins before they enter the police academy. In fact, there has been considerable discussion concerning whether people who possess certain characteristics are more likely to express an interest in police work than others and if this depends upon previous socialization or social environment. If this is the case, applicants for police work share some common interests and characteristics before they become officers. In addition to the question of whether self-selection (deciding to apply for a police job) creates a group with some common characteristics, there is the question as to what extent the complex processes of selection and recruitment add to the uniqueness of the characteristics shared by police officers. Research informs us that applicants with certain characteristics and from a certain background are more likely to be selected from the pool of applicants to attend the police academy than others. These questions can be reduced to: (1) are the recruits unique when compared to the general population, and (2) in which ways do their characteristics differ?

The academy experience is the first *formal* socialization process within the police organization that directly begins to influence recruits' attitudes, values and behaviors and serves to separate them from society at large. On-the-job experiences while performing duties and acting out the role of a law enforcement officer provide the continued socialization that often pulls the officer into a distinct and powerful police subculture. Members of this subculture often view the outside world suspiciously and sometimes as opposing their best interests and activities.

The purpose of this chapter is to answer the two questions regarding recruit characteristics and to discuss some aspects of police socialization and the resulting police subculture. We will begin with a sociological discussion of the processes of socialization and professionalization to provide a background for studying police work. In addition, we will examine the nature of subcultures and apply the concept to the police as a group. The remainder of the chapter will include a discussion of the various aspects of the police subculture and their impact on the quality of police work and crime control.

SOCIALIZATION AND PROFESSIONALIZATION

All social groups have means of teaching their young the norms, values and attitudes that are highly valued by the members of the group. In turn, the young person is expected to internalize these as he or she grows older. This is called the process of *socialization*. It is a complex process of social learning that contributes to the individual's personality, permits participation in group life, and engenders acceptance of the beliefs and values of the group. One of the products of socialization is the individual's personal organization or unique psychological nature. This is commonly referred to as *personality*. Socialization persists throughout the life cycle and continues to shape one's orientation to others and to all experiences.

Various subgroups to which we belong may provide powerful influences that shape our beliefs and values. When vocational subgroups shape our beliefs and values as they train us in the technical skills needed to perform the vocational roles, it is called *professionalization*. Professionalization is really a special type of socialization that involves vocational content. Through professionalization, standards are internalized by each member as part of his or her technical training so that the person's actions are self-regulated.

Not every occupation is defined or accepted as a profession. Even those that are organized may not include certain attributes or maintain standards. The distinction between an occupation and a profession include, but are not limited to, the following: (1) prolonged membership, (2) requirements for higher education, (3) specialized training, (4) controls over training, (5) controls over licensing, (6) developed rhetoric, (7) a shared perspective, (8) belief that work is worthy of high self-esteem, and (9) autonomous command and control of the organization. Police work includes all of the attributes necessary to be called a profession, and the members' standards are regulated through internalized norms and outside controls.

As we discussed in chapter 4, the police have a "tainted occupation." Many citizens feel that the police are just a little above the evil they fight or believe that the police are against them and misuse their right to use force to uphold the law. However, the police often perceive a more extreme negative evaluation by citizens than what really exists. A new recruit quickly recognizes that he or she is different from most others in society and feels that others view police officers as being different from ordinary citizens. As a result of this isolation, the police operate within the context of one of the strongest vocational subcultures in American society. Before we discuss the subculture and its impact on police officers, we will present Chief Bowlin's opinions.

CHIEF'S CORNER
POLICE SOCIALIZATION

To me, there seem to be two types of individuals involved in law enforcement. The first type of individuals become quite cynical in a few years and tend to isolate themselves within the police culture. Their friends are police officers; they talk primarily about job-connected interests and concern themselves to a great degree with the stupidity displayed by anyone who is not a police officer. As a result, a feeling of "us against them" dominates their lives and robs them of any real or prolonged happiness. This officer's frustration many times manifests itself in the beating of a handcuffed prisoner, getting divorced because his or her spouse just doesn't seem to understand, or committing suicide when forced to retire, as a consequence of losing a support network.

The second type of officer is a rather strange person who doesn't seem to completely belong because he or she can't seem to incorporate all the attributes that the first type of officer has developed. This officer's attitude toward work, family, and the community in general, is positive. He or she is able to discern between the good and bad in the world and to keep each in its proper perspective. A firearm is just that—a weapon to be used for self-protection or the protection of others—not a symbol of the ever-present battle of good versus evil. This officer does not feel under constant assault from the crooks, the community and the administration. He or she realizes the need for controls on law enforcement; first-hand observation of peers has demonstrated what will happen if there are no behavior limitations on police officers. Without even realizing it, this officer belongs in the department much more than the dramatized, cynical officer we've become familiar with through the media.

It is this officer, who truly likes people and the opportunity to serve them, that enjoys a successful career, both personally and in terms of positive feedback from the community. The single-most important trait required to be successful in law enforcement is social intelligence—the ability to enjoy and to interact effectively with people.

SUBCULTURE

Culture is the foundation upon which a social group operates within the world around it. It includes knowledge, beliefs, morals, laws, customs, and any other capabilities or habits acquired by its members. Obviously, the police are a part of American culture and share many of the traits and customs of the larger society. However, in many ways, the police develop traditions and survival skills that are unique to their vocational group because of their duties and responsibilities. These distinct differences in culture qualify them as members of a *subculture*, a group that shares a great deal of the dominant culture, but that is set off from general society because of its unique aspects.

Many officers are not aware of the strong influences of the police subculture or how the norms affect their lives and careers. Many do not realize that membership in the group influences how they view the world and, more specifically, how they view and act toward citizens outside of the police subculture. Research has confirmed this observation and has identified some important differences in attitudes and beliefs between the police and other citizens (Burbeck and Furnham, 1985). Officers feel that to be accepted in the police role, they must conform to the norms of unity and loyalty, the code of secrecy, the perceptions of outsiders, and the danger and suspicion that pervade the police profession and subculture.

As with other subcultures, the police subculture involves secrecy and isolation from those who are not part of the group. Police officers even protect one another from outsiders, and sometimes from inside investigations into the wrongdoing of fellow officers. This "blue code of silence," as it has been called, also involves maintaining a tough, macho image, and being distrustful of outsiders. The Fuhrman tapes, revealed during the O.J. Simpson trial, provided an image of the L.A. police subculture that shocked nearly everyone. If true, the attitudes and practices of Detective Mark Fuhrman and a few other extremist officers go well beyond the values and norms of most police subcultures. According to the tapes, some Los Angeles police officers used the police "code of silence" and loyalty to cover up extreme racist practices involving the planting of evidence to convict innocent citizens, extreme forms of police brutality, and even murder. The tapes depicted police authority and "use of force" gone wild. Hopefully, these scenes of "the dark side of the force" are exaggerated and uncharacteristic of other police subcultures.

Some police researchers relate the unquestioned support and loyalty within the typical police subcultures to a survival strategy in the dangerous and often isolated occupation of policing (Bittner, 1980). Michael K. Brown, in *Working the Street*, (1981) illustrates how police officers create their own subculture to deal with the recurring anxiety and emotional stress that are endemic to policing. His analysis of police subculture reveals three important characteristics: honor, loyalty, and individuality. Honor refers to bravery and commitment to fulfilling their duties no matter how much risk is involved. Loyalty is shown toward other officers and the police subculture, especially in backing up each other in difficult situations. Individuality refers to officers being autonomous, aggressive, and able to take charge of difficult situations.

Since a subculture exists, it is important that we understand its effect on the quality of police work. The remainder of this chapter is devoted to a discussion of some of the aspects of the police subculture and their effect on policing.

POLICE PERSONALITY

There has been considerable interest in whether or not there exists a personality type unique to particular professions, especially to the police profession. In other words, are police officers different from average citizens; is there a "police personality"? As a result of this long-standing interest, considerable research has been conducted comparing the personality characteristics of the police with those of citizens in general (Burbeck and Furnham, 1985).

A number of differences have been discovered between the personality characteristics of the police and those of other citizens. The discovery of these differences has led many researchers to conclude that there is a distinct police personality which they call the working personality of the police (Skolnick, 1966; Burbeck and Furnham, 1985). These researchers claim that three important features of an officer's working environment can account for the working personality. These include danger, authority, and isolation from the public.

A very real and important aspect of police work is the constant prospect of *danger* to the officer, to his or her fellow officers and to citizens. This is a continual concern which begins in the police academy, is carried through on-the-job training and continues until retirement. In order to deal with this constant threat of being in a potentially dangerous situation, patrol officers come to view everyone with suspicion. In fact, the public in general and especially members of high-crime minority groups in particular are viewed as "symbolic" assailants. Officers learn through training and often through painful experience that they have the most to fear from young male minority group members in low-income neighborhoods. This fact sets the stage for the development, or at least the claim, of racial prejudice and discrimination.

The second aspect of police work that helps to account for the development of a distinct police personality is *authority*. Because of their role in society as law enforcers, the police are authority figures by definition. New officers learn very quickly that authority enables them to carry out their responsibilities. As a part of the role, an officer must give orders, exercise control in law enforcement and order maintenance situations, place restraints upon the freedom of action, enforce unpopular laws, conduct searches, make arrests, and perform a host of other duties. It would be impossible to perform these duties without the right and ability to use force when needed. Perhaps the foremost concern of police officers is establishing and maintaining authority, especially when involved in difficult situations. This concern over authority is the basis for the authoritarian personality that is often associated with police officers (Neiderhoffer, 1967; Clinton, 1995).

Both the concern over danger and over authority serve to *isolate* police officers from the rest of society. In part, this is due to the public's response to the difficulties, inconveniences and threats posed by police authority and to the officers' detached demeanor. For example, it is not uncommon for an officer to refuse to sit down and accept a cup of coffee in the home of a victim while writing notes or filling out a report. Many officers would rather struggle to fill out a report while standing than to weaken their authoritative posture and detached demeanor. This example illustrates how the officer's concern for maintaining authority isolates him or her from the rest of society in important ways and leads to an intense solidarity among fellow officers to cope with this isolation.

In fact, the process begins in the academy, as John Van Maanen has noted (1978:299):

> The main result of [police] training is that the recruit soon learns it is his peer group rather than the "brass" which will support him and which he, in turn, must support. For example, the newcomers adopt covering tactics to become proficient at constructing consensual ad hoc explanations of a fellow recruit's mistakes. Furthermore, the long hours, new friends and ordeal aspects of the recruit school serve to detach the newcomer from his old attitudes and acquaintances. In short, the academy impresses upon the recruit that he must now identify with a new group: his fellow officers.

This aspect of academy training teaches recruits to maintain a detached attitude when interacting with citizens. This creates an exaggerated concern with authority and control, a power that will never be total. While this position or posture may be helpful in dangerous situations and when an officer finds himself or herself without community support, it is ineffective and often counterproductive in most police-citizen encounters. A relaxed stance, an ability to roll with the punches, and showing some sympathy result in effective police-citizen encounters. The dilemma is to act with the appropriate demeanor in each situation.

Unfortunately, police officers are trained and prepared mentally for the worst and most dangerous situations. They often have a difficult time adjusting their demeanor and responses to the more frequent, less dangerous encounters. Later, we will examine many of the personal problems of police officers and discuss the stressors of police work that are at the root of those problems. A significant amount of stress is directly related to this detached demeanor and the related emotional overreaction.

Before discussing the subject of a working personality among the police, two points of clarification should be made. When the personality characteristics of police recruits have been compared to others of the same age and the same socio-economic status, few differences have been found (Burbeck and Furnham, 1985). In fact, the characteristics of the working police personality are not so different from those of other working-class persons. Authoritarianism, prejudice, conservatism and cynicism are hardly unusual characteristics in American society. Perhaps, the interesting question is why are the police singled out for special attention for having the characteristics common to their social groups? Why is there more interest in their characteristics than in those of other groups? Although this question has not been addressed adequately in the research literature, there are some logical explanations.

Police behavior is public behavior. The police represent the community-at-large and the laws of the community. When a police officer approaches a citizen to issue a traffic ticket, to inquire about the citizen's purpose and intentions for being in the area, or just to pass the time of day, he or she directly brings the power of the state to the situation. As a result, any potential misbehavior can reflect negatively upon the officer, the department, and the state. Because of this, police behavior is subject to more public scrutiny than the behavior of others. The officers' personality characteristics are not only more visible, but also are much more salient to the average citizen. Apparently, prejudice shown by a police officer toward a suspect is much more visible and disconcerting than prejudice shown by a construction foreman toward a worker or by a personnel recruiter when hiring employees.

Another point of clarification is that the police do have some unique personality characteristics when compared to other citizens; yet, this does not mean that all police officers think or act alike. In the aggregate, however, they differ from other citizens in some ways. In chapter 7, we will discuss a typology of working styles of the police, demonstrating how officers develop one of several general styles depending, in part, upon their individual personality characteristics.

In Burbeck and Furnham's (1985) review of the literature comparing the attitudes of police officers with those of the general population, they have indicated that police officers place a higher emphasis on terminal values such as family security, mature love and a sense of accomplishment, while giving lower rankings to social values such as equality. They also found that, as officers gain experience on the job, they appear to de-emphasize what could be called the softer, affective values and place greater emphasis on a harder, more cognitive orientation (see Burbeck and Furnham, 1985). In addition to finding some differences in the general orientation of police officers when compared with the orientation of other citizens, several specific personality traits have been discovered.

Two aspects of personality have been identified with the police personality: authoritarianism and prejudice (see Broderick, 1987). Both of these are highly relevant to the fairness of law enforcement and have stimulated considerable controversy concerning their effect on good policing practices.

Authoritarianism is a complex domain of personality traits that includes an exaggerated concern for authority, punitiveness, conservatism, and rigid adherence to rules and values. Included in this personality constellation is a need for order and routine, inflexibility and a proclivity to stereotype groups different from one's own group. When this personality type is applied to the police working personality, the focus is often upon toughness, aggressiveness and cynicism as its manifestations. Interestingly, studies of police personality have not demonstrated that authoritarian characteristics are the result of the types of people choosing a police career or the result of selection (Burbeck and Furnham, 1985). Apparently, the experience of joining the police force and becoming a part of the police subculture influences individuals to become more authoritarian, prejudiced, closed-minded and conservative than they were before joining the force. Some researchers believe that authoritarian characteristics are related to the nature of policing, are unavoidable and, to some extent, necessary. They believe that the authoritarian characteristics are the result of trying to fulfill their occupational role. These researchers have referred to the police as "occupational authoritarians," a concept that includes occupations other than the police, such as physicians, army personnel and priests, among others. A negative aspect of the authoritarian personality is its relationship to prejudice (see Wilbanks, 1987).

Prejudice is an attitude toward members of a group (often ethnic minorities) that involves unfavorable and essentially unjustifiable beliefs and feelings. Prejudice is closely associated with authoritarian personalities. A person with an authoritarian personality is likely to have an unfavorable attitude toward people belonging to other groups. In addition, this person is likely to stereotype members of those groups. The aspects of the authoritarian personality which result in prejudice have been the basis for considerable criticism of the police working personality and have obvious implications for fair and equal treatment under the law.

Since police officers must be constantly aware of the possible threat of violence, many officers rely on profiles to identify potentially dangerous people. These profiles often identify young minority males as the most likely to pose a threat. Other characteristics included in the profile that the police recognize as antecedents to violence are the use of certain gestures, language and attire. People fitting these profiles are treated with suspicion and discrimination, which is the basis for the claim of prejudice.

In summary, there is some evidence for the existence of a police working personality. Most of the evidence points to the influence of socialization and experiences after becoming a police officer as the main source of the unique traits. This is commonly referred to as the *socialization model*. There is little evidence that these characteristics are present before the recruit joins the police force, which discounts the *predispositional model* or theory that recruits, as individuals, already have these unique characteristics.

POLICE UNITY

Unity among officers pervades the police subculture. It has its basis in the realities of police work and, in its own way, serves a purpose. Policing is a dangerous business and, therefore, unquestioned support and loyalty among officers are important aspects of survival. Another benefit of police unity is that it bolsters the officer's self-esteem and confidence. This confidence and perceived support enable the officer to tolerate the isolation from general society and the hostility and disapproval of citizens.

Loyalty is one of the core values in the police subculture. Michael Brown, in his book *Working the Street* (1981:82), describes the value of loyalty in the police subculture:

> As one patrolman expressed the matter, "I'm for the guys in blue! Anybody criticizes a fellow copper, that's like criticizing someone in my family; we have to stick together." The police culture demands of a patrolman unstinting loyalty to his fellow officers, and he receives, in return, protection and honor: a place to assuage real and imagined wrongs inflicted by a (presumably) hostile public: safety from aggressive administrators and supervisors; and the emotional support required to perform a difficult task. The most important question asked by a patrolman about a rookie is whether or not he displays the loyalty demanded by the police subculture.

A related characteristic of the police subculture is the pressure for conformity among officers (Reiser, 1974:158). Peer influence is one of the most profound pressures operating in police organizations. While it can be helpful, it can also create problems and ethical dilemmas. On the positive side, when making tough decisions or when in trouble, an officer can count on not being alone. Negatively, this sense of unity and loyalty may someday be invoked by an officer to cover a serious mistake or to help him or her out of serious trouble. Even the increasing professionalization of the police role has modified only slightly the value of loyalty, the penchant for secrecy and the willingness of one officer to cover up some misbehavior of a fellow officer (see Van Maanen, 1989). In other words, loyalty is still at the core of the police subculture. The code of secrecy remains very real and influential. However, there is a general accepted limit of what can be tolerated and held secret. In most subcultures, conspicuous corruption crosses that line and calls for some action.

PROFESSIONALIZATION

The professionalization of the police is both organizational and individual. The police, as an institution, must include the specific characteristics outlined earlier. Individual officers must understand and benefit from these organizational attributes in a variety of ways.

The responsibilities of a police officer are so varied and sensitive that some students of the police function have claimed that for an officer to be adequately educated and trained, he or she would need several Ph.D.s. Their work in human relations requires many decisions that are not only difficult but also are critical to a person's life—socially, emotionally, and, sometimes, physically. For example, an unwise decision concerning the handling of a minor situation involving a juvenile delinquent can have devastating effects on a juvenile's life. Settling a domestic dispute can involve complex situations that are very difficult to decipher. Improper or unwise decisions on the part of an officer intervening in a marital dispute can have a terrible impact on the individuals or on their marriage. Crime-fighting situations also call upon the officer to make crucial decisions that have the potential for making a critical impact on the lives of citizens.

In addition to the social or emotional impact of an officer's decision making, there are also many legal and procedural issues involved in everyday police work. A good officer should be capable of considering all of these issues when carrying out his or her duties. It is somewhat difficult, however, for police administrators, given the available resources, to produce officers with these capabilities. One important way of striving to reach this level of efficiency and capability is through police professionalization.

The professionalization of the police includes the drive for more technical training and higher education. Higher education is seen as the route to develop a professional occupational identity, to gain professional social acceptance, and to standardize the working knowledge of the police. As discussed in the history chapter, advanced education for police officers began with August Vollmer, who developed two-year associate degree programs in criminal justice at junior colleges in California in the 1920s and 1930s. Except for California and a few other states, the idea of a college-educated police force had received very little support prior to 1963. However, in 1967, the President's Crime Commission called for a higher standard for educational requirements of police officers. The Commission recommended that all personnel with general law enforcement powers have baccalaureate degrees. This was extremely ambitious considering that, at the time, about one-half of the nation's law enforcement officers had not even finished high school. Further, about 30 percent of the nation's police agencies did not even require a high school diploma as a condition of employment. About two years later, the federal government's Law Enforcement Education Program (LEEP) was established as part of the Law Enforcement Assistance Administration to fund higher education for police officers. In 1974 alone, there were almost 100,000 LEEP recipients attending 1,036 participating educational institutions, at a cost of forty-five million dollars. This funding increased the number of programs offering advanced education in criminal justice eightfold in just five years.

This development brought the goal of a college-educated police force much closer to realization and created a giant step toward nationwide professionalization of police. In 1973, the National Advisory Commission on Criminal Justice Standards and Goals recommended specific time periods for setting higher education as a condition of employment. In the mid-1970s, only about 10 percent of the police possessed four-year college degrees, and 50 percent had not even attended college. The Standards and Goals Commission recommended that a four-year college degree be a requirement of employment in all police departments by 1982; however, we are far from reaching this goal today and, in some cases, have lowered some standards to meet affirmative action goals for minority employment. Some have criticized this inability to reach a goal as a lack of professionalism, while others have acknowledged that the goal was too lofty (see Carter et al., 1989).

UNIONIZATION OF THE POLICE

The 1960s was a time when advancements were made in collective bargaining for public employees. The formation of police employee organizations was a part of this larger movement for collective bargaining. Some of these organizations are called benevolent associations and others are referred to as police unions. Regardless of their title, they represent a formalization of the police subculture. They officially and formally represent the needs and priorities of the police officer which are sometimes in opposition to the needs and priorities of police management. Police officers are usually not willing to accept the rigid control that may be imposed upon them by the often over managed police department. In the past, they resorted to overt acts of sabotage of their department and its efforts to control crime. At times, they deliberately misused departmental equipment or even resorted to the tactic of the "blue flu" to stage unofficial strikes. In any event, when the officers in the police subculture feel that their needs and priorities are not being satisfied by management, they begin to organize associations which are parallel to the police department. These parallel organizations usually take the form of unions or police benevolent associations.

There are several areas of concern among police officers that typically serve as catalysts for the formation of a police officers' association. These are interests that most police officers are concerned about but do not receive much attention from the public or from management. In a sense, these areas of disagreement are much of the substance of the police subculture: specific attitudes and values that differ in some respects from the rest of society.

Historically, the police have felt isolated in their efforts to control crime. We have already mentioned that the police usually perceive a great deal more public hostility and disapproval than really exists. In addition, the police have perceived the due-process movement and the movement to establish civilian oversight of law enforcement as votes of no-confidence concerning their work and their professional standards. Many police officers, particularly patrol officers, have viewed the emphasis on due-process that has been established by the courts as an infringement on their ability to control crime. Many view this as a way of handcuffing the police and a demonstration of weak support from the very institutions that should be joining with them in the effort to increase their effectiveness in controlling crime. Instead, the courts are seen as being at odds with the priorities of the police.

Another area where the police feel that their interests are compromised is the emphasis on the creation of civilian oversight boards. These boards oversee and monitor police work at the community level. From the outset during the 1960s, police organizations have been adamantly opposed to the civilian-staffed review boards for two reasons. First, they have a negative impact on police morale. Second, they have a negative impact on police-community relations. During the 1960s, the police responded to these boards by creating or strengthening already existing police organizations to represent the interests of the police. Civilian oversight boards were seen as a way of dividing the police and weakening their subculture.

Probably the major reason for forming police unions was job dissatisfaction, especially with regard to pay and working conditions. During the 1960s, the police felt that their pay scales were far below what they should be in comparison to other workers. They also felt that the only way they could raise their pay to a reasonable level and ease their working conditions was to organize and to fight collectively. This perception was apparently correct, since, in many areas of the country, police organizations and unions have been successful in bargaining for higher pay scales and better working conditions.

Today, most officers are members of some police organization or association, but, unlike most other unions, police groups have no national organization. Their only national representation is concerned with professional goals and advancement through the International Association of Chiefs of Police (IACP) and the National Sheriff's Association (NSA). Most issues for the police are decided locally and at the state level, so this is where the organizations focus their efforts. As do other unions, police organizations spend much of their effort working toward better pay and retirement, improved benefits, more reasonable hours, and the improvement of other working conditions. However, other concerns include the protection of officers under investigation, input into changes made to law enforcement organization and priorities, and the protection of officers with seniority against the threat of affirmative action policies.

Police organizations and unions are a formalization of certain job-related aspects of the police subculture. These unions have been effective in expressing the interests and concerns of the police subculture and in forcefully representing their interests and priorities to police administrators and supervisors, as well as to municipal officials and the public. However, the movement is best characterized today as fragmented (Hoover and DeLord, 1995:792).

> . . . it has become difficult to identify the major organizations representing the substantial numbers of police officers. With mergers, affiliations, and name changes over the last ten years, it is indeed a confusing picture. . . Much of the turmoil surrounding the police "union" movement revolves around whether it is indeed a union movement. Police officers in the United States belong to every imaginable type of labor union, association, fraternal organization, and professional group.

This situation seems to indicate that police officers cannot agree on which organizations, or even which type of organization, best serve their interests: fraternal or militant, democratic or benevolent, decentralized or centralized (Hoover and DeLord, 1995:795). Perhaps, one day the police will have one dominant organization to be the national voice, as we find for teachers, firefighters, and other public servants.

ORIENTATION TOWARD ACTION

An important and common characteristic among police officers is an orientation toward action. This is somewhat contrary to the often used characterization of police officers as subprofessionals looking for the security of government work. It is true that police work does provide considerable security, but security is just as easily obtained from civil-service jobs that do not have the inherent danger, stress or excitement of police work. It is also true that a great deal of police work is mundane and boring, yet there is that omnipresent possibility that something will require immediate action and crucial decision making and will contain an element of danger. Because of these aspects of police work, some have characterized police officers as calculating, manipulative individuals for whom the real lure of police work is the excitement. Joseph Wambaugh (1977:3–4) provides us with a good example of a police officer's view on the unpredictability of police work:

> Hollywood Division was a good place for police work. It was busy and exciting in the way that is unique to police experience—the unpredictable lurked. Ian Campbell believed that what most policemen shared was an abhorrence of the predictable, a distaste for the foreseeable experiences of working life. . . . No, policemen [were] not danger lovers, they were seekers of the awesome, the incredible, even the unspeakable in human experience. Never mind whether they could interpret, never mind if it was potentially hazardous to the soul. *To be there* was the thing.

It is interesting that the working styles of policing to be discussed in chapter 7 mostly involve an orientation toward action. The four styles of policing that are presented (enforcers, idealists, realists and optimists) all have an orientation toward a different type of action. However, the common thread linking them together is that each style focuses on problems to be solved by acting or reacting pragmatically and resourcefully. There is not a sense in any of the four styles of policing of a laid-back civil servant biding time, avoiding as much work as possible, and craving security. This is not to suggest that there are no lazy police officers who just go through the motions, but this type of orientation to police work is not one of the major criteria for membership in the typology. In any profession, one can find people who approach their jobs in this manner.

While one can often find police officers with a cynical orientation toward their job, the police subculture operates to discourage it. The obligation of loyalty discussed earlier involves dependability and the willingness of each officer to do his or her share of the work and not to shift the burden of work onto fellow officers. This obligation is tied very closely to the atmosphere of unity that protects each officer from danger, isolation, and any type of trouble originating from supervisors or the public. Slacking off too much means alienation from the police subculture and being labeled as unreliable. Fellow officers might refuse to talk to you or go out of their way to get you into trouble. When you are on the police force, you cannot afford to have other officers against you, because there are too many situations in which you might need to depend upon them.

However, it is also common for the subculture to discourage rate-busters in the same manner. Any officer who sets standards of work performance that put pressure on all the other officers to meet those standards will feel the influence of the subculture discouraging this type of "disruptive" behavior.

SUMMARY

Researchers have identified some unique characteristics of the working personality of the police and of the police subculture. These distinct traits are the result of a socialization process that begins when one joins the police force and continues while executing the duties of a law enforcement officer.

It is clear from our discussion of police socialization and the police subculture that the two are linked in important ways. Socialization provides the basis for the subculture, and the subculture influences the socialization process. As students of the police have examined the police subculture and tried to understand its origins, one important conclusion has emerged. This subculture is not so much the result of self-selection to become a police officer or of screening applicants as it is the result of a need to create a social organization to cope with the difficulties and stresses of performing the role of a law enforcement officer. Although many police scholars have looked to the initial selection of police recruits as the source of the characteristics thought to be unique among police, further examination has reduced the importance of this view. In confronting the difficulties, ambiguities and uncertainties of police work, officers have turned inward to their partners and co-workers for survival. While the resulting subculture has been the focus of much debate and criticism, we have come to view it as a coping mechanism rather than simply as a self-interested and irresponsible subculture.

This view of the subculture emphasizes its vocational aspects. As a vocational subculture, the values, attitudes, and behaviors that are inherent to the group are mostly job-related. These characteristics are ways of viewing and reacting to the outside world and to any obstacles that frustrate the group members' role performance. Subcultural identities are perceived solutions to the ambiguities and uncertainties inherent in the police officer's structured role. Perhaps, the message to those who are critical of certain aspects of the police subculture and who call for major structural reform is that the vocational solution cannot be taken away without addressing the problems inherent in the police role, as well as the deviance and corruption that may result.

References

Bittner, Egon. 1980. *The Functions of Police in Modern Society*. Cambridge, MA: Oelgeschlager.

Broderick, John J. 1987. *Police in a Time of Change*, 2nd ed. Prospect Heights, IL: Waveland Press.

Brown, Michael K. 1981. *Working the Street: Police Discretion and the Dilemmas of Reform*. New York: Russell Sage Foundation.

Burbeck, Elizabeth and Adrian Furnham. 1985. "Police Officer Selection: A Critical Review of the Literature." *Journal of Police Science and Administration* 13(1): 58–69.

Carter, David, Allen Sapp, and Danell Stephans. 1989. *The State of Police Education: Policy Directions for the 21st. Century*. Washington, DC: Police Executive Research Forum.

Clinton, Terry W., III. 1995. "Psychological Attributes." In William G. Bailey (ed.) *The Encyclopedia of Police Science*, 2nd ed., pp. 669–74. New York: Garland Publishing.

Cole, Stephen. 1975. *The Sociological Orientation: An Introduction to Sociology*. Chicago: Rand McNally.

Hoover, Larry T. and Ronald G. DeLord. 1995. *Unionization*. In William G. Bailey (ed.) *The Encyclopedia of Police Science*, 2nd ed., pp. 792–96. New York: Garland.

National Advisory Commission on Criminal Justice Standards and Goals. 1973. *Police*. Washington, DC: United States Government Printing Office.

Neiderhoffer, Arthur. 1967. *Behind the Shield: The Police in Urban Society*. Garden City, NY: Anchor Books.

President's Commission on Law Enforcement and Administration of Justice. 1967. *Task Force Report: Police*. Washington, DC: United States Government Printing Office.

Reiser, Martin. 1974. "Some Organizational Stresses on Policemen." *Journal of Police Science and Administration* 2, no. 2 (June): 138–44.

Skolnick, Jerome. 1966. *Justice Without Trial*. New York: John Wiley and Sons.

United States Commission on Civil Rights. 1981 (October). *Who Is Guarding the Guardians?* Washington, DC: United States Government Printing Office.

Van Maanen, John. 1978. "Observations on the Making of Policemen." In Peter Manning and John Van Maanen (eds.) *Policing: A View from the Street.* New York: Random House.

————. 1993. "Making Rank: Becoming an American Police Sergeant." In Roger Dunham and Geoffrey Alpert (eds.) *Critical Issues in Policing*, 2nd ed., pp. 165–80. Prospect Heights, IL: Waveland Press.

Wambaugh, Joseph. 1977. *The Onion Field.* New York: Delacorte Press.

Wilbanks, William. 1987. *The Myth of a Racist Criminal Justice System.* Monterey, CA: Brooks/Cole Publishing.

Wilson, James Q. 1968. "Dilemmas of Police Administration." *Public Administration Review* (September/October): 409.

Chapter Six

POLICE DEVIANCE: CORRUPTION AND CONTROL

The powers given by the state to the police to use force have always caused concern to those against whom the force is used. Where power is given, there is the potential for corruption and misuse or abuse of that power. The discussion of police organization and administration in chapter 4 points out that increasing formalization and specification of rules and procedures is probably the best method available to ensure correct use of discretionary powers and to control police deviance. Over the years, police organizations have become more bureaucratic in an effort to control this high level of power and authority. Although the community policing emphasis has influenced the centralization of control, efforts to eliminate all types of abuses and deviance have improved. However, two elements which allow for corruption will always exist: opportunity and greed.

Any discussion of police corruption must begin with the mention of *ethics* and *morality*. A code of ethics, or a set of values, forms a strong link between behavior and professionalism. Morality can be referred to as making good judgments or using discretionary powers properly. Perhaps, ethics and morality can be understood simply as values defining what is right (Davis, 1995). Police officers experience numerous opportunities to commit illegal and unethical acts. Fortunately, most resist the temptations. As a response to those who have not resisted temptations, agencies have created numerous ways to guard against corruption and the abuse of power.

Improvements have been made to control corruption, but numerous opportunities still exist for deviant and corrupt practices. The opportunity to acquire power in excess of that which is legally permitted or to misuse power is always available. The police subculture is a contributing factor to these practices. The behavior of the officers who choose to act in a corrupt manner is often overlooked, sometimes condoned or reinforced by other members of the subculture. This banding together can create a serious problem for administrators who want to eliminate corruption and deviance in their agencies.

This chapter will focus on some of the factors that explain police deviance and corruption. Both internal and external sources to the police organization will be examined for possible solutions to the problems.

THE OPPORTUNITY STRUCTURE FOR POLICE DEVIANCE

There are two elements that can contribute to occupational deviance and the corruption of an individual: *opportunity*—which will vary depending upon the structure of the organization—and *greed*—which will vary depending upon the individual.

Unfortunately, the first exposure to police deviance may occur at the training academy, where recruits may be convinced to lie in some situations. Lies and deception are often encouraged "... in situations of crisis intervention, investigation and interrogation, and especially with the mentally ill" (Hunt and Manning, 1991:54). This initial instruction may influence how young officers respond to other opportunities for misconduct. Even in the slowest suburban patrol districts, there is the potential to base arrest decisions on extra-legal criteria, to accept money for not issuing a traffic citation, and to deliver street justice to those who do not belong, to overly aggressive citizens, or to those with a perceived attitude problem.

A comparison of work-based deviance committed by police and by employees in other occupations leads one to wonder why there is special concern over the police. Many individuals in various professions become involved in corrupt and illegal practices. However, the occupational setting and structure provide police officers a greater range of deviance-inducing situations when compared to many other occupations. The public's perception of law enforcers leaves little room for criminal behavior. Most importantly, we expect the police to enforce the laws to protect citizens. We do not expect them to violate the laws to benefit themselves or others.

The normal routine of a police officer brings him or her into contact with a vast assortment of social deviants and criminals. Many of these are willing to pay considerable sums of money to avoid arrest. For criminals, payoffs are often viewed as just a necessary business expense. Unfortunately, police officers may find themselves in positions where they can accept more money in one payoff than they make in a year's salary. Of course, payoffs are just one of many types of opportunities that cross the path of the average police officer. Opportunities for all of the following are easily encountered: accepting gratuities, theft or burglary, illegal administrative actions, sexual harassment, lying, use of excessive force, prejudice, discrimination, and more.

Lawrence Sherman, in *Police Corruption: A Sociological Perspective* (1974:12–14), discusses the aspects of the police role that make corruption and deviance possible. The extraordinary *discretion* inherent in police work is an important factor leading to the opportunity for corruption or deviance. Any time an officer is called upon to exercise discretion, the potential for corruption exists. An illegitimate use of discretion can be covered up by a legitimate use. For example, if an officer does not like wealthy African Americans or Jewish people, he or she can detain or arrest them because of this dislike and later devise a legitimate basis for the action. If an officer does not like citizens with bad attitudes, he or she may arrest those citizens because of their attitudes but justify the arrest on other grounds. These are examples of action when action is unnecessary. More common misuse of discretion is when an officer fails to take an action when one is justified. The highly publicized case of Jeffery Dahmer provides an excellent example. After receiving a citizen call about a young boy running naked and bleeding down the street, three Milwaukee police officers returned the fourteen-year-old Laotian to Dahmer. The officers, who were at the end of their shift, found it easier to believe Dahmer's story, which was that the boy was nineteen and that the two were involved in a homosexual relationship. It was only after Dahmer was arrested on multiple counts of murder and dismemberment that any credence was given to the original complaint by the community. Dahmer's neighbors contend that this inaction on the part of the police officers was due to bias: the officers were white; the boy was Asian; Dahmer was white; the callers were black; the neighborhood was poor and deteriorating; the situation was described as homosexual. Considering all of the situations when an officer must exercise discretion and all of the possibilities of misuse, the role that discretion can play in providing opportunities for corruption and deviance becomes apparent (Kappeler et al., 1994).

The high degree of discretion necessary for police work and the *low visibility* of line officers' actions to their superiors often allow abuses to go undetected. As most police operations call for a single officer or a two-person patrol, many decisions are made without a supervisor's input until after the fact. In addition, most incidents of police discretion are neither visible nor known to the public. Most police activities are not seen by citizens other than those involved. Even when the public happens to view the police in action, it is difficult to discern between legitimate operations and police deviance or corruption. A citizen viewing a police officer breaking into a home or a car would not know whether the action was legitimate or not. This low visibility to both supervisors and to the general public is conducive to corruption and deviance.

The *code of secrecy* which is an inherent part of the police subculture further contributes to opportunity for police deviance. A police officer's actions are more visible to fellow officers than to anyone else, yet this does not always create a strong control over police deviance. The sense of loyalty among officers and the code of secrecy prevent this visibility from being an important factor. As we discussed in chapter 5, the unwritten rule of most police subcultures is that one would rarely report a fellow officer's misconduct.

Another aspect of police organization that makes officers especially susceptible to corruption is that *police managers are very much a part of the police subculture*. Police departments recruit police managers exclusively from line officers, which means that the managers have been and often continue to be a part of the police working subculture. Thus, they share in the code of secrecy and loyalty. In fact, the cohesiveness of the police subculture encourages officers and their supervisors to be good friends. This can make it difficult for supervisors to be objective in monitoring police deviance and corruption.

A final factor contributing to the deviance of police officers is the perceived *low status* of the police officer's occupation. Police officers are called upon and given considerable power to perform complex tasks requiring judgment and a wide range of discretion. However, they receive relatively low pay and status when compared to other occupations with similar responsibilities and duties. Although the pay scales of police have improved in recent years compared to those of other occupations, the police officers continue to feel that they are severely underpaid. This creates a ready-made rationalization for corruption and lawbreaking for personal gain. The opportunity is often present, and officers constantly view criminals committing crimes and getting away with them. It is easy for the officers to come to the conclusion that they, too, should share in the benefits of crime.

All of these factors combine to create an opportunity structure that is conducive to corruption and deviance; however, a vast majority of police officers refrain from taking advantage of their position and remain law-abiding citizens.

Recently, the audio tapes of Mr. Mark Fuhrman have forced many citizens to focus on the language and behavior of police officers. It is unclear if Mr. Fuhrman was describing his beatings of African Americans and other minorities, framing suspects, planting evidence, playing God, and other unconscionable actions as he remembered them or as he wanted to be remembered! In either case, his words have raised the question—Is this type of behavior an aberration or a symptom of a broader problem with the police? As many questions are being asked about the behavior of Mr. Fuhrman and the integrity and morality of police in the 1990s, the *Los Angeles Daily News* reported on September 3, 1995, that prosecutors have dropped murder charges against two defendants and are concerned that more than 100 other cases are in jeopardy because a Los Angeles police detective falsified a document in a murder trial and lied about it.

SOCIALIZATION AND PEER GROUP SUPPORT FOR RULE VIOLATIONS

Police officers acquire a major portion of their identity from their occupational role. Being a member of the department, dressing in a uniform and being identified by others as an officer contribute to this role identity. Most of their interaction with influential persons involves other police officers. One important feature of this subculture is social isolation, and part of this isolation is manifested by withdrawing into the subculture for support and approval. As a result the police officer is subjected to intense peer influence and control. This socialization can involve the acceptance of deviant behavior.

Research on police deviance has made several important contributions to our understanding of police officer activities. A study conducted in the 1970s (Savitz, 1971) questioned police recruits at three different time periods and found that they became more permissive toward deviant and corrupt police conduct as they advanced from the police academy to working in the streets and as exposure to the police subculture increased. The officers questioned began to favor less severe punishments for taking bribes, failing to issue a traffic ticket and stealing liquor from a guarded store. The author concluded that the structure for police socialization is a contributing factor in police deviance and corruption. In field training, the experienced officers train the rookie officers, and this training can lead to negative as well as positive consequences. It seems that the patterns of deviance and corruption that develop over the years, and are tolerated by the more experienced officers, are transmitted to the new officers through the process of socializing new recruits.

Police deviance seems to follow many of the same patterns as the deviance of those in other professions. Persistent deviance typically is not a solitary enterprise. It tends to flourish when it receives group support. Further, it is seldom an individual or group innovation; rather, it usually has a history within that social environment.

In the past, research has also supported the conclusion that a substantial amount of police deviance and corruption is unofficially approved by the police at different levels in the organization (Barker, 1976; Kappeler et al., 1994). In one study, it was found that receiving a free meal, services, discounts or liquor was viewed by many police officers as a fringe benefit of the job and that there was little risk of punishment if an officer accepted such favors. There was apparently a greater likelihood of a fellow officer reporting a kickback received by another officer if it was in the form of money, rather than goods or services. Forty-two percent of the officers interviewed reported that kickbacks in the form of goods and services would rarely or never be reported. Twenty-six percent reported that fixing a misdemeanor would rarely or never be reported. Although it has been more than twenty years since many of these studies were conducted, information suggests that things have not changed dramatically.

It is clear that the police subculture reinforces and provides encouragement for certain types of deviance and corruption, and discouragement for other types. It appears that in many departments, a distinction is made between "clean" and "dirty" money, as well as between approved and disapproved corruption and deviance. In most cases, the deviance which is most discouraged includes the more severe types which leave victims who are labeled "dirty." At this point, more specific definitions of police corruption and deviance are presented to help distinguish among these types of behavior.

DEFINING POLICE DEVIANCE AND CORRUPTION

Herman Goldstein defined police corruption as ". . . the misuse of authority by a police officer in a manner designed to produce personal gain for the officer or others" (Goldstein, 1977:188). The terms, *misuse of authority* and *personal gain*, are key elements which need interpretation and evaluation. Others have included terms such as *"illegal use of power"* (Sherman, 1974:30) and *organizational gain* (Klockars, 1983:336) in their definitions of corruption. McMullan (1961:182) adds *improper* and defined corruption in general terms: "A public official is corrupt if he accepts money or money's worth for doing something that he is under a duty to do anyway, that he is under a duty not to do, or to exercise a legitimate discretion for improper reasons."

Whatever the specific definition, several concerns run through each and raise certain issues. Combining the elements of these definitions results in a comprehensive understanding of police corruption.

Understanding police corruption requires a review of improper activities which benefit the officer and those which benefit the organization. An activity which benefits the officer can be clearly identified but one that benefits the organization may be masked or hidden. One example of such an activity is squelching an investigation of a politician or business person who has been supportive of the agency.

An important aspect of personal or individual deviance is that it is not condoned, supported or encouraged by the police organization. This type of deviance is viewed as illegitimate behavior by others in the department. When it comes to the attention of others, it is reported to supervisors who respond by initiating the appropriate investigation and by suggesting disciplinary action when necessary.

This type of misconduct is not unusual in any social organization. The same type of misbehavior happens in virtually every group or organization, whether it be the White House staff, Congress, religious organizations, businesses, or even a university. Many citizens, however, become more disturbed when misconduct is exposed in police departments than when it is uncovered in other organizations, private or public. The irony of police officers violating the very laws they swore to uphold may make police deviance even more intolerable and disturbing to the public.

We become most concerned when this type of deviance and individual misconduct becomes a patterned and accepted part of any organization. When deviance and misconduct are condoned, supported and permitted by an organization, they become *organizational deviance and corruption*. Richard Lundman (1980a:140–141) lists the major factors that distinguish police deviance as organizational deviance or corruption:

First, for an action to be organizationally deviant it must be contrary to norms or rules maintained by others external to the police department. . .

Second, for police misconduct to be organizational rather than individual in origin, the deviant action must be supported by internal operating norms which conflict with the police organization's formal goals and rules . . .

Third, compliance with the internal operating norms supportive of police misconduct must be ensured through recruitment and socialization . . .

A fourth and related condition for organizational deviance is that there must be peer support of the misbehavior of colleagues . . .

Finally, for improper behavior to be organizationally deviant, it must be supported by the dominant administrative coalition of the police organization . . .

Therefore, police misconduct is organizational deviance when actions violate external expectations for what the department should do. Simultaneously, the actions must be in conformity with internal operating norms, and supported by socialization, peers, and the administrative personnel of the department.

Organizational deviance is often patterned in such a way that officers engage in it on a regular basis and do not attempt to hide their actions from other officers or supervisors. Also, peer support or the support of supervisors need not always be active. Active support exists when supervisors or high-level administrators encourage, cover up, or ignore misconduct. In addition, support is active when these administrators are engaging in the same type of misconduct. Support is passive when the supervisors and high-level administrators fail, for whatever reason, to take reasonable measures to control the misconduct. It is passive when the organization has taken all appropriate measures to control the misconduct, and it continues to occur. Lawrence W. Sherman (1974) developed a typology to distinguish different levels of corruption, its organization, and its sources.

TYPE I:
ROTTEN APPLES AND ROTTEN POCKETS

This type of police deviance and corruption corresponds to the individual deviance discussed earlier. It is simply a case of certain individuals failing to abide by the rules of the organization and the law. This type of police deviance has little or no organization. It is not tied to the larger police structure and does not receive any support from supervisors or administrators. As already mentioned, personal deviance exists in most organizations and, to some degree, is omnipresent.

The "rotten apples" theory is often used by police chiefs to explain deviance and corruption discovered in their departments. Using this explanation permits an interpretation that there is no organizational problem. Obviously, the corruption and deviance of a few "rotten apples" among a department of generally conforming and honorable police officers is a much less serious problem than pervasive and patterned corruption that has been condoned or permitted by the supervisory staff. One of the attractive features of this explanation for police administrators is that the lack of an organizational problem alleviates the need for a critical examination of the general procedures and supervision practices within the department. The solution to the problem rests with identifying and removing the bad officers. However, quite often the problems go much deeper into the police organization. Dealing with the problems requires considerable structural and personnel changes. A great deal of police deviance falls into the next two categories.

TYPE II:
PERVASIVE UNORGANIZED CORRUPTION

If Type I deviance and corruption is not identified and punished effectively, it can develop into Type II deviance. This type of deviance can permeate an organization until many of its officers will be involved in corrupt activities, actively or passively. Similar to Type I corruption, Type II corruption does not require organization within the police department. In this case, many officers may be involved in corrupt practices but not jointly. Individual officers and small groups of officers are pushing the limits of what they can do on their own. A majority of officers in the department may be taking bribes when they get the opportunity or participating in other forms of deviance, but doing so individually or in small groups.

TYPE III:
PERVASIVE ORGANIZED CORRUPTION

The most serious problems with police corruption exist when officers acting in an organized fashion are involved in deviant and corrupt practices. A good example of this type of corruption is the systematic payoff for the protection of illegal activities. Sherman (1974) links this type of corruption with organized crime, as it usually takes a well-organized criminal operation to buy adequate protection. This type of corruption requires the involvement of those in the hierarchy of the police department or an absence of any effective control. Sherman (1974:11) distinguishes between Type II and Type III corruption by the way a new recruit is introduced and socialized into the system. In a Type II situation, the recruits learn from peers that there are numerous on-the-job opportunities to make extra money and that it is common to accept or solicit services or money. In a Type III situation, the recruits are told by supervisors where to make regular pickups of money (e.g., whore houses, crack houses, gambling houses, drug distribution locations). In addition, they are told how to distribute the money to fellow officers, to supervisors, and to themselves. The corruption can involve the whole departmental hierarchy. Fortunately, it is seldom that whole departments are involved in corruption.

ANOTHER TYPOLOGY OF POLICE CORRUPTION

Barker and Roebuck (1973) have developed an empirical typology of police corruption. They grouped together many instances of police deviance and corruption into seven conceptual categories that are listed in ascending order by degree of seriousness. These categories provide us with some common examples of police deviance and corruption.

ACCEPTANCE OF FREE OR DISCOUNT MEALS AND SERVICES

The most common and most extensive form of police corruption is the acceptance of small gratuities or tips. Free or discount meals are available to officers in most American cities. Some nationwide restaurant chains and convenience stores have a policy of giving police officers free or discounted merchandise. Similarly, other retail establishments offer discounts to the police. In some cases, the motive behind the gratuity is to show respect and gratitude to the police. In other cases, however, the motive is to buy protection that results from having uniformed officers frequenting the establishment and from the expectation that officers who accept the gratuities will respond more quickly and willingly to calls for help from the establishment. Officers often have a tendency to feel more protective toward an establishment that is good to them than one that is not. This type of corruption is the least serious and seems harmless. However, the expectations for gratuities may grow into demands that, if not met, may result in a lack of protection or even in harassment by the police. More important, an officer who accepts something for nothing could be compromised by the provider. For example, if an officer has been accepting "favors" from a business owner who becomes involved in a situation requiring police intervention, he or she may request the "favored" officer, explaining that this officer would help. Incidents invoking this type of response could range from a traffic ticket to a car that needs to be towed, or something more serious. In any case, it places the officer in a compromised situation—and for what, free coffee and doughnuts?

ACCEPTANCE OF KICKBACKS FOR REFERRALS FOR SERVICES

Another form of police corruption that is common, yet not considered too serious, is accepting kickbacks for referring services. A typical example would be a towing company that gives small kickbacks to officers who call them to the scene of an accident. Another common referral is to a particular ambulance service that will give the officer a kickback. Again, this type of police behavior may not be serious corruption, but it can initiate a pattern of behavior that *develops* into more serious activities (e.g., accepting bribes).

The one feature that distinguishes these first two types of police corruption from others is that the officer is receiving personal compensation from outside sources for fulfilling the normal responsibilities of the job. This does not seem very serious since the officer is fulfilling his or her duties. In some of the following types of corruption, the officer gains compensation either for failing to fulfill a responsibility (e.g., failing to issue a traffic ticket when one is justified) or for altering the response to a situation (e.g., giving extra protection to an establishment or ignoring certain illegal activities).

OPPORTUNISTIC THEFT

It is common for police officers to be in situations where a citizen is helpless or where the premises of an establishment are unsecured. These situations provide an unusual opportunity for theft. One study reported interview data from men in a Seattle jail who had been arrested for public drunkenness. Each was asked if he had personally witnessed a Seattle police officer rolling, clipping, or stealing from a drunk or from someone picked up for public drunkenness (Spradley, 1969:286; also see Kappeler et al, 1994). One-third of the men interviewed had witnessed this type of opportunistic theft. It is all too common to hear about officers who arrest drug dealers and keep part of the money, weapons, or valuable goods for their personal use or to sell for profit. Further, arresting officers have been accused of confiscating and "destroying" narcotics and not arresting the suspect. Similarly, after an arrest, officers have been accused of turning in a smaller amount (or lesser quality) of drugs as evidence than acknowledged by the suspect.

SHAKEDOWNS

A shakedown occurs when an officer extorts money from a citizen with an arbitrary threat to enforce the law. For example, officers might solicit money from a tavern owner by threatening to enforce liquor laws or to harass customers, which would obviously keep them away from the tavern and destroy business.

PROTECTION OF ILLEGAL ACTIVITIES

The most well-organized type of corruption is the systematic payoff for the protection of ongoing illegal activities. The most common forms of crime that need protection are gambling, prostitution and drug operations. This type of protection requires the involvement of more than just patrol officers, although patrol officers may agree to leave the operations alone and not interfere with the illegal activities. However, it may be other divisions such as vice or investigations that have the main responsibility for controlling this type of criminal activity. Thus, it may be necessary for officers to conspire collectively not to get involved.

ACCEPTING MONEY TO FIX CASES

Fixing traffic tickets is probably the most common form of case fixing and the least offensive. The citing officer can just fail to show up in court or can nullify the ticket. The more serious examples of case fixing involve trials of organized crime figures. In Gardiner and Olson's *Theft of a City* (1974; also see Kappeler et al., 1994), Gage reviews numerous studies of police corruption, ranging from fixing traffic tickets to fixing cases involving racketeers. He reports, for example, that the rate of dismissals and acquittals for racketeers was five times that of other defendants.

PLANNED THEFT

Direct involvement by the police in planned theft is not as uncommon as one might expect. Police involvement in burglary and fencing operations has been uncovered in many large police departments. In a number of these situations, the activities are organized and operated by police officers. In most situations, however, these types of direct criminal activities are not supported or even tolerated by police administrators. This type of direct criminal activity is harder for police officers to rationalize since it directly contradicts their mandate to serve and protect the public.

REVIEW OF POLICE DEVIANCE AND CORRUPTION

In the first part of this chapter, we discussed several aspects involved in defining police deviance and corruption. First, police deviance is a type of occupational deviance which is made possible by the opportunity structure unique to members of the police community. In addition, new recruits are socialized into the system of norms and techniques that allow involvement in these deviant activities. The second element in police deviance is greed, whether brought to the job or developed by informal socialization. A distinction was made between personal or individual deviance and organizational deviance. Organizational deviance is generally a more serious threat to the community and requires structural change in the department and possibly in the community to assure effective control. There are three types or levels of police corruption in a police organization. Each type reflects different degrees of involvement in the activities of the organizational hierarchy.

The sources of police deviance and corruption are important to understand because they also point toward the appropriate forms of control. Organizational processes, or organizational "pathologies" if one wishes to view them as such, are the causes of organizational deviance. Contrast this organizational context with the individual pathologies that result in individual misconduct. Each requires a different approach to bring about effective control, the topic of the remainder of this chapter. Before we turn to those controls, it is important to read Chief Bowlin's comments about police corruption.

CHIEF'S CORNER
POLICE CORRUPTION

After more than twenty-six years in law enforcement, I have come to believe that no officer is immune from corruption. Certainly there are officers who have a higher degree of integrity than others, but, under the right circumstances, almost all are susceptible. It doesn't always have to be money. One of the best officers I ever knew sold out completely to a large-scale prostitution ring and was being paid off solely with sex.

In law enforcement we have a saying: "There's two things that will get you: women and booze." To a great degree, this is true, and illicit involvement with each seems to provide the corrupting circumstances that influence a good cop to go bad. Interestingly enough, as women became involved to a much greater degree in law enforcement, this same premise held true. When they go bad, there is usually some male they are involved with romantically, and generally, substance abuse is prevalent. Administrators must understand that corruption is an ever-present threat in their department due primarily to the human beings and personal problems which make up the organization. This is especially true in light of the evolving use of drugs and the increased amounts of money which are available to corrupt officials at every level within the criminal justice system.

The most effective means I know to fight corruption within a department is to build a strong supervisory structure which has an understanding of its importance in the role of curtailing corruption. Additionally, an action-oriented, anti-corruption unit which reacts to the many indicators reflective of an officer going bad is essential. In almost every case of officer corruption, there is a significant change in an officer's lifestyle and personal habits. Such patterns should be known and understood by all responsible supervisors within the department and swift action should occur when these patterns of behavior are observed. While it is true that law enforcement officers generally have an unspoken code of never "handing their fellow officer up," such a code does not extend to criminal corruption cases when the administration reinforces the reputation of the department as a team of hard-working, honest professionals. The only effective means for the administration to accomplish this is through personal example.

CONTROLLING POLICE DEVIANCE
AND CORRUPTION

The efficient operation of a police department requires both internal discipline of officers and external review of their behavior. In the case of most public agencies, especially police departments, it is also important that the public image of the operations be clean and positive. While it is impossible to control a police department from the outside, there are ways to establish guidelines and standards for civilian review and monitoring that will be discussed later in this chapter. First, we will examine methods of internal control of the police.

INTERNAL CONTROLS

Any effective system of internal control must include a clear definition of proper and improper conduct, as well as mechanisms for detecting and punishing improper behavior and rewarding exemplary behavior. As we stated earlier, these rules, policies and procedures must be articulated in a clear and understandable manner. Officers must be trained to comprehend and respond to them. The manner in which the departmental administrators communicate their expectations informs officers what conduct will be accepted and what will not be tolerated. Once the rules are understood by the officers, they must be enforced by some internal mechanism, usually by an inspections unit or direct supervision.

An inspections unit functions to make sure that officers are performing adequately to achieve the stated goals and objectives of the agency. That is, are policies and procedures being followed, do they meet agency goals and are they appropriate and current. Basically, an inspections unit should compare performance against standards. This can be accomplished by reviewing administrative reports and case reports as well as by interviewing officers and consumers of police services. Discrepancies should be reported and corrected. Inspections units can assess policies, equipment and other materials to ensure that the resources are being used properly and are appropriate; they can determine whether there is a need for improvement or replacement. This formal inspection must be augmented by direct supervision.

A study by the International Association of Chiefs of Police (1989) emphasized the importance of management and supervision of the line officers.

It concluded that officers who are engaged in corrupt activities may also be those who exhibit other questionable conduct. Supervisors can compromise integrity by many actions or inactions, including failing to enforce departmental policies and regulations, ignoring problem indicators because of friendship with the officer, overlooking slight irregularities in reports and allowing subordinates to perform personal favors. In fact, the report notes, "Supervisors who fail to audit the activities of personnel fail to perform their jobs, a fact which must be accepted by the officers as well as the supervisors" (International Association of Chiefs of Police, 1989:57). Supervisors must be more than officers "with stripes." They must be trained professionals who are willing to manage their subordinates. In addition to routine supervisory activities, there must be a formal mechanism to receive complaints.

When the strategy of direct supervision proves inadequate, the internal affairs office is asked to investigate. This operation is basically a police department within a police department. Remember, as Chief Bowlin implied, the speed of the boss is the speed of the crew (see Alpert, 1985). The internal affairs unit is designed to serve as a mechanism for internal accountability by receiving, processing and investigating complaints against police officers, whether these complaints are for violations of criminal law, police procedures or policies. The roles of this division can include investigating citizens' complaints or departmental investigations of possible officer misconduct.

The emphasis placed on this unit by the chief and his or her command staff will have a strong influence on the behavior and morale of the officers. If an internal affairs division is merely a mask to approve all police behavior, whether appropriate or not, it provides little or no guidance or deterrence to officers who may violate policy. Just as citizens must be provided the opportunity to make complaints about inappropriate police behavior, officers must be protected when reporting corrupt or unethical actions. Both officers and citizens should be encouraged to bring grievances or complaints against errant officers.

The effectiveness of a complaint-management task depends on the structure of the system and how the officers serving as investigators respond to the allegations. The process must not be intimidating for those who want to report police misconduct. There must be sufficient intake points to make the ability to file a complaint realistic. Once a complaint is filed, it is up to the investigator, usually an internal affairs officer, to handle the inquiry with sensitivity. If the internal affairs officers assume that any complaint made by a civilian or another officer is an attack on policing or a personal attack on the department, they may attempt to shield the individual officer or discourage the person from continuing with the complaint. In this case, the process will fail. If the internal affairs officers honestly investigate and evaluate the merits of each complaint and encourage the complainant to do what he or she thinks is right, the process will succeed. Approaches other than police internal affairs investigations exist which include the incorporation of police complaint-management into a broader city or county-wide complaint-management system. Regardless of the structure, an openness must exist which holds officers accountable for their actions. Kappeler and Kraska (1995) suggest that the police adopt a process used by many private businesses which encourage and solicit consumer attitudes, concerns and complaints. While private industry has been more open than government to soliciting consumer opinions to improve its performance, there is a special responsibility for the police to evaluate their activities. In fact, Wagner and Decker advise us (1993:289): "Certainly few bureaucracies are successful in institutionalizing an instrument of self-criticism. However, the tenuous position of the police in a democratic society demands that such institutionalization occur. To fail to do so jeopardizes the police enterprise."

When internal controls over police operate properly, potential problems can be nipped in the bud by administrators before they develop into more serious concerns. If the process simply masks the problems and keeps important information from administrators, then it is likely that the behavior will continue and possibly become worse.

One innovation that has been used with increasing frequency is called an Early Warning System (EWS). The EWS can be programmed, manually or by computer, to keep track of concerns relating to officers' behavior and performance, officers' reports and absences, or all complaints that have been received, whether substantiated or not. A system can be devised to track these by type, seriousness, location, or any number of variables. After a given number of complaints or other indicators of concern have been received during a specified period of time, that officer will have his or her whole file reviewed for potential problems. For example, an officer could have received numerous unsubstantiated or minor complaints that trigger a review and interview during which the officer states that he or she has been assigned to a very high-crime area and has been tough on crime and alleged criminals. Complaints against the officer may be an attempt to have him or her transferred out of the area so the criminal element can return to its old habits. The same complaints could lead investigators to realize that the officer is experiencing problems at home, excessive use of alcohol or some unrelated stressor or problem that has affected his or her police work. In that way, the internal affairs division and EWS can assist police administrators in providing help to their officers before a problem gets too serious (Kappeler et al., 1994).

Traditionally, most citizen complaints are dismissed as unsubstantiated, which leads to the popular belief that the police refuse to discipline themselves. Samuel Walker (1992) provides an excellent review of the internal affairs unit and explains that to be successful, one needs strong support from the chief, sufficient manpower and independence. Further, he notes that its effectiveness and reputation, both inside the agency and in the community, will be determined by the actions taken on its recommendations. Internal affairs officers are faced with a serious dilemma. Officers working in internal affairs may be viewed with suspicion by other officers, because their roles include policing the police. These internal affairs officers must maintain good relations with the other police officers. Similarly, there is a need for these officers, who often represent the department to the public, to maintain credibility and a good image. If police do not police themselves, or if the public perceives that the police are not policing themselves, there will be a call for the other method of controlling police, external review by citizens.

EXTERNAL CONTROLS

It should be emphasized that formal lines of authority and internal investigations are not the only methods available to review and control police. Both the electronic and the print media can be powerful sources of support for a police department, or they can be devastatingly antagonistic. This influence usually emerges when a serious and newsworthy crime has been committed or some major event has taken place that reflects poorly on the police. The media representatives can color their coverage to make the police appear more efficient and professional than they really are, or they can slant their coverage to emphasize the mistakes, inefficiency or possible police corruption. The particular slant of the media coverage depends upon the perception of a reporter or editor and the relationship between the media representatives and the police chief and administrators.

Community groups and churches can also exert considerable influence over police operations by organizing their members and followers. The problems that are of the greatest concern to these organizations are often vice-related. The interests of these groups usually rally around conservative community standards concerning prostitution, drugs, pornography and gambling. If leaders organize their members on an issue, or set of issues, police administrators must act or face the loss of a substantial source of support. In fact, if sufficient numbers of influential citizens band together, they can demand the development of civilian review boards.

The concept of civilian review of police involves the creation of a group of civilians (often called a civilian review board or civilian oversight board) to review instances of alleged police misconduct. This direct and formal review of police behavior is as popular with critics of the police as it is unpopular with police officers and has experienced both success and failure (West, 1993).

Oversight boards can help bring police abuses and corruption to the attention of the public. They can influence the proper punishment of deviant officers, and they can provide a vehicle by which police policies and procedures may be reviewed. The real question is whether they perform these duties to the satisfaction of both the police and the public. The first civilian review boards were established in the late 1950s in New York and Philadelphia (Walker, 1992; Note, 1964). Other cities, including Kansas City and Detroit, soon followed that lead. The initial review boards were relatively unknown and not truly civilian in nature (Walker, 1992). Due to the severe police-community tensions during the 1960s, there was an explosion of interest in civilian review boards and many cities created them as a direct result of specific problems (Kahn, 1975; Hudson, 1970).

The composition of the review or oversight board usually includes representation of a cross section of the community and is independent of the police department. The members are often selected by the mayor or some other political figure. This method of appointment has been criticized by members of minority communities as one more way to ensure that no action against the police will take place (United States Commission on Civil Rights, 1981). Many patrol officers and police administrators also complain about the composition of the boards. They believe that politicians are attempting to control police behavior.

The traditional hostility of the police toward civilian oversight boards is based upon their opinion of reformers as being soft on crime and not understanding police work. The police view the oversight process as another way to coddle criminals. A common reason given by the police for opposing civilian oversight is that effective policing requires secrecy. Civilian oversight interferes with this needed secrecy and compromises police operations. Police officers also oppose civilian oversight because they claim that police behavior and operations cannot be fairly evaluated if one has never been involved in crime control personally. If one has not directly experienced the hostility expressed toward the police, the danger involved in police operations, and other intricate problems unique to the police, then one cannot truly evaluate police behavior. Any such evaluations will compromise police operations, naively "tie the hands of the police" and interfere with effective policing. More important, civilian oversight negatively affects police morale.

In spite of this opposition, civilian oversight remains an issue and has received a recent resurgence of interest (West, 1993). Many view it as an important vehicle for making the police more democratic and for monitoring the police. In spite of experiencing some success, most of the efforts at civilian oversight have met with failure. Many police researchers have blamed this failure on the fact that the boards serve only in an advisory capacity, having no subpoena power or ability to decide cases and impose punishment. It is also argued that, traditionally and legally, only the police chief has the power to make decisions concerning the discipline of subordinates. Another reason given for the failure of citizen oversight boards is a general lack of resources and insufficient investigative staffs. The police feel that they can do a better job of controlling police deviance and corruption with their own internal investigation divisions without compromising their ability to maintain order and control crime (International Association of Chiefs of Police, 1989).

Because of the problems mentioned above and because many civilian review and oversight panels were established as a result of specific tensions, most of the boards have met with failure. The renewed interest in civilian oversight of government has created a second generation of oversight boards with interests broader than just law enforcement. For example, some jurisdictions are establishing panels that will hear complaints about all government workers and will conduct an investigation of a public works employee in the same way they will conduct an investigation of a police officer. Some of these panels are being given broad powers; others are very limited in their scope and investigatory and enforcement powers. Only time will tell if any are more successful than the first generation of civilian review boards and which model, if any, should be perpetuated (see Roberg and Kuykendall, 1993).

Regardless of the method by which police deviance becomes known to the administration, action must be taken. In chapter 9, we will discuss progressive discipline, but here it is important to explain a disciplinary philosophy that should be a part of every police agency. Chief Darrel Stephens, of the St. Petersburg (Florida) police department, has provided his officers with an excellent approach to discipline (quoted in Kappeler et. al., 1994:249–252). He notes that a disciplinary system must incorporate the positive reinforcement of appropriate values with behavioral standards established by policies and procedures. Violations of that trust must be disciplined in a progressive manner depending upon employee motivation, degree of harm, employee experience, whether the error was intentional or unintentional, and the employee's past record. Chief Stephens has provided his officers with a reasoned and well-balanced notice of discipline.

SUMMARY

Effective internal discipline and external monitoring of police activities are in the best interest of the police department and of the community. It is essential to the efficient operation of the department and to officer morale that these activities be understood by all officers and administrators. Further, it is central to the department's public image to have a system of control that is known and trusted by community members. The public must have confidence in the willingness and ability of the police to police themselves. It is ineffective to focus excessive attention on negative discipline as a means of controlling police deviance and corruption. The word discipline itself does not refer only to reprimands and punishments. The word discipline is derived from the same Latin word as disciple, which refers to a follower or pupil. Its original meaning is not that of a blind follower whose conformity comes out of a fear of punishment. Rather, the concept refers to following a leader or someone in authority because of agreement with common principles. It refers to following a leader or teacher out of respect.

There are three important aspects in the development of an effective system of discipline. First, a department must have a well-formulated and consistent set of rules and procedures. The rules and procedures must be internally consistent and must reflect the moral constraints that are accepted in our society and especially within the community being served by the police. Second, the rules and procedures must be communicated fully and effectively to the officers at all levels of the organization through proper training. To achieve some level of conformity to the rules, officers should internalize them and the general value system within which they are incorporated. The degree to which they do this will determine the level of conformity to the rules. A third factor is proper supervision and leadership within the department to ensure conformity to the rules and to maintain a working environment conducive to following the rules. When all else fails, there should be a system by which officers can be decertified (Alpert and Smith, 1993).

This discussion merely scratches the surface of what can be said about police deviance and corruption. Obviously, it is much more efficient to prevent problems before they arise than to handle them on a crisis basis. The development of a good set of internal rules and procedures, the provision of proper training, and effective supervision and leadership can do more to solve problems than any reactive approach. Kappeler, Sluder and Alpert concluded (1994:289–290):

> . . . police deviance is a complex, multifaceted and multidimensional enigma. Thus, there are no simplistic, quick-fix cookbook solutions for problems of police wrongdoing. Yet, despite these cautionary notes, a complex, interrelated web of remedies are suggested. At the simplest level, the opportunity structure inherent in the nature of policing presents officers with virtually unlimited chances to engage in deviant activity. Hiring well qualified and capable employees, providing appropriate training and education programs, mandating that supervisors hold officers accountable for their behavior . . . are all simple means to thwart deviance in the police organization.

As mentioned in the beginning of this chapter, the problem of police deviance and corruption will never be completely solved, just as the police will never be able to solve the crime problem in our society. One step in the right direction, however, is the monitoring and control of the police and the appropriate use of police style to enforce laws and to provide service to the public.

References

Alpert, Geoffrey P. 1985. *The American System of Criminal Justice.* Beverly Hills: Sage Publications.

Alpert, Geoffrey and W. Smith. 1993. "Policing the Defective Centurion: Decertification and Beyond." *Criminal Law Bulletin* 29:147–57.

Barker, Thomas. 1976. "Peer Group Support for Occupational Deviance in Police Agencies." Dissertation, Mississippi State University.

———. 1977. "Peer Group Support for Police Occupational Deviance." *Criminology* 15, no. 3 (November).

Barker, Thomas and Julian Roebuck. 1973. *An Empirical Typology of Police Corruption: A Study in Organizational Deviance.* Springfield, IL: Charles C Thomas.

Brooks, Laure. 1993. "Police Discretionary Behavior: A Study of Style." In R. Dunham and G. Alpert (eds.) *Critical Issues in Policing: Contemporary Readings*, 2nd ed., pp. 140–64. Prospect Heights, IL: Waveland Press.

Center for Research on Criminal Justice. 1975. *The Iron Fist and the Velvet Glove: An Analysis of the U.S. Police*. Berkeley, CA: Center for Research on Criminal Justice.

Coleman, James. 1985. *The Criminal Elite*. New York: St. Martin's Press.

Davis, Kenneth C. 1975. *Discretionary Justice*. St. Paul, MN: West Publishing.

Davis, Michael. 1995. Code of Ethics. In W. Bailey (ed.) *The Encyclopedia of Police Science*, pp. 83–94. New York: Garland Publishing.

Fogelson, R. M. 1977. *Big City Police*. Cambridge, MA: Harvard University Press.

Gage, Nicholas. 1974. "Organized Crime in Court." In John A. Gardiner and David J. Olson (eds.) *Theft of a City*, p. 165. Bloomington: Indiana University Press.

Gardiner, John A. and David J. Olson, eds. 1974. *Theft of a City*. Bloomington: Indiana University Press.

Goldstein, Herman. 1977. *Policing in a Free Society*. Cambridge: Ballinger.

Hudson, James. 1970. "Police-Citizen Encounters that Lead to Citizen Complaints." *Social Problems* 18 (Fall): 179–93.

Hunt, Jennifer and Peter Manning. 1991. "The Social Context of Police Lying." *Symbolic Interaction* 14:51–70.

International Association of Chiefs of Police. 1989. *Building Integrity and Reducing Drug Corruption in Police Departments*. Arlington: International Association of Chiefs of Police.

Kahn, Ronald. 1975. "Urban Reform and Police Accountability in New York City: 1950–1974." In Robert Lineberry and Louis Masotti (eds.) *Urban Problems and Public Policy*, pp. 107–27. Lexington: Lexington Books.

Kappeler, Victor and Peter Kraska. 1995. "Citizen Complaints in the New Police Order." In W. Bailey (ed.) *The Encyclopedia of Police Science*, pp. 75–80. New York: Garland Publishing.

Kappeler, Victor, Richard Sluder, and Geoffrey Alpert. 1994. *Forces of Deviance: Understanding the Dark Side of Policing*. Prospect Heights, IL: Waveland Press.

Klockars, Carl. 1983. "Introduction to Chapter Six: Police Corruption." In C. Klockars (ed.) *Thinking About Police: Contemporary Readings*, pp. 332–37. New York: McGraw-Hill.

Lundman, Richard L. 1980. *Police Behavior: A Sociological Perspective*. New York: Oxford University Press.

Lundman, Richard L. 1980a. *Police and Policing: An Introduction*. New York: Holt, Rinehart and Winston.

McMullan, M. 1961. "A Theory of Corruption." *Sociological Review* 9, no. 2 (July): 181–201.

Roberg, Roy and Jack Kuykendall. 1993. *Police & Society*. Belmont: Wadsworth Publishing Co.

Savitz, L. 1971. "The Dimensions of Police Loyalty." In Hahn Harlan (ed.) *Police in Urban Society*. Beverly Hills: Sage Publications.

Sherman, Lawrence W. 1974. *Police Corruption: A Sociological Perspective*. Garden City, NY: Anchor Books.

Spradley, James P. 1969. *You Owe Yourself a Drunk*. Boston: Little, Brown.

United States Commission on Civil Rights. 1981. *Who is Guarding the Guardians?* Washington, DC: United States Government Printing Office.

Wagner, Allen and Scott Decker. 1993. "Evaluating Citizen Complaints Against the Police." In R. Dunham and G. Alpert (eds.) *Critical Issues in Policing: Contemporary Readings*, 2nd. ed., pp. 275–91. Prospect Heights, IL: Waveland Press.

Walker, Samuel. 1992. *The Police in America*, 2nd ed. New York: McGraw-Hill.

West, Paul. 1993. "Investigation and Review of Complaints against Police Officers: An Overview of Issues and Philosophies." In T. Barker and D. Carter (eds.) *Police Deviance,* 3rd ed. Cincinnati: Anderson Publishing.

Chapter Seven

STYLES OF POLICING

Earlier discussions regarding police organizations (chapter 4), police sub-cultures and personalities (chapter 5), and controls (chapter 6) have established a sufficient baseline of information about police to analyze their different styles. To understand why styles of policing differ between officers and departments, it is necessary to recognize the political demands made on the organization combined with the many methods, procedures and limitations of police work as practiced by individuals. In this chapter we will first examine *institutional* characteristics and styles of policing, and then proceed to see how they are translated into *individual* styles. Our focus will be upon the different styles, their formation, and how each becomes a part of the various police organizations. Further, we will discuss the types of departments in which the various styles are practiced and the interrelationships among the police departments' styles and the communities' evaluations of police services.

Before we turn to our review of police styles, recognizing the usefulness of studying them is important. Understanding these styles can inform political leaders and the public about the priorities of the police. This information will also help police administrators reorient policing by altering priorities and by encouraging and rewarding a specific style. This is especially important when there is a lack of harmony between police officers and the consumers of their services. Each of these goals has its own merit and its own utility. The first goal is to understand the functioning of the police and the relationship between the police and the community they serve. The second goal is to create the ability to redirect policing into a style or styles that benefit the police and are accepted by the politicians and members of the community. The first study of police styles was conducted in the late 1940s by William Westley (1953). Since then, many social scientists have studied both institutional and individual adaptations to police work.

INSTITUTIONAL BEHAVIOR

Institutional styles of policing had been a topic of limited debate until James Q. Wilson's study of how police departments, and not individual officers, adapt to the environment of the communities they serve. Wilson created a general typology of police behavior based upon the needs and demands of the community (Wilson, 1968). One of Wilson's major theses was that various police departments can be classified into several types, each of which is influenced by the attitudes, beliefs and actions of members of the communities served. In a fashion similar to individual typologies, these institutional typologies are not mutually exclusive and are subject to overlap and generalizations. However, Wilson gives us a starting point and some thought-provoking interpretations of the watch style, the legalistic style and the service style of policing.

Police departments that use the *watch style* of policing follow the basic rule of watchers or observers in maintaining order. The major role of the officers is to reduce the law enforcement aspect of their jobs by avoiding confrontations and many minor law violations. Problems that do not amount to threats to the public peace are routinely ignored. Criminal activities, such as gambling and prostitution, that include willing victims and participants will be tolerated if that is the wish of the members of the community, or at least the powerful members!

In most situations, domestic problems will be viewed as private issues, and police will be encouraged to follow the path of least resistance. Matters that affect the public peace or threaten the social fabric of the community will not be tolerated and may be handled formally with coercion. Policies and practices that are generated from the watch style have dramatic consequences, both positive and negative. First, minor offenses are tolerated and their penalties are rarely enforced. Second, target populations, such as minorities and the poor, often receive the blunt end of justice. In sum, the watch style lives up to its name and keeps the order, but it is the order of the community leaders and power brokers at the expense of the silent weak majority.

Police departments that emphasize the *legalistic style* maximize enforcement of laws as their dominant characteristic. Activities, such as gambling and prostitution, that are interpreted as garden-variety to the watch-style officer are seen as threatening actions requiring formal intervention. Juvenile delinquents and prostitutes will be arrested because they violated the law. Because of these guidelines, legalistic departments generate large numbers of citations and arrests. The impact on the community of the legalistic style of policing is a strict requirement to follow the letter of the law. Discrimination will be reduced but so will discretion. The financial costs of this style are extensive; officers will enforce most laws, arrest most law violators and, as a result, will fill the courts and the jails. These departments generate more arrests and therefore, higher crime statistics than other agencies.

Departments with a *service-oriented style* take all requests for police assistance seriously. The major goal of these departments is community service. Officers in these departments tend to be proactive or to take action, as opposed to officers with the reactive nature of the other styles of policing. Although police intervention is frequent, most is informal. Alternatives to formal intervention are stressed and, when appropriate, include referrals to social-service agencies for assistance. Service-style policing and community relations go hand-in-hand. The major emphasis of this type of policing is on service and protection.

INDIVIDUAL STYLES

Styles of policing are based on a number of influences that range from personality variables to organizational imperatives. William Ker Muir (1977) generated one of the more interesting theories on the effects of organizational, political and social environment on police work. Basically, Muir analyzed the nature of coercive power, how it affects the police personality and how these personality "types" encourage and discourage behavior. That is, what are the conditions that influence unacceptable policing and what are the conditions that encourage appropriate and moral policing. Following Muir's lead, Michael Brown conducted research on individual styles of policing and provided us with a good way to understand and define the notion (Brown, 1981:223): "A patrolman's operational style is based on his responses to . . . the difficulties and dilemmas he encounters in attempting to control crime . . . [and] the ways in which he accommodates himself to the pressures and demands of the police bureaucracy."

Brown explains further that the officer's style derives from the specific choices made about how aggressively and selectively he or she chooses to work the streets. Aggressiveness includes both the initiation of crime-control activities and the ability to outsmart the offender by legal or, sometimes, almost legal activities. Selectivity is the ordering of priorities. In police work, this includes the use of discretion in balancing crime control, order-maintenance and service calls. It also means ordering responses by the seriousness of crimes and criminals. A police officer's style can range from behaviors made popular by Dirty Harry to Joe Friday's by-the-book actions.

These ideas form an excellent foundation for understanding how police types are formed and how individual styles of policing impact the communities the police serve.

As we discussed in detail in chapter 5, a working police personality is multi-faceted. There have been several important studies on types of police officers and police styles. John Broderick (1987) has written one of the most informative books on police officer types. His personality schema reflects patterns of values, attitudes and beliefs that officers rely upon to adapt to the job of policing. He has classified police personalities into four ideal types that can be identified by an overall pattern of dominant characteristics. Broderick warns us that characteristics common to one type may be found in other types and that "no claim is made that police officers must fall neatly into this set of categories or any similar set, but this scheme provides a useful and convenient way of examining a very complex area of human behavior" (1987:4). It is important to keep in mind that stereotypes do not exist in a vacuum and that they are interrelated with their social systems.

Typologies are classification schemes that simplify complex phenomena. They are usually based upon several characteristics of the most important ideas to be classified. As Broderick informs us, police personality characteristics and styles overlap and do not form neatly distinct groups. Other research conducted on police types and their enforcement styles report findings similar to Broderick's (Coates, 1972; White, 1972; Muir, 1977; Brown, 1981; Hatting et al., 1983; and Walsh, 1986). Any one of the typologies could have been chosen for review, as each has some worthwhile information to offer and may be applied as a generalization to other police officers and departments. Since Broderick has analyzed his study within the context of the other researchers, we will briefly review his types and the accompanying styles of policing.

Broderick has created general groupings from his study of, and participation in, several police departments. He has labelled his types according to common and prevalent characteristics. His study includes a complex analysis of police styles and reports both general comments and specific examples from real-life experiences. His categories include enforcers, idealists, realists, and optimists.

Enforcers are those types of officers who place a high value on the safety of the streets and the social fabric of the community, and a low value on individual rights and due process of law. In other words, the officers who fit this type have strong subcultural ties and view their jobs as keeping the streets safe by removing those who threaten the public.

Idealists are police officers who believe that they can solve the problem of crime by following closely the procedural laws established for them. They place a high value on individual rights and due process and incorporate as their mandate the responsibility to protect citizens from criminals and to preserve the social order. Idealists hold education as very important but report a low level of commitment to law enforcement.

Realists place a relatively low emphasis on the individual rights of citizens and the maintenance of the social order. They report extreme dissatisfaction with the criminal justice system but often compensate by withdrawing into their own world and avoiding difficult decision making. Cynicism is a part of this reaction and helps to protect the officers where frustration and failure run high.

Broderick's final type, the *optimist*, views his or her job as one that helps people in trouble. These officers conceive of their job as people-oriented. This focus gives the officers great satisfaction. The priority of fighting crime is placed after the job of providing service to the public. Optimists generally appreciate the relatively high level of education they have received and report a correspondingly high level of commitment to law enforcement.

Most recently, Worden (1995) has reviewed, compared and contrasted the various typologies in a study of police officers' belief systems. His synthesis reveals five types, including the professional, the tough-cop, the clean-beat crime-fighter, the problem-solver and the avoider. To Broderick's types, he has added the problem-solver which was included by White (1972) as the problem-solver and Muir (1977) as the reciprocator. Worden (1995:59–60) notes that problem-solvers do a great deal more than crime control:

> . . . for them, in fact, law enforcement is incidental to their responsibilities. They focus on outcome, and particularly on the outcomes connected with individual problems. Thus, they resist bureaucratic controls and efficiency norms, preferring instead to resolve problems through means appropriate to the situations . . . they feel free to prioritize criminal offenses . . . on the preferences of the community.

The importance of recognizing these types is the acknowledgment that police officers do not all think or act alike. While police officers have many characteristics in common, each individual does not react to the decisions and difficulties of the job in the same fashion. The manner in which each reacts represents his or her individual style. Although individual officers can be classified into one or more categories of a typology, this information is not sufficient to predict responses or behavior. Individual style coupled with and controlled by the requirements of the organization lead to institutional behavior or what the consumers of police work receive.

CHIEF'S CORNER
POLICE STYLES AND THE COMMUNITY

Many police administrators have come to believe that members of the public want a close, personal and friendly relationship with their police department, 100 percent of the time. It has been demonstrated to me again and again that this is just not the case. When there is danger, disorder, or something that causes a citizen to become uneasy about safety, he or she will both desire and demand control, authority and a military-like regimen which reassures them that knowledgeable, trained, well-equipped professionals, who are strong enough to defeat the problem, are willing and available. I know of no other model than the traditional military organizational structure that fulfills this public need. To this end, the personnel working within such a model must be trained to be kind and understanding in their general dealings with the public, yet firm and in control when there is danger. To do so requires situational behavior which many officers do not seem to be able to adopt. They attempt to make one type of behavior fit all situations (generally a tough-guy attitude) and find themselves at odds many times with those they want to please.

This lack of ability to adapt the behavior to the situation is also a major cause of stress among police officers. Many come into police work with set personalities and behavior patterns which have been successful throughout their lives to that point. When they enter the academy, it is reinforced that they should be ever cautious, detached from the emotions of any situation, and should carry themselves with military bearing. In many ways, this type of behavior can be successful. But it most certainly won't be successful at those times when the citizen needs compassion, understanding and someone whom they believe really cares about their problem. It is in this situation that the police officer needs to drop the military demeanor and change behavior to fit the needs of the customer, the citizen. When the officer can't do this because he or she has become so rigidly frozen in an unemotional, just-the-facts role, it causes a great deal of confusion and stress. While the officer came into police work wanting to help people, it is difficult to do so because he or she has been trained to believe that such empathy by police officers is unacceptable behavior.

BEYOND TYPOLOGIES

Several years after the importance of typological research had been established, The National Advisory Commission on Criminal Justice Standards and Goals (1973:13) emphasized the importance of community characteristics to policing when it reported:

> Because the responsibility of law enforcement and the provision of police services to meet local needs are properly borne by local government, it would be unrealistic to establish rigid criteria for all police agencies in the United States. Priorities regarding the police role are largely established by the community the police agency serves.

Although the complex nature and importance of the various styles of policing have been established, more questions have been asked than answered. It is difficult to create categories, even ones based on important and identifiable criteria. It is more difficult to place officers and departments correctly into the proper category. The more careful and precise the research, the higher the probability that proper placements will be made. Unfortunately, there is always a chance that a round peg will be placed in a square hole. It is important to consider typologies only as a way to explain general concepts and themes, not finite details. The best available typologies for both individual and institutional policing have been mentioned; the sources of variation will now be considered.

SOURCES OF VARIATION

Why one police department or community will support or even require one style of policing over another depends upon several determinants, including internal and external pressures. Individual officers may fit into one type or another based upon backgrounds or upon the incentives offered by the department. In other words, how a department structures its institutional rewards may determine an officer's style. For example, a legalistic department may encourage its officers to fit the enforcer style, while service-style departments might reward an optimist-type officer. From these differences, the pressures and influences from the communities can be determined. As in all organizations, money and power can determine the fate of a police department and must be considered the bottom line. Police departments differ from other organizations only in how they generate and control power and money. Police must be accountable to the legal system under which they operate and must account for the local rates of crime. In many ways, these two elements—the legal system and crime statistics—determine the department's power and money.

There are other considerations for police agencies, but accountability for laws and crime have been the most traditional. For example, all the positive thinking in the world cannot substitute for competent police officers whose style and performance are consistent with the philosophy of the department and the communities served. In addition, if dissatisfaction exists, politicians can change the philosophy of a department with a quick wave of a magic wand that can replace the police chief or diminish his or her ability to govern the department.

THE LEGAL SYSTEM

As we learned in chapter 1, substantive laws refer to specific behavior to be controlled or to the rights and duties of citizens. Procedural laws, as well as the agencies' policies and procedures, define how the substantive laws can be applied or how the substantive laws are enforced in the courts. This idea of enforcing laws sets the scene for a dilemma in policing: protecting the public from crime while doing so within the law and its due process protections. Jerome Skolnick has discussed these inherent conflicts and has noted (1966:6):

> The police in democratic society are required to maintain order and to do so under the rule of law. As functionaries charged with maintaining order, they are part of the bureaucracy. The ideology of democratic bureaucracy emphasizes initiative rather than disciplined adherence to rules and regulations. By contrast, the rule of law emphasizes the rights of individual citizens and constraints upon the initiatives of legal officials. This tension between the operational consequences of ideas of order, efficiency and initiative, on the one hand, and legality, on the other, constitutes the principal problem of police as a democratic legal organization.

As we have seen, police officers, police departments and communities may view substantive laws and due process protections differently. The balance between the rights of the government (police) and the rights of the citizens hinges on the interpretations and applications of these procedural laws. The issue boils down to a not-so-simple question: should the police have the ability to control what they consider the dangerous class, or should citizens have every possible ounce of protection from an unjustified arrest? In other words, should some criminals be set free so we are assured that we do not convict an innocent person?

One event summarizes the issues we face. A man nicknamed "Dirty Dog" was being interrogated by police detectives. While one detective provided the Dog with a sandwich and cold drink, the other detective pounded on the table near the accused's injured head. After more than ten hours of interrogation, Dirty Dog confessed to a murder. The defendant was neither touched, hit, nor beaten, but he was scared and confused. There was no criticism of the police behavior at the community level. In fact, newspaper reports indicated the public's pleasure that a criminal had been arrested and that he had confessed. At a hearing, however, a judge ruled that the confession, the only strong evidence against the defendant, was inadmissible. Dirty Dog is free because the police used methods that may have been permissible to the community but were inappropriate to the legal system.

This example of a police trickery which resulted in a coerced confession illustrates the complexities of procedural law and how police practices which may be approved by many community members may not be considered reasonable by the courts. A comprehensive analysis of police practices reveals that the courts are often called upon to balance effective law enforcement with the need to protect individuals' rights. In this example, there exists a thin and blurred line between a voluntary and involuntary confession. As this need to balance effective law enforcement with individuals' rights encompasses many police tactics and practices, it is instructive to review the legal issues affecting interrogation as an example.

Although reviewing courts often refuse to consider deceptive police conduct as unconstitutional in the same way they regard certain other forms of psychological and physical force (see *State v. Jackson*, 1983; Note, 1984), it is important to understand when such a tactic becomes unreasonable and illegal. As the essential goal of a police interrogation is to obtain a legal confession, police are instructed to make the suspect want to confess voluntarily. Inbau, Reid and Buckley wrote an authoritative text in 1986 which organized tactics and techniques for successful interrogations, or "selling the suspect on the idea to tell the truth" (159) into "nine steps to effectiveness" (77–84). This process begins with methods used to "disarm" the suspect (84–85), moves to the "critical stage" when the apprehensive suspect becomes indecisive about his answers (159) to the suspect's first admission of guilt (165–170) and concludes with a detailed oral and written confession (171–178). Specifically, interrogators are encouraged to develop a "theme" which will provide the suspect with a moral excuse for the crime. Examples of possible themes include that anyone under the same circumstances would have done it, the victim deserved it, and that the whole report must be exaggerated. The purpose of a theme is to "establish the psychological foundation to achieve an implicit, if not explicit, early, general admission of guilt" (97).

Inbau, Reid, and Buckley's text includes a twenty-page appendix, "The Psychological Principles of Criminal Interrogation," authored by Brian C. Jayne, Director of the Reid College of Detection of Deception. The section notes that the goal of the entire process of interrogation is "to decrease the suspect's perception of the consequences of confessing" (332). The bottom line of this process is to convince a suspect to abandon a false denial and to admit to the truth, whether or not the suspect is inclined to do so. Obviously, the most intelligent course of action for any suspect is to refuse to answer questions, as telling the truth may not be in the best interest of a guilty suspect.

Two general concerns emerge from this process. First, is "the best interest of the suspect" in the best interest of criminal justice? In other words, should police be empowered to trick criminal defendants into revealing the truth and "cleansing one's soul"? The underlying question is that of "voluntariness" (Note, 1985). Second, can these tactics force or compel a suspect into making a false confession? The concern over the best interest of the subject and criminal justice can be answered by both the philosophical balancing of the protection of individual rights with effective law enforcement and the legal analysis of the Fifth and Sixth Amendments (Saski, 1988).

Perhaps the most confusing procedural law is that of search and seizure. The process of stopping, frisking and questioning people or searching their surroundings is closely tied to the process of arrest. Since stopping and searching a person may constitute a seizure of the person, the Fourth Amendment of the Constitution protects the rights of the citizen. While the Constitution protects citizens against unreasonable searches and seizures and formally controls the actions of the government, the guidelines it provides are vague and difficult to put into practice.

In most situations police require a search warrant to search a person or his or her effects. If a search and subsequent seizure are conducted legally, all items seized can be used in a court of law. If a search is conducted illegally, or in bad faith, no items seized can be used in a court of law. To obtain an arrest warrant, probable cause that a crime has been committed and that the specific individual named committed the crime must be demonstrated to a neutral magistrate. To obtain a search warrant, probable cause that evidence or contraband is being stored in a specific place must be demonstrated to a magistrate.

In emergency situations, a warrantless search or seizure may take place. What constitutes an emergency, what constitutes probable cause, and what constitutes a search are among the most confusing areas of American jurisprudence (Alpert and Haas, 1984). It has often been said that we expect police officers to make split-second decisions that must stand up to hours of arguing and years of litigation. For our purposes, it is sufficient to understand that these terms are difficult to define, have meanings that change periodically, and can be applied differentially (see *California v. Hodari D.*, 1991). Police officers and police departments can interpret these laws in such a way to justify their own philosophy and behavior. Which procedural laws police officers follow, how closely they follow them, and whether or not they are applied equally determine part of the legal environment in which the department operates and which influences styles of policing.

CRIME STATISTICS

Law enforcement policies are often influenced by resources and political pressures. One consistent measure of the emphasis of law enforcement is the Federal Bureau of Investigation's *Uniform Crime Reports* (UCR). As we mentioned in the chapter on the history of police, these reports help define traditional success or effectiveness for the police department. This measuring rod has changed only slightly during the past fifty years. The UCR includes the crimes of homicide, rape, aggravated assault, robbery, burglary, auto theft, larceny and arson. These are the crimes that most often make headline news, are pointed to by politicians who want to take credit or place blame, and are most often committed by the poor. The FBI's crime report does not include white-collar crimes such as tax fraud, housing-code violations, or computer crimes. Many white-collar crimes are investigated by state and federal agencies, but the bulk of law enforcement, and especially local law enforcement, is directed toward specific types of criminal behavior and, consequently, a specific class of persons. Crimes are reported together by the UCR as a rate (number of reported incidents or arrests divided by the population of the jurisdiction multiplied by 100,000). The "rate of serious crime" is a compilation of the eight crimes mentioned above.

Any discussion of crime statistics includes the fact that police policies directly affect the crime rate, and the crime rate affects police policies and budgets. Police are placed in an awkward position. Too much crime could be interpreted as scarce resources not being used efficiently; too little crime could be interpreted to mean that the current levels of funding are unwarranted.

The official FBI *Uniform Crime Reports* often are mistakenly interpreted as reflecting most of the serious crimes that are committed. This is a misunderstanding that is reinforced by the media that report crime rates as if these statistics represent all crimes committed. The fact that approximately 85 percent of police work is reactive to calls for service, rather than proactive, allows many crimes to go unnoticed by the police. Other problems with the collecting, analyzing and reporting of national crime data have compelled the publishers of the *Uniform Crime Reports* to place the following disclaimer in each issue of the Report: "The final responsibility for data submissions rests with the individual contributing law enforcement agency. . . . The statistics' accuracy depends primarily on the adherence of each contributor to the established standards of reporting" (*Uniform Crime Reports*, 1985:3). In addition, users are warned not to compare statistics across jurisdictions or within jurisdictions over time. Even with these disclaimers, most media report crime statistics as though they reflect an exact measure of crime. The media continue to provide comparisons that they are warned against presenting. In fact, the media interpret crime statistics in ways that are too simple, too plain, and often inaccurate (Garofalo, 1981). This type of sensational reporting without alternative explanations can create an unwarranted fear of crime (Galvin and Polk, 1980). Those who interpret and use data in the *Uniform Crime Reports* encounter not only the problems above but must consider how a police officer's discretion or a department's policies shape the crime statistics.

Although the reporting and editing of information, offense estimation, and crime trend analysis have improved, the UCR data must be interpreted with great caution. In 1989, Congress passed the Uniform Federal Crime Reporting Act, requiring all federal law enforcement agencies to participate in the UCR. As participation among the state and local agencies grows, the UCR becomes more meaningful. During the 1990s, the UCR is attempting to transform its format from summary to incident-based statistics. This new program, called the National Incident-Based Reporting System (NIBRS), will collect data on every incident and arrest for twenty-two crime categories. Each incident will incorporate data on victim, offender, property, injury and circumstances. This will greatly enhance the meaning, interpretation and usefulness of UCR data.

For example (with the exception of armed robbery), it has been found that approximately 70 percent of violent crime is perpetrated against acquaintances while only 30 percent is against strangers. Statistics generated from the 1992 South Carolina NIBRS data revealed that 72 percent of all murder victims knew their killer, 76 percent of all aggravated assault victims knew their assailant, and 71 percent of all rape victims and 86 percent of other forcible sex crimes knew their assailant. Nineteen percent of the victims of robbery reported knowing their attacker (Alpert et al., 1994). Further, the data showed that more than one-half of the murders (57%), aggravated assaults (58%), rapes (68%) and other forcible sex crimes (76%) occurred in places of residence. The NIBRS report noted that robbery is the only crime studied in which the traditional police approach could have an impact. However, the clearance rate for robbery is the lowest of the five crimes. These statistics suggest that we can have more police protecting the citizens. It has been said that society needs a police officer on every corner. Perhaps, it might be more effective to have one in every bedroom! The ability to review the relationships among criminals and their victims, place of crime, weapon use and injury, etc., has widespread implications for those in academics as well as for criminal justice planners. Coyle et al. (1991) conducted a survey of individuals involved in the production, collection or analysis of incident-based crime data. Their study found that victim and offender relationships, drug and alcohol involvement in criminal incidents, and the tracking of offenders through the criminal justice system ranked as the most important applications of the new data.

The implementation of NIBRS on a national level has begun, albeit at a slow pace. The FBI has been able to accept NIBRS data since January, 1989. In April of that year, Alabama was the first state to submit a tape for analysis. During the 1990s, many states will have converted from the summary data to NIBRS format.

The politics of policing also has an effect on crime statistics. Whether a police administrator wants to demonstrate the efficiency of his or her operation or a serious need for further funding, crime statistics can provide the ammunition. Examples of this political maneuvering are frequent and present in most jurisdictions (see Galvin and Polk, 1980). For example, during a convention of the American Society of Travel Agents in Miami, Florida, police were instructed to rid the streets of prostitutes, vagrants and other undesirables. This change of policy was made to demonstrate the safety of Miami's streets and to attract an increased number of tourists. Several hundred arrests were made during the period when the travel agents were looking over Miami. The efforts faded at the end of the convention, but the arrests had a lasting effect on the official crime statistics. Another example comes to our attention from Thomas and Hepburn (1983). They reported that the crime rate at the University of Florida was one of the highest in the country and that university officials were livid and anxious to do something to reduce the criminal behavior. As Thomas and Hepburn reported, something was done (1983:92):

> In February of 1982, the Chief of the University of Florida Police Department announced that his department would no longer report any crime that his personnel could not fully verify. In effect, for example, students reporting thefts of personal property had to substantiate their reports to the police by providing some evidence that they really owned the item being reported as stolen.

As one can imagine, this action lowered the crime rate, and Thomas and Hepburn (1983:92) reflected:

> The volume of crime at the University of Florida now seems to be under control. It now seems that we can walk the streets and paths of our campus in safety. Recent statistics "prove" this to be the case. The parents of our students, the alumni and the state legislature will no doubt react in a properly grateful manner.

Perhaps the most important crime statistics are gathered by the National Crime Victims Survey (NCVS), which provides data on crime rates and the characteristics of crime based upon national household interviews. In other words, NCVS reports information from victims of crime. The data are generated from interviews of all persons twelve years of age or older in a sample of households (Bureau of Justice Statistics, 1990). Information collected in the NCVS included details about the characteristics of victims, the victim-offender relationship and the criminal incident, including the extent of loss or injury. These data, when supplemented by the information provided in the UCR, can help create a comprehensive picture of crime in the United States. In fact, if the victim data are not part of a crime analysis, the overall picture of crime will be incomplete.

Although crime statistics are the most unreliable of the social statistics and can be manipulated for multiple purposes, they are relied upon for some very serious budgetary and police policy decisions. Crime, as it is interpreted from the statistics, can have a strong influence on the individual and institutional styles of policing. The legal environment in which a police department operates, along with the need to produce results and justify one's existence, can explain the differences among police departments and how each handles its discretionary decisions.

DISCRETION

Since police work is so complex, official responses to situations cannot all be alike. Rather, they must follow some reasonable pattern for predictability and social order. However, police officers are not robots and must have some degree of authority to vary a response. Kenneth Culp Davis (1975:1) has observed that:

> The police make policy about what law to enforce, how much to enforce it, against whom, and on what occasions. Some law is always or almost always enforced, some is never or almost never enforced, and some is sometimes enforced and sometimes not. Police policy about selective enforcement is elaborate and complex.

Davis's comment informs us that it is impossible to implement a policy of full enforcement of the law and that police must have written guidelines that outline what is expected of them, both individually and collectively.

Written guidelines or policies direct police officers' behavior. As we have discussed, departments that operate without the benefit of policies place themselves and their officers in a precarious situation. Policies based on relevant laws serve to provide guidance from the agency administrators or command staff to the officers. These guidelines must provide members of the organization with sufficient information so that they can successfully perform the day-to-day operations. Some agencies have gone into great detail to specify the exact behavior which is permitted and specific behaviors that are not permitted. Other agencies have opted for a more generalized style of guidance. As a result, discretion is available to officers in varying amounts.

As we have learned from our review of individual and organizational types, there are many options from which officers may choose. While we know that discretion exists, and often know the results of discretionary decisions, we are unable to pinpoint the exact reasons police exercise it they way they do. However, we know in general terms that police discretion is partially determined by a combination of several factors, including the interests and styles of individual officers, the nature of the law and the legal system, and the institutional work environment. These factors converge and produce patterns of police discretion (see Brooks, 1993 and Brown, 1981). Laure Brooks has written an exhaustive review of the literature on police discretion and has concluded (1993:161):

Since police exercise so much discretion, it is important to understand the factors which affect their choices in how to behave. It appears as though organizational characteristics, neighborhood factors, situational cues, officer characteristics, and lastly, officer attitudes, all play some part in the decisions that police make regarding their behavior. While we know a great deal about the determinants of police discretionary behavior . . . much is still left unexplained. . . . [M]ost research attention has been focused at situational cues which officers confront, with less attention paid to other levels of analysis. One area which seems to offer promise as an enhancer to our understanding of police behavior, but which has received little empirical examination, is that of police officer orientations or attitudes.

Different patterns of discretion develop among different police departments. These patterns can be observed in many facets of police work, including the most common and visible police function: police patrol.

POLICE PATROL

As O. W. Wilson argued, patrol "is the backbone of policing" (Wilson and McClaren, 1977:320–321). Traditionally, the majority of police officers are assigned to the patrol unit or division and are the most visible to the public. Additionally, the patrol function often doubles as traffic control in many departments and serves to train individuals for supervisory and other administrative tasks, as virtually every police officer begins with "street experience" on patrol. Career advancement begins with a promotion out of patrol duty. The few who advance without this experience on the streets have missed out on shared experiences and socialization with fellow officers. This void increases the chances that an officer will be labelled as one who does not know what policing is really all about, regardless of future assignments. Today's police departments are returning to foot patrols and moving away from reliance on the automobile. However, each type of patrol serves different functions, promotes different relationships and creates different problems. Regardless of the type, or of how the officers get around, patrol is an important aspect of policing, as it brings the officers and citizens together in some form of interaction.

The National Advisory Commission on Criminal Justice Standards and Goals (1973:189) has pointed out that "the patrolman is usually the lowest paid, least consulted, most taken for granted member of the force. His duty is looked upon as boring and routine." For these reasons, it is argued that enhancing the status of patrol and improving conditions of patrol are critical problems facing police administrators.

One of the difficulties experienced by police administrators is finding a consensus among patrol officers and between those officers and members of the public concerning the purposes, objectives, procedures and functions of the police. Many lists of police activities have been created, yet none includes all of the tasks performed by the police. Certainly there is no "one best way" to accomplish the tasks. The following list identifies activities that are typically conducted by patrol officers:

1. deterring crime through routine patrol;
2. enforcing the laws;
3. investigating criminal behavior;
4. apprehending offenders;
5. writing reports;
6. coordinating efforts with prosecutors;
7. assisting individuals in danger or in need of assistance;
8. resolving conflicts;
9. keeping the peace;
10. maintaining order;
11. keeping pedestrian and automobile traffic moving; and
12. studying criminal behavior and analyzing possible responses.

These activities serve several purposes and are both proactive and reactive. Additionally, administrative issues related to the allocation and distribution of patrol officers (foot, bicycle, horse, or one- or two-person car patrols, etc.) are important but secondary to the success and effectiveness of patrol. The differential distribution of these resources can affect the success of patrol and must be considered as supportive to that function of policing.

Patrol can be divided into three related outcomes. First, the presence of an officer on patrol may eliminate the opportunity for someone to commit a crime successfully. In other words, the presence of a police officer may frighten the offender away or influence him or her to wait until the officer leaves the area. Additionally, the presence of an officer allows observation of traffic violations that may turn into investigative leads. Second, patrolling provides an officer with the opportunity to determine the probabilities of criminal behavior and, through preventive strategies, to reduce or eliminate those probabilities.

Patrol officers are in the best position to understand crime in a given area and to suggest possible responses and remedies. These proactive duties can be achieved by becoming familiar with communities and those who live or work in them. By encouraging cooperation and fostering trust, a patrol officer can learn about possible criminal behavior and offenders and intervene before it is too late. Finally, patrolling provides officers with the opportunity to respond or react to calls for assistance in a timely manner. This reactive policing is the most common method of serving the public, whether for crime control or service calls. Response time may be a matter of life or death.

The success or effectiveness of patrolling depends upon the specific patrol strategy. Again, patrolling by foot, horse, automobile, or any combination can influence the effectiveness or perceived effectiveness of patrol. Perhaps the most comprehensive evaluation of traditional police patrol was the Kansas City Patrol Experiment (Kelling et al., 1974). Although there have been serious concerns about the methods and results, the study has raised our level of consciousness about patrol (Larson, 1975).

THE KANSAS CITY PREVENTIVE PATROL STUDY

This study has an interesting history and ranks as one of the first scientific experiments designed to measure the effectiveness of a police function. The experiment began in July, 1972 but was suspended as the experimental conditions were not being maintained. The experiment started again in October and continued for twelve months, ending in September, 1973. Fifteen beats in the South Patrol Division of Kansas City were chosen and computer matched based on crime data, police calls for service, ethnicity, income, and transiency. The beats were divided into three different groups:

1. *Reactive*—no preventive patrol. Police vehicles entered these areas only when answering calls for service.
2. *Proactive*—these beats were assigned two or three times the normal number of patrol vehicles.
3. *Control*—these five beats were assigned the normal number of police patrol vehicles (one per beat).

Data were collected from multiple sources concerning a wide variety of issues. The sources included public opinion and victimization surveys, observations of police-citizen encounters, and official police records. The issues included information on police behavior, criminal behavior, victimization, community attitudes toward police, crime, and crime deterrence.

The results of the Kansas City Experiment were contrary to conventional wisdom. The study concluded that variations of the level of patrol made very little difference in any of the areas tested. Specifically, no significant differences were found in the rate of victimization among reactive, proactive or control beats. Citizen fear of crime was not significantly affected by the three levels of patrol. Citizen attitudes toward police were not significantly affected by the various patrol strategies, and response time (the time taken by police to answer calls) for service was not affected by variations in the level or strategy of patrol.

Any implications that can be drawn from this study for policing must be tentative. Although a great deal of information was analyzed, there was an even greater amount of information that was not even collected. For example, the impact of police presence on the decisions of potential offenders in specific situations could not be measured, nor could more complex problems of police service be evaluated by this study. In any case, the three levels of patrol made very little difference on crime rates and had very little effect on citizens' attitudes toward police or satisfaction with the police. One significant benefit was the acceptance of the experimental research design for police services.

BEYOND THE KANSAS CITY STUDY

Police departments have been experimenting with patrol strategies for years and have responded to the various problems and issues with some innovative programs. Many types of strategies have been attempted, ranging from the original foot and horse patrols to different levels of motorized patrols. The Kansas City Study demonstrated that sometimes the obvious is not always correct and that conventional wisdom needs to be tested. Since the results of that study have been disseminated, many departments have returned to strategies of the past or have combined ideas practiced in earlier years with newer ones to improve the effectiveness and efficiency of patrol.

Some departments are deploying their patrol units based upon previous criminal patterns; others are moving to a problem-solving approach to detect and deter crime. In addition, some departments are opening storefront police stations and using bicycle, horse and foot patrols. Unfortunately, we do not know how to increase the efficiency or effectiveness of patrolling, but we have learned how to improve the citizens' perceptions of safety. The major findings from The Newark Foot Patrol Experiment (Police Foundation, 1981) demonstrated that, while crime levels were not affected by different types of patrols, foot patrol did have a significant impact on the attitudes of the people served by such patrols. "Consistently, residents in beats where foot patrol was added see the severity of crime problems diminishing in their neighborhoods at levels greater than the other two areas" (Police Foundation, 1981:4–5). Wilson and Kelling offer some valuable insights into the results of this study (1982:29):

> These findings may be taken as evidence that the skeptics were right—foot patrol has no effect on crime; it merely fools the citizens into thinking they are safer. But in our view, and in the view of the authors of the Police Foundation study [of whom Kelling was one], the citizens of Newark were not fooled at all. They knew what the foot-patrol officers were doing, they knew it was different from what motorized officers do, and they knew that having officers walk beats did in fact make their neighborhoods safer.

There are many ways to bring the police officer closer to the community and to establish rapport with the community residents. There are also a number of strategies that have been attempted without positive results. In a very influential and thoughtful study, Skolnick and Bayley (1986) identify a number of negative research findings that must be addressed before we guide our future policies and practices.

The research reports data from recent empirical studies and warns us that ". . . the primary strategies followed by American police departments are neither reducing crime nor reassuring the public. The police often devote resources to traditional but bureaucratically safe approaches that no longer work if they ever did" (Skolnick and Bayley, 1986:5). These strategies include an increase in the number of police, motor patrol (with set or randomized patterns), saturation patrolling and reduced response time to emergency calls. Skolnick and Bayley conclude that four elements of innovation exist. These include: police-community reciprocity, decentralization of command, reorientation of patrol, and civilianization. We will discuss some of these elements below and others in our final chapters.

The development of a good relationship between police and citizens is a necessary first step that will ultimately foster a two-way exchange of information. This interaction will promote the officers' ability to help residents sharpen their crime-prevention skills and to receive information that can help prevent and solve crimes, as well as to maintain an orderly community. Other techniques can also be used to patrol communities. Regardless of the specific technique, it should be used as part of a larger patrol strategy which incorporates Skolnick and Bayley's elements of innovation. One good way to develop successful policing is to combine the traditional methods of evaluating law enforcement productivity with an interactive method of community feedback.

Many police departments determine their own organizational goals, form a style, and control their officers' discretion without the benefit of information and suggestions from outside sources. The most successful and progressive departments, however, rely upon structured feedback from the consumers of police services. Projects conducted by the Police Foundation have identified specific methods to improve policing (Pate et al., 1986:3).

> The most successful programs (neighborhood police centers, door-to-door contacts, community organizing by the police, and the coordination of several such approaches) had two characteristics in common:
>
> 1. they provided time for police to have frequent discussions with citizens who were encouraged to express their concerns about their neighborhoods; and
>
> 2. they relied upon the initiative and innovativeness of individual officers to develop and implement programs responsive to the concerns of the public.

The final section in this chapter will expand upon these and other findings and look at how police departments can benefit from the community's evaluation of police services.

EVALUATING POLICE SERVICES: A CONSUMER'S PERSPECTIVE

Each community requires policing that is consistent with its own needs. The typologies we have reviewed provide a snapshot of police officers and departments that operate in different communities. While these typologies are a useful tool to help study the police, they are only of limited use to police administrators. An integral part of good policing is the supervision and control of officers to provide protection and service that is within the acceptable bounds of the community. As we have seen above, police can use foot, bicycle, horse, automobile, or a combination to patrol. Officers can also act in different ways. The key element that has not been discussed is the *linkage* between the community and the police—to determine the style and patrol that will be most beneficial to the specific community.

Perhaps the most detailed study of police at work is the Police Services Study. Data were collected from twenty-four local police departments in sixty neighborhoods in three metropolitan areas. On the basis of the more than 26,000 calls for police service, the findings report that 19 percent of the calls involved crime (only two percent involved violent crime), and 33 percent of the calls were for information or assistance (Scott, 1981:28–30). As these data demonstrate, calls for information and assistance are the most frequent requests from the public and form the primary function of the police. The issues mentioned earlier including response time and arrests may reflect the most serious concerns voiced by citizens, but they are not the ones most often heard. In fact, only a small fraction of crimes committed are observed and no more than 6 percent of calls to police report crimes in progress (Bureau of Justice Statistics, 1988:62). Moreover, the police respond to only 28 percent of the reported violent crime within five minutes and less than 10 percent on nonviolent crime within five minutes (Whitaker, 1989). These facts and figures are presented to demonstrate the issues that will affect the perception of police performance by the public.

Ironically, when police departments converted calls for service into a 911 emergency telephone number and began focusing on the time it took to respond as a measure of police effectiveness, it forced policing further into a reactive system. The focus of the police shifted from community concerns to how quickly an officer could respond. A great deal of the pressure for this change of focus came from the public which voiced a preference for a rapid response rather than a need for proactive or problem-solving police strategies.

There are several methods available to politicians and police administrators to assure that the police services are within the limits of what the community will tolerate. Several important bits of information must be used to determine what is acceptable. First, the relevant audience or consumers of police service must be identified. Second, police agency performance must be measured by that audience. In other words, a set of subjects must be selected to help guide the police. This set, or sample, can include police administrators, politicians or members of the community. In addition, some method for evaluating police services must be devised.

The most convenient and possibly the most commonly used approach is an informal, key-informant method by which politicians and high-ranking officials hear from their friends and colleagues what is best for the community or jurisdiction. This information is provided to the decision makers who influence policies and procedures. Officials can make a key-informant system more formal by having representatives from the business community meet with government officials to provide information on police performance. Another approach is to seek information from citizens with a periodic open house, formal town meeting, or a public opinion poll.

The importance of the various measures of police performance differ according to the audience that is being questioned. For example, a business person who lives in a well-protected community may be more concerned about the appearance of crime or an image rather than actual arrest figures. A middle-class person may be more concerned about the protection of his or her home and family than about crime in the ghetto. A lower-class person may be more concerned about the personal interest and demeanor police officers show than about the crime rate. In other words, the sample of respondents and how certain types of questions are asked will generate different results. There must be some police-community reciprocity among all levels of citizens. The police must communicate that they are genuinely interested in the public's welfare and that the public has a substantial role in the design of policing priorities.

One important aspect of the public's influence is the feedback it can provide to police administrators. First, there should be some institutionalized method for all citizens to evaluate the police; the indicators or measures used should be meaningful to both police and the community. What is called a community or a neighborhood refers to the different forms of social organization and the different levels of identity possessed by the members of that organization. In today's world, some people may have no more in common than shared boundaries. Others who live in some proximity may share many common characteristics. The importance of these differences to policing is that effective policing in a given community may require significantly different tactics, strategies and styles from what is desired and necessary within another community under control of the same police department (see Alpert and Dunham, 1988; Taub, Taylor and Dunham, 1986).

Linking neighborhood and policing requires a major effort on the part of the police and a concern on the part of the public. As we have seen, there is little disagreement that some changes must be made in police work and that appropriate styles of policing must be used in the right communities. Larry Sherman has summed up the theoretical evidence quite well (1983:163):

> One point seems clear. We should not change the current numbers of public police. Instead, we should redirect their efforts away from waiting and

responding toward analyzing, coordinating, and watching. Police should spend more time on foot talking to citizens, and do more to stimulate and guide volunteer watching efforts. They should focus special attention on repeat offenders and illegal gun-carrying. They should gain the time to do this by refusing to handle certain kinds of requests, despite the political storm it may provoke.

Although Sherman's statement deserves serious attention, he leaves the reader wondering how, what, where and why. His thoughts are important but they do not provide specific direction. Others have made the same general suggestions (see Thibault et al., 1985; Skolnick and Bayley, 1986), but there is little to guide the formation of the linkage between the appropriate police style and the specific community.

Perhaps the best method for linking police with the community requires that we move beyond our general theoretical suggestions to empirical analyses of our police and the consumer of police services, the public. One empirical study has evaluated the needs of different neighborhoods and the officers who patrol the neighborhoods (Alpert and Dunham, 1988). This study examined community preferences for and responses to different styles of policing, as well as police officers' perceptions of policing in the various neighborhoods. The results of this study suggest that different communities should evaluate their own specific preferences and those of the police department and officers. Alpert and Dunham warn that while studies of typologies may suggest some general guidelines, neighborhoods and communities may differ significantly from each other and warrant periodic monitoring and evaluating. They conclude (Alpert and Dunham, 1988:221–222):

Both civilians and police officers want differential policing based upon neighborhood characteristics. In areas that acknowledge this need or may desire policing which relates to their neighborhoods, it is important that the police departments respond and determine the most appropriate style and limits of police in each neighborhood. . . . Police officers should be educated and trained in the expectations of the communities they serve. They must recognize differences that may exist between gender or ethnic groups or between social classes so they can bring their own style of policing into line with the expectations of the community and the department. . . . Members of the community should be encouraged to provide feedback to the police department on its individual officers and on general department performance.

Most recent research and commentary on policing indicate a need to integrate the police into the community or to return to police strategies that previously incorporated police in the community. The original community policing movement rested on the basic assumption that the police had a responsibility to seek solutions to problems that may be only indirectly related to criminal behavior.

Police-community relations units were established in the 1950s as a result of the widening of the net of police functions. The St. Louis Metropolitan Police Department is credited with establishing the first permanent unit in 1957 (Brown, 1971). Most units were issue-oriented and focused upon specific targets such as youths, minorities, or social service functions. The major responsibilities of these units included acting as liaisons with community groups, developing good police-community relations, acting as communication links for citizens who want to complain about the police or to make suggestions, and identifying the training needs of the police. The strengths of police-community relations units were also their weaknesses. As they were peripheral to basic police functions, they were perceived as outside the central police mission. Today, community policing refers to the process by which police identify and solve social problems affecting crime.

COMMUNITY-BASED POLICING

What exactly is community policing? What types of policing strategies are advocated by community policing advocates? How would a change to community policing affect a traditional police department and its programs? It is important to answer these and other questions to understand the essence of community policing and its dimensions.

Police-community relations divisions exist for several reasons: to handle public relations, to establish a formal avenue for addressing social and police issues, and to help the department maintain a high profile and a positive image. If these units were dissolved, police departments would probably be criticized as being insensitive to community needs and problems. In recent years, these programs have been phased into larger, more autonomous and powerful community policing divisions and applied as an overlay to the departmental philosophy (Kennedy and Moore, 1995; Cordner, 1995; Normandeau and Leighton, 1990; Greene, 1989; Alpert and Dunham, 1988; Greene and Mastrofski, 1988; Skolnick and Bayley, 1988; Reiss and Tonry, 1986).

Police officers must be familiar with the surroundings in their jurisdiction. In fact, they are trained to know not only where buildings are located within an area but also where the fire escapes are located within buildings. When an officer moves from one precinct, beat, or division to another, he or she learns about the new environment. Unlike the physical landmarks, the community residents are not often studied or understood. In many police departments, it is business as usual regardless of the type of community.

BREAKING FROM TRADITIONAL STYLES

Fortunately, there have been changes in that particular policing philosophy. Police departments are beginning to view their mandate as a contribution to the larger social fabric. Before this vision becomes a reality, however, many changes must take place. First, police officers must know more about the neighborhood and people they serve and protect. Second, major police departments must decentralize their administration to allow for regional and community differences. Third, the officers assigned to an area should remain for an extended period so they can learn more about the people, their ways and their problems. Fourth, police officers have to be evaluated on performance measures with which they agree. In other words, officers should not be evaluated by similar criteria regardless of their patrol assignment. An officer in a high-crime housing project should not be evaluated by the same criteria as an officer in a quiet suburb. The officers and the command staff should all agree upon and understand the criteria for evaluation. Finally, there must be an institutionalized informational feedback loop. Information from the consumers of police services can keep administrators apprised of individual officer and general departmental success.

The key to a successful community-oriented policing program is understanding and adjusting to the social fabric of the community (see Alpert and Dunham, 1988). One method that can expand the traditional attempts to understand the community is to identify the appropriate social indicators of unrest, perhaps by formally or informally speaking with people familiar with a neighborhood about their personal observations and feelings. For example, the extent of gang activity, the increase in the number of abandoned vehicles, the apparent establishment and use of "crack houses," and the general deterioration of an area which can be observed by residents can also be systematically reported by municipal workers, including sanitation workers, mail carriers and others whose employment routinely brings them to the area. As selected indicators in various areas begin to change, police or other agencies can address what could be negative results from those changes.

This approach was made popular by James Wilson and George Kelling (1982) in an article titled "Broken Windows," based upon Herman Goldstein's concept of problem-oriented policing (see Goldstein, 1977). The Wilson and Kelling article summarized the limits of the police in fighting crime and used the symbol of "broken windows" to illustrate that no one cares about the area. When decay begins and is allowed to continue, it encourages others not to care. This process permits deterioration and a resulting increase in crime (see Wilson and Kelling, 1989).

The Metro-Dade Police Department in Miami began an analysis of social indicators of unrest (IOU) in 1980 shortly after the McDuffie riot (see Porter and Dunn, 1984). This department initiated a process by which the officers and others would report IOU and identify, to use their own terms, "Hot Spots" of crime. The exceptional feature of this approach is the focus on specific target problems and the unobtrusive nature of the information which is gathered by individuals who are merely going about their ordinary business (see Sherman, 1990 and Sherman et al., 1989). Skogan (1990) has provided and analyzed a list of concerns that contribute to neighborhood decline and disorder which can be utilized in any locale:

1. public drinking
2. corner gangs
3. street harassment
4. drugs
5. noisy neighbors
6. commercial sex
7. vandalism
8. dilapidation and abandonment
9. rubbish

Many police departments are gaining a more complete understanding than they have in the past of the areas for which they are responsible and the characteristics of the communities they serve. As a result of this knowledge, the progressive administrators are dedicating patrol activities to designated areas and focusing investigations on specific types of offenses. The purpose is to match a method or design to a specific objective.

This emphasis on community-based policing has evolved into what many police analysts refer to as a paradigm shift from the traditional style of policing or the professional style to community-based policing (Kennedy and Moore,

1995; Alpert and Moore, 1993). Further, there has been a strong political commitment at the federal level to community policing as evidenced by the 1994 Crime Bill and the emergence of community policing on the national agenda. More and more, it is viewed as a solution to police-related problems. While there are certainly critics of community policing and those who think it needs much more evaluation and refinement, it appears that it will be the dominant policing strategy for the foreseeable future.

DIMENSIONS OF COMMUNITY POLICING

Gary Cordner, a prominent researcher and former police chief, has identified three major dimensions of community policing (Cordner, 1995). The first is a *philosophical dimension*. He emphasizes that community policing is a new philosophy of policing. One of the central ideas is that policing should entail a broad view of the police function. Policing is more than the traditional focus on crime fighting and law enforcement. He argues that the professional model actually has narrowed the focus of policing in recent decades. Community policing broadens the focus to include order maintenance, social service, and general assistance functions.

Another central idea of community policing is that in a free society, citizens should have open access to police organizations and have the ability to give input into police policies and decisions. There are a number of ways citizens can have meaningful input into police decisions. Citizens have some access through elected officials, open forums or town meetings, citizen advisory boards, minority group representatives, and business leaders. However, Cordner emphasized that the police must be open to this input and should seek and consider carefully the ideas of citizens when making policies.

Neighborhood variation is another central idea of community policing. The police must consider the "will of the community" when deciding on which laws to focus enforcement efforts and resources. Cordner argues that policing should be tailor-made to the norms and values of a particular neighborhood or community. Obviously serious offenses will always be a focus of the police, but the handling of minor criminal infractions, violations of local ordinances, and public disorder involves considerable discretion. This is where neighborhood values and norms should be considered.

The second major dimension of community policing, according to Cordner (1995), is the *strategic dimension*. This includes "key operational concepts that translate philosophy into action" (Cordner, 1995:2). Strategies based on community policing emphasize a geographical focus. For example, the fundamental unit of patrol accountability is shifted from time of day (shift), to place (neighborhood). Rather than being responsible for a shift, officers are responsible for a neighborhood. Obviously this requires some decentralization of command.

Community policing strategies also emphasize prevention. Rather than just waiting for calls for service and reacting, police are encouraged to be proactive by being involved in specific crime prevention efforts, problem solving, and interaction with citizens. While traditional policing involved some prevention efforts, community policing shifts the emphasis to a better balance of enforcement and prevention. Under community policing, prevention is given a more central role. The police are expected to have a modified social welfare orientation especially with respect to juveniles. The crime prevention focus involves officers as mentors and role models, and has them involved in educational, recreational, and counseling services with community residents.

Another major aspect of the strategic dimension, according to Cordner, is a *substantive* focus. This involves a more careful and deliberate focus on substantive problems in the community, in addition to law enforcement concerns. Under the traditional or professional model, the bulk of training, policy, and programs are focused on enforcement of laws. Under community policing, law enforcement is viewed as just one of the tools to accomplish the police goals of protection of life and property, the maintenance of order, and the protection of rights. Other tools that can help reach those goals are emphasized as well. For example, in a dispute among acquaintances or family members, enforcing the law may not always be the best way to maintain order. Thus, a police officer called to the scene of a domestic dispute may calm the disputing parties and refer a counselor or social worker to help resolve the problem rather than arresting the disputants.

The third major dimension of community policing is the *programmatic dimension*. Cordner (1995:4) defines this dimension as what "ultimately translates ideas, philosophies, and strategies into concrete programs, tactics, and behaviors." Some police analysts have criticized community-based policing as being merely philosophical or rhetorical rather than actual solutions to the problems of policing in the modern age (Greene and Mastrofski, 1988). Others suggest community-based policing is just a new marketing strategy for all the old components of policing (Manning, 1988). These may be misplaced criticisms that say more about the lack of implementation and evaluation of community policing than about the actual strategies or their potential.

Cordner (1995), however, argues that there is a programmatic dimension to community policing. He claims that community policing has reoriented police operations by emphasizing "less reliance on random motorized patrol, immediate response to all calls for service, and follow-up investigations" (Cordner, 1988:4). These traditional police strategies have given way to increased use of foot patrol, door-to-door policing, and other strategies that stress police-citizen interactions. Instead of stressing immediate response to calls for service by sworn officers, community policing has reoriented responses to match the needs of the caller. Some agencies are taking crime reports over the phone, or referring the callers to other agencies for help. Some are dispatching civilians to handle certain situations that do not need a fully trained and armed police officer. Some new community policing strategies rely more on the patrol officer to follow-up with investigations, rather than having specialized detective units spend time on the less serious crimes.

Another programmatic element of community-based policing involves shifting the emphasis from response-based policing to problem solving (Goldstein, 1990). Cordner (1995) suggests that whenever possible, attention should be directed toward solving underlying problems and conditions. While the police must respond to serious calls for service, and respond to crimes after they happen, strategies should exist that focus attention on solving the underlying problems leading to the crime. Each community will need special and unique strategies to deal with the underlying problems. Cordner argues that the problem-solving approach should be the standard method of policing, rather than an occasional special project. It should be practiced by officers of all ranks, and not just by specialists or administrators. It should be systematic and involve community leaders and other citizens, as well as other governmental and private agencies that are relevant to the specific problems.

Perhaps, the most central programmatic dimension of community policing is community engagement in its own protection. This opens many possibilities including neighborhood watch, citizens reporting suspicious persons and situations, advisory boards for police policy, and even citizens patrolling the streets. Citizen involvement is especially critical to the problem-solving and prevention aspects of policing. The police, however, cannot just sit by and wait for citizens to volunteer or to come up with ideas for citizen involvement. Police departments should actively plan for citizen involvement, educate citizens concerning the need for their participation and how they may get involved, and actively solicit citizens for their help.

While empirical evaluations of community-based policing do exist, the results are preliminary and mixed. Many criticize the methodologies and appropriateness of the evaluations (Kennedy and Moore, 1995). While traditional policing can be evaluated by analyzing the police organization and police operations, evaluations of community policing must change the focus to accounting for community analysis and creative and often unique solutions to the problems underlying crime. Police adaptability to the unique environments of specific neighborhoods and communities is difficult to measure for evaluations.

"We believe that community policing is located in *creative and responsive organizations* and that the proper dependent variable is *these organizations' production of innovative operations that are, in aggregate, effective* not only in controlling crime but also in preventing crime, reducing fear, and increasing community confidence in the police" (Kennedy and Moore, 1995:284).

Alpert and Moore (1993) suggest several major themes inherent in community policing that need to be evaluated. One of these is the theme of building a strong relationship with the community. This is justified as a way to make enforcement more effective, and a way to prevent crime by making the community co-producers of justice. Another theme emphasizes attacking the communities' problems on a broader front than traditional policing. While serious crime is important, other things need to be addressed as well. For example, fear of crime is often independent of actual chances of victimization. The police can attack fear of crime independent of victimization. Focusing on customer satisfaction is another way of expanding the focus of evaluations.

When all the dust settles, it seems that community-based policing is here to stay. However, we are a long way from adequate implementation of the strategies, and still further from effective evaluations of the strategies. It remains to be seen how strong our commitment is to the new policing, and exactly how it will affect the nature and focus of modern policing.

SUMMARY

In recent years, there has been a call for changes in police style and performance. Primary measures of improvement include the increase of social order and satisfaction with living in the community, the reduction of fear and incidents of crime, as well as an increase in positive evaluations of the police. This is best achieved by linking the style of policing to the specific communities served. There is no doubt that different communities want and deserve different styles and levels of policing, but each can follow the same pattern of interactive research and evaluation to determine what is likely to be the most appropriate and the most successful. The desired result can be competent police officers who are neither defensive nor tentative and who will adapt well to their surroundings. They will serve as the best police-community relations representatives, as they are best able to deal responsively with the numerous and varied concerns of the public. It is insufficient that this competence extend to departmental procedures or even laws alone. The officers must understand conceptually, as well as technically, the reasons for their actions and omissions.

Jerome Skolnick and David Bayley have analyzed the most important elements of community policing including community-based crime prevention, reorientation of traditional patrol activities, increased accountability and decentralization of command. They note that (1988:17) "[C]ommunity policing is a package whose parts are integrally related." This integrated approach is necessary but not sufficient. Without strong individual and departmental commitment, the police are likely to produce unwanted and negative results. The inclusion of an ongoing feedback mechanism and a system to reward officers for exemplary behavior will assist both the police and the public (Alpert and Dunham, 1988:137).

Although many scholars and police practitioners have attempted to define or describe community policing in a simplistic manner, Cordner (1995) describes community policing as having several common dimensions. These include philosophical, strategic and programmatic dimensions. Programmatic elements of community policing have produced benefits to community members, such as specific programs, tactics, and behaviors. Although departments have adopted different approaches, it is the commitment to change and incorporation of community input that drives the programmatic elements.

References

Alpert, Geoffrey P. 1985. *The American System of Criminal Justice*. Beverly Hills: Sage Publications.

Alpert, Geoffrey and Roger Dunham. 1988. *Policing Multi-Ethnic Neighborhoods*. Westport, CT: Greenwood Press.

———. 1986. "Community Policing." *Journal of Police Science and Administration* 14:212–22.

Alpert, Geoffrey and Kenneth Haas. 1984. "Judicial Rule-Making and the Fourth Amendment: Cars, Containers, and Exclusionary Justice." *Alabama Law Review* 35:23–61.

Alpert, Geoffrey and Mark H. Moore. 1993. "Measuring Police Performance in the New Paradigm of Policing." In *Performance Measures for the Criminal Justice System*. Washington, DC: U.S. Department of Justice, pp. 109–40.

Alpert, Geoffrey P., Merrill Adkinson, Melvin Allen, Lowell Bailey, Terrance Hunter and Kimberly Pass. 1994. *Violent Crime in South Carolina: A Secondary Analysis*. Columbia: College of Criminal Justice, University of South Carolina.

Black, Donald. 1980. *The Manners and the Customs of the Police*. New York: Academic Press.

Broderick, John. 1987. *Police in a Time of Change*. Prospect Heights, IL: Waveland Press.

Brooks, Laure. 1993. "Police Discretionary Behavior: A Study of Style." In R. Dunham and G. Alpert (eds.) *Critical Issues in Policing: Contemporary Readings*, 2nd ed., pp. 140–64. Prospect Heights, IL: Waveland Press.

Brown, Lee. 1971. "A Typology of Police-Community Relations Units." *Police Chief* (March): 16–21.

Brown, Michael. 1981. *Working the Street*. New York: Russell Sage.

Bureau of Justice Statistics. 1990. *BJS Data Report, 1989*. Washington, DC: Bureau of Justice Statistics.

Bureau of Justice Statistics. 1988. *Report to the Nation on Crime and Justice*, 2nd ed. Washington, DC: United States Government Printing Office.

Chaiken, Jan, Peter Greenwood, and Joan Petersilia. 1983. "The Rand Study of Detectives." In Carl Klockars (ed.) *Thinking about Police*, pp. 167–84. New York: McGraw-Hill.

Coates, Robert B. 1972. "The Dimensions of Police-Citizen Interactions." Ph.D. dissertation, University of Maryland.

Cordner, Gary W. 1995. "Community Policing: Elements and Effects." *Police Forum* 5, no. 3 (July): 1–8.

Coyle, Kenneth, John Schaff, and James Coldren. 1991. *Futures in Crime Analysis: Exploring Applications of Incident-Based Crime Data*. Washington, DC: United States Government Printing Office.

Davis, Kenneth C. 1975. *Police Discretion*. St. Paul: West.

Fortson, Sanna and Stewart Stephenson. 1986. "Police on Beats." *Law and Order* 34, no. 3 (March): 48–52.

Furstenberg, Frank and Charles Wellford. 1973. "Calling the Police: The Evaluation of Police Service." *Law and Society Review* 7:393–406.

Galvin, Jim and Kenneth Polk. 1980. "Any Truth You Want: The Use and Abuse of Crime and Criminal Justice Statistics." *Journal of Research in Crime and Delinquency* 19:135–65.

Garofalo, James. 1981. "Crime and the Mass Media." *Journal of Research in Crime and Delinquency* 20:319–50.

Goldstein, Herman. 1977. *Policing a Free Society*. Cambridge, MA: Ballinger.

———. 1990. *Problem-Oriented Policing*. New York: McGraw-Hill.

Greene, Jack. 1989. "Police and Community Relations: Where Have We Been and Where Are We Going?" In R. Dunham and G. Alpert (eds.) *Critical Issues in Policing: Contemporary Readings*, pp. 349–68. Prospect Heights, IL: Waveland Press.

Greene, Jack and Steve Mastrofski (eds.). 1988. *Community Policing: Rhetoric or Reality*. New York: Praeger.

Hatting, Steven H., Alan Engel, and Philip Russo. 1983. "Shades of Blue: Toward an Alternative Typology of Police." *Journal of Police Science and Administration* 3:319–26.

Inbau, Fred, John Reid and Joseph Buckley. 1986. *Criminal Interrogation and Confessions*, 3rd ed. Baltimore: Williams and Wilkins Publishers.

Kelling, George, T. Pate, D. Dieckman, and C. Brown. 1974. *The Kansas City Preventive Patrol Experiment: Final Report*. Washington, DC: Police Foundation.

Kennedy, David M. and Mark H. Moore. 1995. "Underwriting the Risky Investment in Community Policing: What Social Science Should Be Doing to Evaluate Community Policing." *The Justice System Journal* 17, no. 3: 271–89.

Larson, Richard. 1975. "What Happened to Patrol Operations in Kansas City? A Review of the Kansas City Preventive Patrol Project." *Journal of Criminal Justice* 4: 271–277.

Manning, Peter K. 1988. "Community Policing as a Drama of Control." In Jack Greene and Stephen Mastrofski (eds.) *Community Policing: Rhetoric or Reality?*, pp. 27–46. New York: Praeger.

Muir, William K. 1977. *Police: Streetcorner Politicians*. Chicago: University of Chicago Press.

National Advisory Commission on Criminal Justice Standards and Goals. 1973. *Police*. Washington, DC: United States Government Printing Office.

Normandeau, Andre and Barry Leighton. 1990. *A Vision of the Future of Policing in Canada: Police-Challenge 2000*. Ontario, Canada: Solicitor General.

Note. 1985. "The Compelled Confession: A Case Against Admissibility." *Notre Dame Law Review* 60:800–15.

Note. 1984. "*State v. Jackson*: Police Use of Trickery, Threats and Deception—What Price Confession?" *North Carolina Law Review* 62:1240–51.

Pate, Antony, et al. 1986. *Reducing Fear of Crime in Houston and Newark*. Washington, DC: Police Foundation.

Police Foundation. 1981. *The Newark Foot Patrol Experiment*. Washington, DC: Police Foundation.

Porter, Bruce and Marvin Dunn. 1984. *The Miami Riot of 1980: Crossing the Bounds*. Lexington, MA: Lexington Books.

Reiss, Albert. 1971. *Police and the Public*. New Haven: Yale University Press.

Reiss, Albert and Michael Tonry. 1986. *Communities and Crime*. Chicago: University of Chicago Press.

Saski, Daniel. 1988. "Guarding the Guardians: Police Trickery and Confessions." *Stanford Law Review* 40:1593–1616.

Scott, Eric. 1981. *Calls for Service: Citizen Demand and Initial Police Response*. Washington, DC: United States Government Printing Office.

Sherman, Lawrence. 1983. "Patrol Strategies for Police." In James Q. Wilson (ed.) *Crime and Public Policy*, pp. 145–63. San Francisco: Institute for Contemporary Studies.

———. 1990. "Police Crackdowns." *NIJ Reports*, March/April.

Sherman, Lawrence, P. Garten, and M. Buerger. 1989. "'Hot Spots' of Predatory Crime: Routine Activities and the Criminology of Place." *Criminology* 27:27–55.

Skolnick, Jerome. 1966. *Justice Without Trial: Law Enforcement in Democratic Society*. New York: John Wiley and Sons.

Skolnick, Jerome and David Bayley. 1988. *Community Policing: Issues and Practices Around the World*. Washington, DC: United States Government Printing Office.

———. 1986. *The New Blue Line*. New York: The Free Press.

Skogan, Wesley. 1990. *Disorder and Decline: Crime and the Spiral of Decay in American Neighborhoods*. New York: The Free Press.

Spelman, William and Dale Brown. 1984. *Calling the Police: Citizen Reporting of Serious Crime*. Washington, DC: United States Government Printing Office.

Taub, Richard, D. Garth Taylor, and Jan Dunham. 1984. *Paths of Neighborhood Change*. Chicago: University of Chicago Press.

Thibault, Edward, Lawrence Lynch, and R. Bruce McBride. 1985. *Proactive Police Management*. Englewood Cliffs, NJ: Prentice-Hall.

———. 1990. *Proactive Police Management*, 2nd ed. Englewood Cliffs, NJ: Prentice-Hall.

Thomas, Charles and John Hepburn. 1983. *Crime, Criminal Law and Criminology*. Dubuque, IA: W.C. Brown.

Trojanowicz, Robert, Marilyn Steele, and Susan Trojanowicz. 1986. *Community Policing: A Taxpayer's Perspective*. East Lansing, MI: The National Neighborhood Foot Patrol Center.

Uniform Crime Reports. 1986. *A Crime in the U.S.—1985*. Washington, DC: United States Government Printing Office.

Walsh, William F. 1986. "Patrol Officer Arrest Rates: A Study of the Social Organization of Police Work." *Justice Quarterly* 3, no. 3 (September): 271–90.

Westley, William. 1953. "Violence and the Police." *American Journal of Sociology* 49:34–41.

Whitaker, Catherine. 1989. *The Redesigned National Crime Survey: Selected New Data*. Washington, DC: Bureau of Justice Statistics.

White, Susan. 1972. "A Perspective on Police Professionalism." *Law and Society Review* 7:61–85.

Wilson, James Q. 1968. *Varieties of Police Behavior*. Cambridge: Harvard University Press.

Wilson, James Q. and George Kelling. 1982. "Broken Windows: The Police and Neighborhood Safety." *The Atlantic Monthly* 249, no. 3 (March): 29–38.

———. 1989. "Making Neighborhoods Safe." *The Atlantic Monthly* 249, no. 2 (February): 46–52.

Wilson, Orlando W. and Roy McClaren. 1977. *Police Administration*. New York: McGraw-Hill.

Worden, Robert. 1995. "Police Officers' Belief Systems: A Framework for Analysis." *American Journal of Police* XIV(1): 49–81.

Cases

California v. Hodari D., 499 U.S. 621 (1991), 111 S. Ct. 1547 (1991).

State v. Jackson, 308 S.E. 2d 134 (1983).

Chapter Eight

HAZARDS OF POLICE WORK

Our focus now turns from an objective study of the functions and duties of police officers to the impact of police work on the individual officer. Without extensive research, it is difficult to assess the short- and long-term effects of this or any occupation on the life and health of its members (Nekin and Brown, 1984). The difficulty lies in isolating just which characteristics of the working and nonworking environments contribute to the problems. Is it the occupation or other factors in one's life that are most responsible for an individual's personal problems?

In spite of the limitations on quantifying occupational hazards, police work does seem to exact a special toll on those who choose it as their profession. The working environment and the subculture to which police belong seem to affect physical and mental health in distinctive and important ways. Over the past decade, law enforcement administrators have increasingly become concerned about the personal hazards of police work and have focused on the identification and treatment of many of these problems.

Police work incorporates several characteristics that present an unusual set of personal hazards. The most obvious is the threat of personal assault involving injury or even death. Another less obvious hazard that has caused increasing concern is the stress involved in police work. This stress originates in the ever-present threat of danger to oneself or to others and involves the potential or actual use of deadly force. A mistake in job performance in most occupations creates a minor inconvenience; a mistake by a police officer, whose discretion has important implications for the community as well as the department, may result in suspension, an arrest for stepping beyond the scope of his or her authority, or a civil lawsuit.

The legal liability inherent in the job is an unsettling source of stress. Officers may be sued for excessive use of force, improper searches, false arrest, false imprisonment, invasion of privacy, unreasonable emergency driving, and other actions. If the officer is acting within the policies, practices or customs of the department and is found to have violated the rights of a defendant or a third party, the department and municipality may be held responsible to the injured party. In some instances, individual officers can be held liable, both criminally and civilly, for their actions. This places officers' personal belongings and family security at risk (Kappeler, 1993). One unintended consequence of the legal liability is a possible decrease in activities taken by police officers. This use of the law may tend to restrict police behavior and has created another source of citizen control over the police. At the same time, however, it has added another personal hazard and source of stress to police work. A more detailed discussion of legal liability is included in chapter 9.

This chapter discusses the threat of personal assault resulting in injury or death, the sources of stress, the effect of the police occupation on family life, the physical and mental consequences of stress on the officer, and possible solutions to the problems associated with stress.

PERSONAL ASSAULT

There is always the danger of being assaulted or killed while carrying out one's duties as an officer. Routine tasks such as traffic stops, answering disturbance calls and arresting suspects all involve some degree of danger. It is indeed a tragedy when an officer is injured or killed in the line of duty. Fortunately, and contrary to popular belief, the killing of police officers is rare considering the number and type of interactions they have with citizens and the potential for violence (United States Department of Justice, 1990).

LAW ENFORCEMENT OFFICERS KILLED AND ASSAULTED

The trends of police killings indicate a decline since 1968, when 134 officers were killed by felonious assault. This number includes federal, state, and local law enforcement officers. Between 1980 and 1989, 801 officers were feloniously killed. The trend of decreasing numbers of officers killed continued throughout the 1980s, with a high of 104 officers killed in 1980 and a low of 66 deaths in 1989 (Maguire and Pastore, 1994:401).

In 1992, the most recent year for which data are available, sixty-two law enforcement officers (the lowest total since the 1960s when the Federal Bureau of Investigation began collecting these statistics) were killed feloniously in the line of duty (Maguire & Pastore, 1994:401). Twenty-six officers (42%) were slain while they were in the process of arresting suspects. The attempted arrests involved burglaries and robberies in progress, drug-related matters, and other crimes. Eleven officers (18%) were killed while responding to disturbance calls. Nine of the eleven officers were killed when called to a family domestic disturbance while the two remaining officers were killed responding to other disturbance calls, including bar fights and "man with a gun" calls. Two of the sixty-two officers killed (3%) were killed while handling and transporting prisoners in custody. Seven officers (11%) were killed while investigating suspicious persons or circumstances, six (10%) were killed in ambush situations, and ten (16%) were killed in traffic pursuits or stops. No officers were killed by mentally deranged suspects or in a civil disturbance. Officers assigned to patrol were the ones most often slain, accounting for nearly two-thirds of all the deaths. This figure underscores the potential hazards of patrol duties.

It is interesting to note that generally as many, or more, police officers are killed each year accidentally as are killed feloniously. In 1992, more officers lost their lives accidentally than feloniously (Maguire and Pastore, 1994:405). Sixty-six officers lost their lives due to accidents that occurred during the course of their duties. Thirty-four (52% of the accidental deaths) were killed in automobile accidents, five (8%) in motorcycle accidents, and five (8%) in aircraft accidents. Six (9%) officers were struck by vehicles during traffic stops or road blocks, and five (8%) were struck by vehicles while directing traffic or assisting motorists. Three (5%) were killed by accidental shootings, including a cross-fire, mistaken identity, and firearm mishap. The eight remaining accidental deaths (12%) were due to a number of other causes, such as falls and drownings. These data indicate that it is about as dangerous for officers to be on the road as it is to face dangerous criminals. Still, in a recent review of the research literature on the mortality of police officers, there is general agreement that police officers have lower than expected accident mortality risks and that there is some evidence that the police are less likely than the average person to die from motor vehicle accidents (Reviere and Young, 1994).

An ironic finding of other studies of police shootings is the frequency that police personnel unintentionally shoot themselves or other officers. Several studies conducted in New York City and Chicago revealed that an alarming proportion of the police officers who were shot were shot either by themselves (accidental discharges or suicides) or by other police officers (accidental discharges or accidentally hitting another officer) (Geller and Scott, 1992). Over a ten-year period, 43 percent of the officers who were shot were shot by themselves or by other officers. The researchers conclude that "It is the armed robber and, paradoxically, the armed policeman who are the threats to the life of the police" (Geller and Scott, 1991:453).

Obviously, the death of a police officer is the most serious consequence of a confrontation with a citizen. However, in many cases a suspect's attempt to murder an officer might fail. For example, the officer could receive quick, life-saving medical attention. In other cases, an officer might be assaulted by a person who is merely attempting to escape custody, injuring the officer only slightly to achieve a successful escape. More than 81,000 law enforcement officers reported on-duty criminal assaults during 1992 (Maguire and Pastore, 1994:406). The trends for assaults have been just the opposite of the trends for officers killed. During the past twelve years there has been a variable, but increasing trend for officer assaults. In 1992, 29,657 law enforcement officers reported personal injuries resulting from criminal assaults. Approximately 35 percent of assaulted officers receive personal injury. This rate has remained fairly constant over time (Maguire and Pastore, 1994:408).

In 1992, assaults on officers occurred more often when responding to a disturbance call (32%) than in any other circumstance. Twenty-four percent of the assaults occurred while officers were attempting to arrest suspects. Twelve percent occurred while handling or transporting prisoners; 9 percent while making traffic stops or involved in pursuits; and 8 percent while investigating suspicious persons or circumstances. The remaining 15 percent of the assaults took place while the officers were performing other duties (Maguire and Pastore, 1994:407).

Contrary to the impression left by media representations, relatively few law enforcement officers are killed in the line of duty, assaulted with a deadly weapon, or receive any physical injury. This does not minimize the *threat of danger* and the emotional impact of being assaulted with a deadly weapon, even if no physical injury results. In most cases, the significant impact of these experiences is the emotional toll they take on the officer.

STRESS CAUSED BY FEAR OF INJURY OR DEATH

Although the actual chance of being killed or of sustaining serious physical injury while performing police duties is less than one might expect, there is the constant threat of danger each time an officer is sent out on a call or investigates a suspicious situation. An officer must prepare emotionally each time he or she gets a call or stops to investigate someone. During a normal tour of duty for a patrol officer, five typical situations arise that present some degree of danger. These include traffic and felony stops, emergency and pursuit driving, answering disturbance calls, investigating suspicious circumstances and persons, arresting suspects and handling or transporting prisoners (U.S. Department of Justice, 1990). Again, only a few of these result in actual danger, but the constant emotional preparation creates tremendous stress. Each call presents the possibility of danger, so the officer must prepare for the worst. This situation results in an emotional roller coaster that can contribute to the personal problems experienced by police officers.

In one study of the police officer's perception of danger, it was found that the police officer's role is characterized by two paradoxes, or conditions with seemingly contradictory qualities, which can cause stress (Cullen et al., 1983). The first paradox is that police officers view their job as being both safe and unsafe. Officers were aware that physical injury occurred only occasionally to those with whom they worked; however, they were equally conscious of being employed in an occupation that requires them to enter into many dangerous situations. This realization of the potential for danger is part of the informal socialization a new recruit experiences when he or she becomes a police officer. Recruits are taught that policing is a physically demanding and dangerous occupation. The potential for armed confrontation shapes training, patrol strategies and operating procedures. It also shapes the relationships between the police and citizens by creating a mutual apprehension. The officer must always remember that any individual with whom he or she comes into contact may be armed and dangerous. The authors conclude that this apparent inconsistency can be understood when a distinction is made between officer perceptions of how much injury is actually sustained as opposed to the potential harm inherent in their work (Cullen et al., 1983).

The second paradox found among officers' perceptions of danger is that these perceptions are both functional and dysfunctional (Cullen et al., 1983). On the one hand, the reality of the danger inherent in police work makes it essential that officers remain constantly prepared for the potential risks of their

CHIEF'S CORNER
HAZARDS OF POLICE WORK

It seems to me that too much emphasis is sometimes placed on certain experiences that a police officer may encounter in the line of duty. Consequently, the general population has a perception of police work as an extremely dangerous profession. I say this knowing full well that many of my peers' beliefs are quite contrary to mine, and they will make a point to cite statistical data they feel support the perception of law enforcement as the most dangerous of all professions.

After so many years in law enforcement, however, I have come to believe that, while schooling in "street survival" is important, training in the ability to understand and to interact with people is much more important. The ability to deal with people successfully is important for a police officer from a preventative standpoint. Armed with the skill to determine if a person or situation is potentially dangerous, a good police officer is most often able to deter any threat of assault. But many police officers reject this approach, because it often involves giving up their "control of the situation," something they have been trained never to do or, in fact, are personally unable to do because of their egos. If a police officer has the strength of character to stand by, to be cursed by an irate husband (who is really engaged in face saving), and to deal patiently and calmly with that person, he or she is much more in control of the situation than one who feels each threat must be dealt with immediately in order to keep the situation from escalating. This is not to say that a police officer should not react and react quickly when the situation is deteriorating and the threat potential is becoming dangerous. What it does mean is that police officers may reduce their personal hazards many times by understanding people, especially their egos and needs. By dealing successfully with people, officers in turn do not become inducers of possible violence in a situation.

Of all of the police officers I have seen shot over the past twenty-six years, almost every one was caught in a situation that was already out of control prior to the officer arriving at the scene (for example: walking directly in on a robbery in progress or confronting a mentally unbalanced person without adequate warning or time to prepare). However, given time to plan alternatives, well-trained police officers can generally resolve almost any situation without violence. I have seen this demonstrated over and over again. The best illustration is provided by our Special Response Officers who, while well-trained to respond to violence, have used time and negotiation skills repeatedly to successfully resolve a myriad of dangerous situations, such as search warrant service on drug houses, hostage situations, and the execution of arrest warrants on dangerous felons who have sworn not to be taken by police. Any one of these officers can tell you about the value of time, patience, and the ability to communicate effectively in controlling potentially violent situations. However, it seems to me that the greater emphasis of police training in many departments is on response with firepower rather than with word power. This misplaced emphasis only serves to increase the danger to the officer.

work. Forgetting the danger and becoming careless can have fatal consequences. On the other hand, this sensitivity to danger is not without its
negativepersonal effects. While it is functional for officers to be aware of the
dangers, such feelings contribute to heightened work stress and, more generally,
to the manifestation of depressive symptoms.

It is not easy to resolve these paradoxes. The functions of perceiving and
preparing for danger make it essential that, for safety, this feature of policing
be emphasized. Policies to minimize the sensitivity of officers to the dangers
they may face could actually increase their real danger. There may not be a
feasible solution to the problems associated with the dysfunctional aspects,
because the functional aspects are so necessary. As a result, considerable stress
and its consequences may be a permanent feature of policing.

The effects of stress can be both positive and negative. The beneficial
aspect of stress is especially important for police officers in that it prepares them
for any emergency (Dempsey, 1994:115). Dempsey explains that the body's
reaction to stress, called the "flight-or-fight" response, involves quantities of
adrenaline being released into the blood stream. This stimulates the liver to
provide the body with stored carbohydrates for extra energy, which in turn
quickens the heartbeat and respiration in addition to increasing blood pressure
and muscle tension. Thus the normal reaction to stress prepares the body for
extraordinary physical and mental exertion. While this reaction is very helpful
for dealing with dangerous situations, it also takes its toll; the body reacts to
the stressful situation and then becomes exhausted. The body's resources
become depleted. This is especially true for police officers who tend to go
through repeated stressful episodes over relatively short periods of time. In
other words, the process takes its toll even if the actual danger does not
materialize. An officer may realize after the fact that responding to a particular
domestic call involved little danger, but it is the mental preparation for the
possible danger that sets the stress reaction process in motion. Over time,
repeated stressful episodes can weaken and disturb the body's defense mechanisms, leading to various mental and physical disorders.

OCCUPATIONAL STRESS ON POLICE OFFICERS

Discussions of police stress usually divide the topic into four sets of
stressors: external, internal, task-related, and individual (Terry, 1981).
All contribute in some way to the problems of the police officer. External

stressors include frustration with the criminal justice system for its leniency in punishing criminals. Negative attitudes about police and policing found in the media and in minority groups also add to the stress factor. All of these stressors come from outside of the police organization. Internal stressors come from within the police organization. They include insufficient or inadequate training, substandard and outdated equipment, poor pay, ambiguous job-evaluation criteria, inadequate career development guidelines, excessive paperwork and intra-departmental politics. Task-related stressors include role conflicts, the rigors of shift work, boredom, fear, danger, association with depressing and brutal human conditions, and work overload. This category of stressors relates to the duties and responsibilities of police officers. Individual stressors involve individual inadequacies of officers that are magnified by the police role. They include fears about job performance, competence, individual success and personal safety. In addition, other problems such as marital discord and divorce, alcoholism, and health problems contribute to job stress as well as result from it.

David Carter (1991:204) has developed a causal model to explain the stress inherent in police work and some of the subsequent problems resulting from it. The model is based on the concept of "cumulative interactive stressors." He claims that there are a number of generic stressors that interact with a police officer's job performance, decision making, and organizational membership. The stressors do not always cause dysfunctional behavior per se, and may have functional benefits such as heightening alertness. Carter thinks the problems arise when multiple stressors begin to accumulate. If there are no legitimate release mechanisms for the stress, then illegitimate or deviant means will surface. Carter identifies seven generic stressors.

1. *Life-Threatening Stressors*. These involve the constant potential of injury or death. An important aspect of these stressors is the knowledge that violent acts against officers are intentional rather than accidental. Because the threat is constant, these stressors are cumulative.

2. *Social Isolation Stressors*. Carter defines these stressors as isolation and alienation from the community, differential socioeconomic status between the police and their constituency, authoritarianism, cynicism, and cultural distinction, prejudice, and discrimination.

3. *Organizational Stressors*. This significant set of stressors involves all aspects of organizational life—both formal and informal. Specific stressors include: peer pressure, role models, performance measures, promotions, poorly drawn or inconsistent policies and procedures, morale,

inadequate supervision and administrative control, inadequate training, internal politics, and leadership styles.

4. *Functional Stressors*. These stressors specifically involve the performance of assigned policing duties. Included are role conflict, the use of discretion, knowledge of the law and legal mandates, and the decision-making responsibilities, including when to stop and question people, when to use force, or how to resolve domestic disputes.

5. *Personal Stressors*. According to Carter, these stressors have their primary origin in the officer's off-duty life. They include family problems and financial constraints. Particularly noteworthy are marital discord, problems with children, and family illness.

6. *Physiological Stressors*. A change in an officer's health or physiology may generate stress on the job. Fatigue from working different shifts (which disrupts one's body clock), changes in physiological responses to critical incidents, and illness all are physiological stressors.

7. *Psychological Stressors*. All of the above stressors may cause psychological stress, but Carter maintains that these stressors can have an additional direct impact on the officer's performance. The fear generated by the constant threat of injury or death can become internalized and upset one's psychological balance. Constant exposure to the worst side of humankind and dealing with homicides, child abuse, and fatal traffic accidents can have a traumatic effect on officers. The cumulative effect of these stressors may result in psychological conditions such as depression and paranoia.

Carter emphasizes that these stressors are not mutually exclusive. It is the interactive nature of the stressors which creates the cumulative effect and leads to problems. If the effects are prolonged, they may manifest themselves in many forms: increased heart rate, elevation of blood pressure, secretion and depletion of adrenaline and other hormones, and mobilization of glucose and fatty acids. Over time the condition may progress to tissue damage and have serious debilitating effects on the officer, physiologically, psychologically, and behaviorally.

VULNERABILITY TO STRESS

Data from one study of police officers (Russo, Engel and Hatting, 1983) reveal that different types of police officers respond differently to different types of stress. These researchers found that three main orientations to police work help account for the differences. While each officer incorporated some degree of all of these orientations, most ranked the characteristics of one category as more influential than the other categories. Similarly, officers are affected by the environmental and professional concerns which brought them to law enforcement. One group of police officers reported that they chose police work as an occupation because of *people-oriented* values. These officers tend to view police work as an opportunity to derive satisfaction from working with people.

The second type of police officer was labeled *professional self-oriented*. This type of officer viewed police work as an opportunity to achieve self-perceived potential and to utilize self-perceived talents. The development of a career and movement up the career ladder are the most important aspects of his or her work, even if it means accepting a lower ratio of rewards for effort expended.

The third type of officer ranked *personal reward-oriented* values as the reason police work was selected as an occupation. These officers tend to view police work as a means to personal reward; their major concern is not career advancement as much as gaining the maximum reward in terms of salary and security for their efforts.

Each of these types of officers tended to respond with greater stress to circumstances and issues relevant to the occupational values they ranked highest. For example, the stress of the people-oriented officers revolved around providing service to citizens, working with people and protecting the public. Pressures arising from the conflicting job demands of a police officer were ranked highest by people-oriented officers. The source of the stress felt by the professionally oriented officers was more likely to be associated with concern over advancement to positions of authority, the use of professional skills, independence, and prestige. These officers cited insensitive supervisors as their greatest problem. The stress of the officers with a personal reward orientation centered around a lack of recognition and economic gain.

Stress usually results in, or is manifested in, some type of personal or family problem. Each group of officers seemed to have certain types of problems that prevailed in that group. The officers with people-oriented occupational orientations reported the highest rates of divorce and arguments at home. In addition, they reported slightly above-average feelings of loss of self-esteem, but were below the average with respect to three stress symptoms: alcoholism, ulcers and moodiness.

The highest rates of stress symptoms with respect to moodiness, nervous anxiety, and feelings of loss of self-esteem were reported by the officers with a professional orientation. Their reported rates of these stress symptoms were well above those of the two other groups. However, professionally oriented officers reported comparatively low rates of such stress symptoms as home arguments and ulcers.

The last group studied, officers with a personal reward orientation, reported comparative rates of ulcers and alcoholism well above those of the other two groups. They also reported above-average rates of nervous anxiety.

Indeed, stress builds up from many sources and affects different types of officers in different ways. In addition to the unpleasantness of experiencing stress, there are a number of personal and family problems that have been linked directly to stress and have been associated with police officers. The next sections will discuss the effect of the police occupation on family life, investigate several symptoms or consequences of stress and review both empirical and theoretical information.

FAMILY LIFE AND DIVORCE

The police profession has been referred to as a "jealous mistress, intruding in intimate family relationships, disrupting the rhythms of married life" (Blumberg and Neiderhoffer, 1985:371). The potential for danger looms heavy over police marriages and arouses fears for the safety of loved ones. The constant changing of shifts and around-the-clock tours of duty complicate family relationships. Indeed, a law enforcement career is much more than a job or a profession. It becomes a way of life for the officer and for his or her family. Police wives and husbands have to cope with the tension of knowing their spouses are constantly in danger. They find that they must block out the anxiety over the possible death or injury of their spouse in order to carry on normal lives. They coordinate their social and sexual timetables to conform to the rigid schedules involved in police work. Police spouses often become in-house therapists, showing support and compassion to their husbands or wives when they are at home. Even though they seem to adapt to being a police officer's spouse, they complain about the strain and sometimes resent the "secret society" of police work (Blumberg and Neiderhoffer, 1985:371).

One prominent psychologist, who is the director of the Psychological Services Division for a major police department and president of the Psychologists in Public Service Division of the American Psychological Association, outlined job-related factors that contribute to family problems in police families (Scrivner, 1991).

1. *Family Disruption Due to Rotating Shifts.* Rotating shifts create numerous problems in a family organization, including planning family meals and events, providing child care, and participating in holiday celebrations. Police families seem to be organized around the officer's work, and even then the unpredictability of hours and overtime create family disruption.

2. *Unpredictable Work Environment.* Much of police work involves responding to crisis situations which creates unpredictable hours and expectations. In addition, the constant fear of death or injury, being the target of internal investigations, or retributions from criminals takes its toll on the officer and family members.

3. *Job-related Personal Change.* The psychological effects of being involved in so much human tragedy can be psychologically disrupting to the officer and in turn to family relationships.

4. *Community Expectations and Demands.* Being a police officer places considerable demands on the officer while off-duty. Neighbors expect the officer to solve neighborhood problems and provide various other services not expected of others. Also it puts all family members in a special role involving strict behavioral expectations. For example, the delinquency of the child of an officer creates unusual embarrassment, and may even affect the officer's respect in the department.

5. *Intrusion into Family Life.* The police officer often must bring aspects of his or her job home. Officers bring their weapons home. Some officers bring their police cars home. They must be available twenty-four hours a day for emergencies. These and other intrusions can put strains on the family.

There has been a prevailing misconception that divorce is rampant in police marriages. The list of researchers who have commented on the high divorce rates found among police officers is extensive (see Terry, 1981). Many of these reports suggest that it is the police occupation that contributes most to marital conflict; however, empirical research that compares the rates of divorce among police officers to the rates among other professionals or members of other occupations indicates that the rates among the police are not that high when compared to the rates for other workers. In fact, some research indicates that the rates among the police are lower than rates found among other professionals. While the conflicting results and the methodological problems prevalent in many of the studies make it difficult to come to any precise conclusion, the best evidence available leads us to believe that the divorce rate among police officers is lower than originally predicted (See Neiderhoffer and Neiderhoffer, 1978).

There are some possible explanations for police marriages having a lower divorce rate than commonly perceived. The structure of the relationship and the expectations of the officer and his or her spouse are two contributing factors. For example, some recent police marriages involve both partners as officers; some couples reverse the traditional husband-officer relationship, and some marriages include second-generation police wives. In addition, some police spouses have coped better than expected with the demands placed on police families; they have been prepared for the inevitable strains. In fact, one study indicates that marriages entered into before the husband joined the police force had a much higher rate of divorce (26%) than marriages formed after one of the spouses was already a police officer (11%) (Blackmore, 1978). Another reason for the possible exaggeration of the extent of police divorces is the tendency to associate police divorces with the job demands. It may be that when marital problems and divorce appear in a police marriage, the strains of the police occupation provide an easy scapegoat, as evidenced by the commonly heard statement: "It was the job's fault." This scapegoating may result in the characterization that more police divorces are job-related than other divorces.

A recent development that may also contribute to the success of police marriages is the establishment of support groups and group counseling for police officers and their spouses. It appears that these types of programs that acknowledge marital problems and provide support are helpful to officers and their spouses who are having trouble coping with the unusual tension present in police marriages.

CONSEQUENCES OF STRESS

The personal consequences of stress and its relationship to a wide variety of physical and psychological illnesses have been well documented and are now supported by social science research (Farmer, 1990). Cardiovascular diseases, hypertension, digestive diseases, alcohol and drug abuse, chronic depression and suicide attempts are all seen as life-threatening illnesses that are linked to stress. While there are many occupations and professions that generate high levels of stress in workers, policing traditionally has been viewed as among the most stressful.

HEALTH PROBLEMS

A review of the literature on police stress indicates the presence of numerous physiological effects (Terry, 1981; Farmer, 1990). Studies have examined the physiological health of police officers in comparison with workers in other occupations by comparing the incidence of health problems, mortality rates, and hospital admissions. Among the conclusions is that no occupation exceeds that of police officers in combined standard mortality ratios for coronary heart disease, diabetes mellitus, and suicide. Further, police officers usually rank among the top twenty occupations (out of 130) for health problems when different occupational groups are compared. However, any interpretation of the data which demonstrates serious health-related problems among police officers must be cautious, as most police officers are from working-class backgrounds. This type of background predisposes them to a higher incidence of health problems and a higher mortality rate than the middle class (Kasl, 1974).

There is increasing evidence that police officers suffer a broad range of physical symptoms linked to the stressful nature of their job, including cardiovascular diseases, ulcers, indigestion, hemorrhoids, headaches and hypertension. Individuals involved in law enforcement have a 10 percent higher diastolic blood pressure than age-matched controls in other occupations. Additionally, law enforcement personnel suffer from increased mortality risk from cancer of the colon and liver, diabetes, and heart disease than others not involved in law enforcement (Norvell et al., 1988). These researchers conclude that there is a strong relationship between job-related stress and the physical illnesses experienced by law enforcement personnel.

ALCOHOL ABUSE

Normal social drinking does not raise much anxiety in our society. Drinking becomes an issue when it starts causing problems in the drinker's life. When job responsibilities involve making important decisions about the lives of others, including life-and-death decisions, the concerns are even greater.

Recently, several important studies examining alcohol use among police officers have been conducted. Most references to alcoholism among police indicate that their rate of alcohol problems far exceeds the rates of other workers. Police chiefs usually admit that alcohol is a severe problem among officers, indicating that as many as one-half of their force drink heavily. Administrators often refer to the existence of alcohol-related problems in police departments, including the practice of officers getting together after work and drinking heavily, drinking on the job, and absences due to hangovers.

A recent study on the effects of death trauma, the use of excessive force and use of firearms, found that officers involved in these activities drank more alcohol than officers who avoided them (Carson, 1987). Interestingly, research findings suggest that heavy drinking is viewed as a socially acceptable coping mechanism for stress among both male and female officers (Farmer, 1990). In a study examining alcohol use among the police, male and female officers report consuming more alcohol than the general population, and female officer drinking patterns approached that of the male officers (Pendergrass and Os-grove, 1986). This finding differs from the lower drinking patterns among females when compared to males in the general population.

Alcohol has the property of relaxing the drinker and giving a sense of well-being. Alcohol can be used as a way of coping by deadening one's feelings and senses so that stress seems non-existent. Of course, this is not a very effective means of dealing with stress. Once the effects of the alcohol wear off, the stress resurfaces. What begins as normal social drinking (to have a good time and to loosen up in a social situation) can easily turn into utilitarian drinking; the drinker begins to drink to feel the effects and to cope with problems. The combination of high levels of stress and an environment of frequent drinking can result in a pattern of utilitarian drinking that develops into psychological dependence on alcohol. In more extreme cases, the psycho-logical dependence can lead to drinking that is heavy enough to result in physical dependence. Both psychological and physical dependence are forms of alcoholism and usually interfere with one's ability to function appropriately in social roles, such as one's job. Since there is a heavy drinking norm in the police subculture and because this is coupled with an occupation that generates an unusual amount of stress, police officers are at considerable risk for alcohol-ism.

One study found that stress in police work increases the need for effective coping mechanics (Violanti et al., 1985). These researchers found that officers' attempts to cope with stress by cynicism were ineffective. Further, officers' attempts to keep emotional distance between themselves and their work did not help in coping with stress. Instead, they found that alcohol use had the strongest correlation to stress. The failure of the officers' attempts to cope with stress by creating emotional distance from their work or by becoming cynical increased their use of alcohol as a coping mechanism. The researchers suggest that drinking problems among police officers are closely related to the perceived absence of alternative coping strategies. They conclude that police officers are in a high-risk category for developing serious drinking problems.

Because of this high level of risk and an apparent high rate of alcohol problems among police officers, many departments have created programs to detect alcoholism and to help officers with their alcohol problems. Some of these programs encourage alcoholism treatment or attendance at Alcoholics Anonymous, while others have their own form of counseling to help officers find more appropriate ways to cope with the unique stress inherent in police work.

SUICIDE

Police suicide, like the other consequences of stress, is closely linked to the unique nature of police work. When comparisons have been made, studies indicate that suicide rates are higher among police officers than among workers in other occupations (Lester, 1983; Labovitz and Hagedorn, 1971; Friedman, 1967). One study analyzing the effects of social class, shift differentials and the physical dangers of specific types of employment found that the police do not die at significantly younger ages than those in other occupations. However, police are more likely to commit suicide and be killed than those employed in occupations other than law enforcement (Hill and Clawson, 1988).

More recent studies have found that police have almost three times the rate of suicide compared to those in the general population (Violanti, Vens and Marshall, 1986). The National Fraternal Order of Police conducted a study of police suicide through their Center for Criminal Justice Studies (Law Enforcement News, 1995). They studied the cause of death among 38,800 FOP members between 1992 and 1994 and found that 37 percent of accidental police deaths were the result of suicide. The study involved mostly small- and medium-sized police departments, all with fewer than 3,000 officers. They found that younger officers were more likely to be victims of homicide than suicide, whereas older members were more likely to be victims of suicide. They concluded that younger officers were more likely to have dangerous assignments, and older officers have difficulty making the transition to retirement and civilian life.

John Violanti, a criminal justice professor who has been researching suicide among the police for years, concludes that there is a continuing and dramatic upward trend in police suicides since 1980 (Violanti, 1995:19). In fact, suicide rates today may be twice the pre-1980 rates. Violanti has found that the desire to shield victim officers, their families, and their departments from the stigma of suicide, investigators often overlook evidence intentionally during the classification process. Several studies have estimated that 30 percent of police suicides over a 40 year period had been misclassified as accidental or natural deaths (Violanti, 1995:20).

A number of reasons have been provided to explain why police officers have such high rates of suicide (Nelson and Smith, 1970). First, although more women are entering the field, police work is a male-dominated profession, and males have demonstrated a higher rate of successful suicide than females. Second, the use, availability and familiarity with firearms by police in their work provide them with a lethal weapon that affords the user little chance of surviving a serious suicide attempt. Another reason given for the high suicide rate among police officers is the psychological repercussions of constantly being exposed to death and serious injuries. In addition, long and irregular working hours do not promote strong friendships outside of the police subculture and often create a strain on family ties. Some analysts have claimed that the officers' constant exposure to public criticism and to the public's perceived dislike for "cops" is another contributing factor to the rate of suicide among police. Other contributing frustrations are the judicial contradictions, irregularities and inconsistent decisions that tend to negate the value of police work. Suicide has been found to be more common among older officers, and to be highly related to alcoholism, physical illness, and retirement (Violanti, 1995:20). When officers feel like they no longer have the ability to cope in normal ways, they may turn to the ultimate solution to cope with their problems.

Unfortunately, many police officers with concerns are reluctant to seek or accept help or counseling. They feel that their fellow officers and supervisors are not tolerant of their problems and do not understand them. These officers fear that others will believe that they are no longer useful to the public or to the profession. This feeling may be a result of exposure to so many behaviorally different and mentally ill citizens and of witnessing intolerance toward these types of people as part of their police duties. In addition, police officers traditionally subscribe to a myth of indestructibility and view suicide as particularly disgraceful for officers and for the police profession (Skolnick, 1975:21).

CHIEF'S CORNER
RECOGNIZING AND COMBATING STRESS

Stress within law enforcement work is much more of a personal danger to a police officer than violence will ever be. It Is also one of the most misunderstood of all health factors with which police officers deal. Much stress is the result of police officers not having a clear understanding of their roles or of what realistic expectations should be placed on them both personally as well as by the organization. A good healthy understanding of the police role can turn a stressful job situation into an interesting, "can't wait to get to work" career.

A great deal of information is directed at police officers by the courts, the media, their personal contacts, and the organization. Many officers interpret such information to mean that they should be rigid, unemotional, totally without fear, strong and able to handle critical situations within seconds without making a mistake. As they interpret this data and begin to impose it as standards on their performance, they quickly learn that they cannot live up to their own benchmarks. They compare themselves to their peers who seem very comfortable in their roles. What these officers do not understand is that the officer who unemotionally rationalizes a suicide he or she handled by making light of it is actually acting out his or her need to share with someone the very emotional experience he or she has just undergone. This is just one example of how faulty interpretation compounds stress problems for police officers. Court failures, human mistakes and a relentless search by the media for the sensational all serve to magnify the problem.

I believe that enlightened management can do much to assist police officers in assuming a more realistic role identification. First, the supervisory structure within the organization needs to be educated regarding the fact that the employee's health is one of their primary responsibilities and that they should take an active role in protecting it. Employees who are experiencing difficulties are not hard to identify. In every case, there are signs, such as increased use of sick time, tardiness, citizen complaints and use of force that indicate that the employee is having trouble. While most officers occasionally have such work-related problems, if the problems increase in frequency and duration, they are generally reflective of deeper personal problems. At these times, enlightened supervisors should step in and take meaningful corrective action.

Second, mandatory periodic attendance at group de-escalation sessions led by trained psychologists can do much to relieve the unnecessarily harsh standards police officers inflict on themselves. Such sessions will place the officers in a controlled situation where identification of sources and relief of stress can be discussed. Here, they will see that it is quite normal to experience emotions, to make mistakes, to be afraid or to be unable to control every situation in which they are placed. Therefore, they may build a more realistic set of personal performance criteria.

Third, the values of the organization should be transmitted clearly to the employees and then supported regularly by management. These values should be realistic and should include such personal behavior standards for the employees as the maintenance of health and weight, refrainment from substance abuse and adherence to moral conduct. Values such as these, which can permeate the organization through effective training and supervision, can serve as a preventative to many serious problems. Standards based on these values also have a way of aiding management in the identification of officers who act contrary to such values and, therefore, in the weeding out of officers who are not suited to the organization.

It should be made clear that the organization supports an employee's marriage. I have observed that, tragically, divorce has many times been the final act preceding a suicide by a police officer. Organizations should make counseling and spouse awareness programs available. Supervisors should be trained to use them as a resource rather than to offer off-the-cuff advice which many times does more damage than good. I have seen numerous marriages break up simply because the police officers felt no one, including wives or husbands, understood them. The truth is that most often they did not understand themselves and had no place in which to turn in order to repair the relationship they really did not want to see fail.

I sincerely believe that while police work does have a great deal of hazards, the hazards inherent in the profession are treatable and preventable and that law enforcement offers the most interesting and fulfilling career in the world. By its very nature, the work poses hazards due to violence and factors which can adversely affect personal health for the officer involved. The best organizations recognize this and take meaningful action on behalf of their employees.

Fortunately, police officer associations provide anonymous assistance to officers identified by supervisors as demonstrating symptoms of stress. Additionally, officers are often encouraged to seek assistance on their own, if so needed. Administrators and rank-and-file officers are becoming more sensitive to emotional problems associated with policing. Departments are beginning to develop effective interventions to save officers' lives, and to spare departments from the devastating effects of suicide. Perhaps the best countermeasure is to train officers to cope with professional and personal problems. Most officers commit suicide when they feel like they have no other way of coping with problems. Another effective intervention is to train supervisors to recognize the warning signs of suicide and to intervene before it is too late (Violanti, 1995:23). The National Fraternal Order of Police recently launched a major police suicide prevention program (Law Enforcement News, 1995). It involves plans to conduct retirement seminars to ease the transition to civilian life. Also they plan to set up a hotline to inform officers about programs to help them cope with problems, and to provide them with a sympathetic ear. This is especially important for officers in small departments that do not have employee assistance programs for troubled officers.

SOLUTIONS AND PROGRAMS

There are no simple solutions to the complex problems discussed in this chapter. The most reasonable approach is to work toward the prevention of these problems by reducing stress and changing the stress-producing features of the police bureaucracy, procedures and operations. Obviously, an ounce of prevention is worth a pound of cure. While there have been some attempts to work on prevention strategies, the most common response has been to react to the problems after they occur.

One type of prevention strategy is to administer psychological tests to police applicants. The test results can be used to screen out applicants who may have trouble coping with stress. While this is common practice in most states, much more needs to be done. Some agencies have used the Officer at Risk Examination to detect individual officers who tend to be over-aggressive or under-aggressive on the job (Dempsey, 1994). The results can be used to refer officers to counseling or relevant programs. Other psychological tests have been used to identify officers on the job who may have mental problems or who may have trouble coping with the stress inherent in certain specialized assignments.

Because of the difficulty of instituting prevention strategies, most departments have focused more on developing programs and services to help the officer cope with the stress or with problems resulting from the stress. There are numerous types of programs and services that have been developed to help officers cope with stress and to understand and solve personal problems. Some examples of these programs and services are:

1. training programs for spouses so that they can be better prepared to understand and to cope with potential problems;
2. mandatory alcohol information and treatment programs;
3. liability insurance to relieve officers of having to second-guess their decisions;
4. psychological services for employees and their families;
5. immediate consultation with officers involved in traumatic events, such as shootings; and
6. group discussions where officers and perhaps their spouses can ventilate and share their feelings about problems.

One example of recent initiatives is the announcement of the National Fraternal Order of Police (FOP) that it will launch a major suicide prevention program (Law Enforcement News, 1995). Fraternal Order of Police officials plan to conduct retirement seminars to ease the transition to civilian life, and to set up a hotline that police officers can call to receive information about programs, and which will provide officers with a sympathetic ear. The FOP programs are especially important for officers in small law enforcement agencies that do not have employee-assistance programs of their own. In addition, many mental health programs of police agencies are tied to disciplinary actions, which creates mistrust between officers and employee-assistance programs (Law Enforcement News, 1995). Their idea is to have trained, volunteer listeners who could offer a confidential source of help and referral to programs.

While these are just a few of the more common additions to police departments, they indicate an increased awareness of the problems associated with police work and an attempt to help officers cope with them. All of these services require a firm commitment from both the individual officer and the department. Often, it is difficult to create an atmosphere of openness where an officer need not feel ashamed or embarrassed by a problem or for receiving help. An important part of increasing the awareness of these needs is to train administrators and officers to view these needs as legitimate and not as weaknesses that indicate that a troubled officer has lost his or her usefulness for police work.

SUMMARY

While it is always a difficult and risky task to assess the personal hazards of an occupation or profession, some of the major concerns about the hazards of police work have been introduced. It is difficult to determine exactly how much of a specific personal problem can be related directly to the job, to the working environment, or to nonoccupational factors. Whether or not these individuals would have suffered from similar symptoms had they not entered police work is impossible to predict; however, it is believed that police work increases the risk of having many of these problems. The seriousness of damage to the individual appears to be greater in police work than in other occupations.

Police administrators are becoming more sensitized to the personal hazards of police work and their effect on the individual officer. Although these problems are complex and without obvious or simple solutions, increasing awareness and the accompanying efforts to establish programs to assist troubled officers are movements in the right direction. Most of these programs and services are responses to problems after they have occurred rather than preventive approaches to possible problems. Solutions at this stage usually are more difficult and challenging.

References

Blackmore, John. 1978. "Are Police Allowed to Have Problems of Their Own?" *Police Magazine* 1, no. 3: 267–73.

Blumberg, Abraham and Elaine Neiderhoffer. 1985. "The Police Family." In Abraham Blumberg and Elaine Neiderhoffer (eds.) *The Ambivalent Force: Perspectives on the Police*, 3rd ed., section eleven. New York: Holt, Rinehart and Winston.

Carson, S. 1987. "Shooting, Death Trauma and Excessive Force." In H. More and P. Unsinger (eds.) *Police Managerial Use of Psychology and Psychologists*. Springfield, IL: Charles E. Thomas Publishers.

Carter, David L. 1991. "Theoretical Dimensions in the Abuse of Authority by Police Officers." In Thomas Barker and David L. Carter (eds.) *Police Deviance*, 2nd ed., pp. 197–217. Cincinnati: Anderson Publishing.

Cullen, Francis T., et al. 1983. "Paradox in Policing: A Note on Perceptions of Danger." *Journal of Police Science and Administration* 11, no. 4: 457–62.

Dempsey, John S. 1994. *Policing: An Introduction to Law Enforcement*. New York: West Publishing.

Dietrich, J. and J. Smith. 1988. "The Non-Medical Use of Drugs Including Alcohol Among Police Personnel: A Critical Review." *Journal of Police Science and Administration* 14 (December): 300–306.

Duncan, J. T., Robert N. Brenner, and Marjorie Kravitz. 1979. *Police Stress: A Selected Bibliography*. Washington, DC: United States Government Printing Office.

Farmer, R. 1990. "Clinical and Managerial Implications of Stress Research on the Police." *Journal of Police Science and Administration* 17 (September): 205–18.

Friedman, P. 1967. "Suicide Among Police." In E. Schneidman (ed.) *Essays in Self-destruction*. New York: Science House.

Geller William A. and Michael S. Scott. 1992. *Deadly Force: What We Know*. Washington, DC: Police Executive Research Forum.

Henry, A. and J. Short. 1954. *Suicide and Homicide*. Glencoe, IL: Free Press.

Hill, K. and M. Clawson. 1988. "The Health Hazards of 'Street Level' Bureaucracy: Morality Among the Police." *Journal of Police Science and Administration* 16 (December): 243–48.

Hitz, Danielle. 1973. "Drunken Sailors and Others: Drinking Problems in Specific Occupations." *Quarterly Journal of Studies on Alcohol* 34:496–505.

Kappeler, Victor. 1993. *Critical Issues in Police Civil Liability*. Prospect Heights, IL: Waveland Press.

Kasl, S. V. 1974. "Work and Mental Health." In J. O'Toole (ed.) *Work and the Quality of Life*, pp. 171–96. Cambridge: MIT Press.

Kroes, W. 1976. *Society's Victim, the Policeman: An Analysis of Job Stress in Policing*. Springfield, IL; Charles C. Thomas.

Labovitz, S. and R. Hagedorn. 1971. "An Analysis of Suicide Rates Among Occupational Categories." *Sociological Inquiry* 41, no. 1 (January).

Law Enforcement News. 1995. vol. XXI, no. 422 (April 30).

Lester, David. 1983. "Stress in Police Officers: An American Perspective." *The Police Journal* 56 (April): 184–93.

Maguire, Kathleen and Ann L. Pastore, eds. 1994. *Sourcebook of Criminal Justice Statistics—1993*. Washington, DC: U.S. Department of Justice, Bureau of Justice Statistics.

Nekin, Dorothy and Michael Brown. 1984. *Workers at Risk*. Chicago: University of Chicago Press.

Nelson, Z. and W. Smith. 1970. "The Law Enforcement Profession: An Incidence of Suicide." *Omega* 1, no. 4 (November): 293–99.

Neiderhoffer, Arthur and Elaine Neiderhoffer. 1978. *The Police Family: From Station House to Ranch House*. Lexington, MA: Lexington Books.

Norvell, N., D. Belles, and H. Hills. 1988. "Perceived Stress Levels and Physical Symptoms in Supervisor Law Enforcement Personnel." *Journal of Police Science and Administration* 16 (March): 75–79.

Pendergrass, V. and N. Ostrove. 1986. "Correlates of Alcohol Use by Police Personnel." In J. Reese and H. Goldstein (eds.) *Psychological Services for Law Enforcement*. Washington, DC: United States Government Printing Office.

Skolnick, Jerome. 1972. "A Sketch of a Policeman's Working Personality." In G. F. Cole (ed.) *Criminal Justice: Law and Politics*, pp. 20–42. Belmont, CA: Wadsworth Publishing.

Reviere, Rebecca and Vernetta Young. 1994. "Mortality of Police Officers: Comparison by Length of Time on the Force." *American Journal of Police*, vol. 13, no. 1: 51–64.

Russo, Philip A., Jr., Alan S. Engel, and Steven H. Hatting. 1983. "Police and Occupational Stress: An Empirical Investigation." In Richard R. Bennett (ed.) *Police at Work: Policy Issues and Analysis*, pp. 89–106. Beverly Hills, CA: Sage Publications.

Scrivner, Ellen. 1991. "Helping Police Families Cope with Stress." *Law Enforcement News* 15 (June): 6.

Skolnick, Jerome. 1975. *Police in America*. Boston: Educational Associates.

Terry, W. Clinton, III. 1981. "Police Stress: The Empirical Evidence." *Journal of Police Science and Administration* 9, no. 1: 61–75.

United States Department of Justice. 1990. *Law Enforcement Officers Killed and Assaulted*. Washington, DC: United States Government Printing Office.

Van Raalte, R. C. 1979. "Alcohol as a Problem Among Officers." *The Police Chief* 44:38–40.

Violanti, John. 1995. "The Mystery Within: Understanding Police Suicide." *FBI Law Enforcement Bulletin* (February).

Violanti, John M., James R. Marshall, and Barbara Howe. 1985. "Stress, Coping, and Alcohol Use: The Police Connection." *Journal of Police Science and Administration* 13, no. 2: 106–10.

Violanti, John M., J. Vena, and James R. Marshall. 1986. "Disease, Risk and Mortality Among Police Officers—New Evidence and Contributing Factors." *Journal of Police Science and Administration* 14 (March): 17–23.

Wagner, M. and R. Brzeczek. 1983. "Alcoholism and Suicide: A Fatal Connection." *FBI Law Enforcement Bulletin* 52: 8–15.

Chapter Nine

CRITICAL ISSUES IN POLICING

Policing has emerged from a political activity to what is considered by many as a profession. The transition has gone through many stages and continues to ebb and flow. The plans on which this progress was based originated from a combination of reform movements, governmental task forces, research findings, changes in law, changes in public opinion and creative leaders in the field. Rather than examine all aspects of policing, our approach will be to take several critical issues and discuss each as a dilemma. The history of dealing with and attempting to resolve these issues has been summarized by Dr. John Bizzack, who has had more than twenty years experience as a police officer: "The quick fix has been the staple of most police management, and serves as a host to the value system of most organizations. Issues in policing are often so overwhelming to an ailing agency, or to an ill-prepared police chief, that merely surviving becomes a noble management science" (Bizzack, 1991:8). This unfortunate and haphazard approach has kept policing mired in the past.

The issues facing police as we move into the twenty-first century continue to grow. Some become less important and receive less attention, but very few are totally resolved. Most of the issues facing police leaders in the previous decades remain, while new ones continue to appear. In the late 1990s, community policing and problem solving are being heralded as the strategies that are going to redirect the police effort. Only time will tell what real impact community policing will have on the management of crime and the fear of crime. Of course, one of the most important consequences of good policing is a peaceful and untroubled lifestyle; a goal that is nearly impossible to achieve. If we treat community policing as a "quick fix" and install programs or even department-wide strategies without knowing what works, and under what conditions and for whom, then we are merely reliving the past without learning from it and community policing, as most other reform movements, will be doomed to failure.

Our discussion will focus on a limited number of important issues that have plagued police for years. Unfortunately, space limitations do not permit discussions of all critical issues. The police response to domestic violence, youths and drugs, gang violence, among others, all merit consideration. However, we have selected minority hiring and promoting, women in policing, use of force, pursuit driving, and lawsuits against the police as our critical issues. The approach to these issues will include two concerns: first, the various needs of the communities served by the police and, second, the needs of law enforcement.

MINORITY HIRING AND PROMOTING

The United States Commission on Civil Rights report, *Who Is Guarding the Guardians* (1981), found that police agencies were underutilizing minorities and women and that this underrepresentation was hampering the ability of police departments to function at their most effective levels. In addition, police departments that do not reflect the ethnic characteristics of the communities they serve have a difficult time earning the respect of community residents and thereby increase the possibility of trouble and violence. This finding by the Commission and similar conclusions drawn by other panels, study groups and advisory boards are not unique to police departments, but they underscore the fact that police have been and are traditionally white and male.

By 1973, many individuals and groups were making the point that minority representation in police departments was an important factor in improving relations between the police and members of the minority communities. For instance, cities such as Baltimore, Newark, Memphis, Miami, and New Orleans had populations with approximately 40 percent minorities but had less than 7 percent minority membership in their police departments. Friction was common between the police and the public in these cities (United States Commission on Civil Rights, 1981 and Florida Advisory Committee to the United States Commission on Civil Rights, 1976). Many other cities, including San Francisco, Dallas, Detroit, Houston, and Philadelphia, have been criticized for having too few minorities in the police department and in positions of authority. There is more to hiring and promoting members of minority communities than the positive public relations a department may receive. It is worth the effort.

Research has demonstrated that recruiting, selecting and hiring minority members can be especially difficult in areas that have traditionally presented limited opportunities for minorities (see Bayley and Mendelsohn, 1969). Although a department may receive a large number of applicants, only a limited number will be accepted. As we discussed in chapter 4, the city of Miami responded to demands from the minority communities by consenting to hire 80 percent minorities and to start that process selecting only minority residents from the city. This was a decision that pleased the minority citizens but frustrated and outraged police administrators.

The city of Miami placated the complaining public by hiring hundreds of minority officers and promoting others. However, the city and its police department are suffering from a variety of problems in the 1990s, and it is suspected that those earlier decisions are to blame (Dade County Grand Jury, 1982). Corresponding consequences of this change have been the lowering of morale among the members of the department and constant administrative change. More than two dozen city of Miami police officers have been arrested for crimes ranging from burglary to murder.

In some respects, Miami is no different from many other cities that have moved too quickly to right a wrong that has been ongoing for years. Decisions were made at one point to correct an imbalance without realizing the full implications. On the one hand, this may have led to the hiring and promoting of individuals who were not the most qualified. On the other hand, if these decisions had not been made and implemented, there could have been greater discord between the minority groups and the police. As Jess Maghan has informed us (1993:348): "The recruitment and hiring of minority police officers has been approached by many police administrators with less than genuine enthusiasm." Perhaps, the campaign to involve more minorities in the police force has been fueled by factors other than a realization that an integrated force is more effective and efficient than a segregated one.

Aligning ethnic and other characteristics of police officers and those of the general population is an important goal. Beyond the factor of public relations, it is important to provide the best policing possible to the community. If that requires the hiring of blacks, Hispanics, females, homosexuals, or any other minority group, it is important to consider all possible ramifications and methods to achieve a balance (see United States Commission on Civil Rights, 1981 and Hongisto, 1980).

Unfortunately, what is "best" for the community is often decided behind closed doors by representatives of interest groups. Even when these decisions are made in an open court, they are often based on opinions and wishes without the benefit of certain facts, including the reported needs of various segments of the community. Borrowing a comment from an analysis of court-ordered reform in prisons can clarify this confusing issue:

> Judges must become more familiar with complex organizations if they are to improve their record of decree implementation. . . . Greater weight must be given to the prevention of dysfunctional, unintended consequences such as collective violence. The incremental introduction of change, carefully based on organizational analysis and knowledge of organizational behavior, would represent a more productive approach to decree implementation. (Alpert, Crouch and Huff, 1984:303)

Unintended consequences can take place both within the organization or police department and in the society it serves. Specifically, dysfunctional, unintended consequences can affect the internal organization of a police department by destroying the established reward structure. When hiring, making assignments or promoting officers is done for affirmative action reasons and not as a reward for competence and performance, an increase in confusion and a decrease in officer morale is likely to occur. Similarly, a decrease in the level of loyalty to and trust in the department will be apparent. Outside of the department, some groups will claim fair treatment and others will claim unfair treatment. Claims may be nothing more than mild protest, but some instances have developed into serious problems for the police department and the community (United States Commission on Civil Rights, 1981). It is apparent that the short-term and long-term consequences may be different.

The hiring and promoting of minorities, or affirmative action, is a dilemma for police administrators. Each group (including the minorities, the majority group, and the politicians of the community) may all have separate goals. Those who claim past discrimination often want the wrong corrected even at the expense or in spite of resulting discrimination against a member of another group. Affirmative action plans for hiring are being encouraged and upheld by the courts. Plans dealing with promotions are more complicated, but are also receiving judicial support (McCoy, 1985). In the future, it is hoped that all sides will proceed with knowledge and caution by negotiating change in an appropriate and timely manner.

Each agency that has faced these problems operates under similar rules and regulations. Each must move ahead and face progress, but different types of progress may come more quickly to some areas than to others. Social, political and economic considerations must be weighed and analyzed before jumping ahead with short-term plans. It is important to prepare for the internal and external consequences of change so that unintended consequences are kept to a minimum.

WOMEN IN POLICE WORK

Until the early 1980s, the few females who were involved in police work were assigned to desks or juvenile details. Women were, for all intents and purposes, kept off the streets and away from "real" policing (Price and Gavin,

1982). The male police officers and administrators kept the ranks closed to females. It was, apparently, the traditional view of the roles of men and women in society that fostered intense resistance to hiring and utilizing female police officers (Hale, 1992). Most male officers held views similar to males in other occupations. Gerald Caiden points to several specific reasons why women were kept out of policing. First, the men did not want to put up with the social inhibitions placed on them by the presence of women. Second, they did not want to be overshadowed or even to take orders from women. Third, most men did not want to be supported by a female in the performance of potentially dangerous work (Caiden, 1977).

Many reforms require judicial intervention; the integration of ethnic minority and female police officers into the force is no exception. In the late 1960s, several lawsuits were filed which attacked the constitutionality of discrimination by gender. This attack brought about another dilemma for law enforcement: the closed nature of policing was acceptable to those already involved but unacceptable to those wanting to enter. Many politicians and community members tried to balance the issue by protecting the traditional view of policing, while also providing opportunities for women to prove themselves. Policymakers were able to base their decisions on a limited amount of research that concluded that the assignment of female officers to a broader role would achieve the following (Milton, 1980):

1. reduce the incidence of violence between police and the public;
2. increase crime-fighting capabilities by using female officers as detectives and decoys;
3. improve the patrolling function, as well as the service aspect of police;
4. increase the responsiveness of the police to the community; and
5. improve the image of the department.

The most frequently heard argument voiced against utilizing female officers is that they will not respond well in dangerous or violent circumstances. Specifically, it was believed that females would react improperly and could not apprehend suspects in violent or dangerous situations as well as their male counterparts. Also, some male officers voiced concerns that, as a back-up, a female officer was inferior. This gender-based criticism has been contradicted by a number of subsequent studies (Sichel et al., 1978; Kizziah and Morris, 1977; and Bloch and Anderson, 1974). As noted below, female officers are often better than male officers at avoiding violence and de-escalating potentially violent situations.

In anticipation of court orders, some departments began to integrate females into the force before being taken to court; others waited until they were forced to integrate their departments. As a result of both voluntary and involuntary actions, females have made steps toward parity but have not reached total equality (see *United States v. City of Philadelphia*, 1980 and Sulton and Townsey, 1980). A Vera Institute study summarizes the evaluation of female officers (Sichel, 1974:iii):

> The findings add to the growing literature justifying assignment of women to patrol. In general, male and female officers performed similarly: they used the same techniques to gain and keep control and were equally unlikely to use force or display a weapon. However, small differences in performance were observed. Female officers were judged by civilians to be more competent, pleasant and respectful than their male counterparts, but were observed to be slightly less likely to engage in control-seeking behavior, and less apt to assert themselves in patrol decisionmaking.

Women have become an accepted, integral part of policing in major cities. In these larger jurisdictions, it is a common sight to see female patrol officers respond to calls with the same effectiveness as their male counterparts. Although women have earned the confidence of the public and of many of their peers, female police officers are still fighting for institutional equality. Few females have served sufficient time to qualify for high level administrative positions. The first woman to head a major United States city police department, Chief Penny Harrington from Portland, Oregon, served only a short tenure and resigned in June, 1986. While other women have been promoted to chief officer in Houston (and now Austin), Texas, and Fort Myers, Florida, it will take more time to tell if female officers are accepted by the institution as well as they have been accepted by their fellow officers (see Belknap and Shelley, 1993).

For decades, females were assigned only to a limited number of positions and were not promoted at the same rate as their male counterparts. Although the female sergeant, lieutenant and captain are relatively common in the 1990s, evaluations of their roles are not readily available. Martin warns us that even though women are being promoted, they "are not likely to assume policymaking positions for many years" (1993:330). In a review of the literature, Martin noted that "The available evidence presents a mixed picture: there has been slow but steady growth in numbers of women officers and supervisors nationwide and an expansion of their assignments into all aspects of policing. Nonetheless, women continue to be underrepresented in police work" (1993:328).

A very serious concern involves the pregnant police officer. Obviously, only women can enjoy that status and as Martin tells us, " there is no way within our legal framework to treat men and women equally and equitably at the same time" (1993:343). The "disability" created by pregnancy and the potential for injury raise several policy issues which must be addressed by departments. First, agencies must have provisions for "light duty." Second, agencies must identify when women become unable to perform normal duties and must be assigned to "light duty." Third, provisions must exist for pregnant officers to take an extended leave.

One of the most critical inquiries into the problems of women in male-dominated work environments was reported by Judith Laws in 1975. Her study, although written over two decades ago, unfortunately remains applicable. Susan Martin reinforces Laws's findings and concludes from her own extensive research that (1993:344):

> . . . the status of women in policing today is uncertain. Clearly, the most blatant barriers that kept women out of police work for more than half a century have fallen and women are entering policing in increasing numbers. Gaining admission to the occupation, however, is only a first step. Women officers still face discriminatory treatment that limits their options and opportunities for advancement. Nevertheless, as more women enter the occupation, move slowly into positions of authority, and serve as role models and sponsors for other women, there is reason for guarded optimism about the future of women in law enforcement, as well as a large number of questions waiting to be addressed.

Our next issue is one that apparently is handled in a more appropriate fashion by many female officers than by male officers. The use of force by police officers is a highly charged issue that has no definite solutions but many workable suggestions.

THE USE OF FORCE

Unlike the hiring of police officers and the utilization of various minorities, police use of force has an immediate and direct effect upon citizens, especially those who are beaten, kicked or shot. Use of force, particularly deadly force, traditionally has been one of the most controversial aspects of police work. In the 1990s, the issue continues to surface with the video taping of the police beating Rodney King (see introduction). Before exploring our information on police use of force, we have included Chief Bowlin's views on police brutality.

CHIEF'S CORNER
POLICE BRUTALITY

In early 1991 an incident occurred in Los Angeles, California, that was the type that shakes the cornerstone of a profession so hard that you know it will never be quite the same. A black motorist was being pursued by a group of officers from the Los Angeles Police Department (LAPD) and the California Highway Patrol (CHP). Upon apprehending the suspect, some of the LAPD officers besieged the motorist—beating him with nightsticks, shooting him with an electric Taser gun, as well as kicking and assaulting him with their fists. While this was taking place, as many as 12 other officers stood by and watched or left. What the officers did not know was that the incident was being videotaped by a nearby resident. Having documented the incident, the person sold the tape to a local news station; the rest is history.

The tape was shown over and over on national television for months. The aftermath of such intense and prolonged media coverage has caused a negative reaction across the country. People are looking at police brutality allegations in a new and even more negative light. Where police brutality was only spoken about before, with little sympathy for the victim, it has now been visualized, and everyone can see for themselves that it is real and repugnant.

Having viewed the tape several times, it continues to astound me how police officers could act like a pack of wild dogs. Thankfully, almost every one of my colleagues with whom I have discussed the matter feels the same sense of concern as I do. But this has not been the case in every instance. Some misguided law enforcement officials and citizens have taken the position that because the motorist had an extensive past criminal record he got just what he deserved.

This type of thinking makes me happy that we have controls on police behavior. As in other occupations, a few individuals take advantage of their position, are unable to deal with the stress of the job, and are bullies using violent behavior to protect their conception of manhood; some are simply dishonest. Certainly no good law enforcement officer wants a situation where police are feared and have unlimited power to treat their citizens in any manner.

There is no doubt that this incident will have an impact on police operations for years to come. However, I believe that in the long run it will be a positive factor for policing. Those police departments that have quietly ignored the problem for years will be forced to take action to correct the small minority of individuals whose behavior is cruel and defiant to the policies of the department. Maybe the incidents are not as serious as what occurred in Los Angeles, but they are nonetheless just as dehumanizing.

Statutes and departmental policies allow police officers to apply force to effect an arrest, maintain order or keep the peace. Although vague, these conditions are the ones that justify force. We will focus our discussion on how an officer takes control of a situation. Force is a necessary tool of law enforcement, but how it is executed comes in many forms and must be controlled.

Reforms in this area have consisted of minor adjustments to a system that needs an overhaul. We need to think differently about all of the aspects involving police use of force, not just tinker with the timing and degree. Too much attention has been placed on specific beatings or shootings, while insufficient attention has been paid to the ways in which police control citizens. In order to eliminate or check the excessive use of force, attention must be focused on police officer interactions with citizens.

We know from prior research (Sykes and Brent, 1980) that a continuum of police control exists. Levels on the continuum include officer physical presence, verbal commands, compliance holds, intermediate force applications, such as side-handle baton and chemical spray usage, and deadly force. In other words, an officer most often attempts to take control of a confrontation by defining the situation. If this strategy does not work, the officer may command or order the suspect. Finally, an officer may resort to increasing levels of physical force and finally to the use of deadly force to terminate a confrontation. It is this final level of control that must be seen as a last resort, and not as a normal method of policing. Unfortunately, not all officers act appropriately in their attempt to control citizens verbally. Often, the verbal confrontation escalates too quickly and without provocation. A situation that could be resolved easily, or certainly without force, can erupt into a violent one. It is important that the officer understand that the best weapon is the voice, not the gun (Alpert, 1985). To complicate matters, the same words spoken by different officers to different suspects in different surroundings can have different meanings. In any case, use-of-force or control-of-persons reports must be completed and analyzed to determine trends and priorities.

Unless and until a change in training philosophy takes place and police officers accept the need to control without force, we will continue to see misuse of force as a dilemma in policing. While some use of force is a legitimate and necessary police activity, the use of excessive force is unacceptable, and its application is one of the worst forms of police misconduct (Kappeler et al., 1994). Most use-of-force policies have a generic phrase that suggests officers can use "force that is reasonably necessary" to apprehend a suspect. Unfortunately, what is "reasonably necessary" is not easily defined and depends on a variety of factors, including the suspects offense and level of resistance (Alpert and Smith, 1994). In addition, most officers are not trained to know what "reasonable" force means. Training that provides officers with a method to assess the threat posed by a suspect and the alternatives available, should be mandatory in all agencies. Recently, police trainers have focused attention on defusing potentially violent situations and providing officers with alternatives to traditional applications of force (Fyfe, 1995). When the force used by police officers is reasonable and necessary, they are merely performing their job. When the amount of force becomes excessive or unnecessary, then police officers must be responsible for the consequences of their actions.

The Rodney King incident (see Alpert et al., 1992 and Independent Commission on the Los Angeles Police Department, 1991) must be understood as an event that is not isolated, but has brought the issue of police use of force back into the focus of public attention in the 1990s. It is not that this case was the most brutal or even the most shocking use of force, but it was the fact that it was videotaped and became such a media event, that it could not be ignored. It is tragic that such an event is necessary to force the police to review their own use of force policies and practices. Hopefully, the Report of the Independent Commission on the Los Angeles Police Department (1991) will serve as a warning for other agencies to review their own policies, training and practices before such a tragedy occurs. It is fortunate that Mr. King did not die as a result of his injuries. As we discussed in the introduction, a similar beating of Arthur McDuffie resulted in a death, an investigation of deadly force and a major civil disturbance in the 1980s.

The use of deadly force is the most critical action a police officer will ever have to take. Police departments have been criticized for allowing officers to use electronic stun guns, certain choke holds, and other weapons that could be considered tools of excessive or deadly force without proper certification or training. Regardless of the specific criticisms, weighted flashlights, PR-24 batons and other legal tools exist for those who want to use them improperly. The service firearm, however, is still the most powerful weapon that serves to protect the police officer, but its use created one of the most controversial police behaviors: the application of deadly force.

DEADLY FORCE

The legal use of force refers to the amount of force lawfully available to local, state or federal law enforcement agents. Excessive force, by definition, exceeds what is reasonable. While police officers are sworn to uphold the law and must attempt to apprehend law violators, they must protect the general citizenry within reason. In other words, when an officer takes someone into custody or attempts to recapture someone who has tried to avoid arrest, only reasonable force is permissible. A good rule of thumb is "the amount of force that you may use is in direct proportion to that force or degree of injury you believe is about to be used on you" (Adams, 1990:365). Excessive force is force that is beyond that which is necessary (Adams, 1995:62). This guide also applies to the defense of other persons and requires an analysis of the threat created by the suspect.

Since force is measured in terms of severity, the most serious force a person can use is deadly force. The standards regarding the use of deadly force by the police have been revised greatly since they were first applied. In the Middle Ages in England, the law enforcement officials were permitted and even expected to use deadly force against any fleeing felon. It was not until the 1980s that the fleeing-felon doctrine was abandoned and replaced with a standard that permitted the use of deadly force only in a modified defense of life situation. Most recently, progressive police officials have gone to a preservation of life standard. The following discussion will outline the theory and practice related to these standards.

During the Middle Ages, police officers had the authority to use deadly force under the "fleeing-felon" doctrine to apprehend any suspected "fleeing" felon. During this time period, and as the common law developed, the fleeing-felon doctrine was reasonable. First, all felonies were punishable by death in England, and second, defendants did not possess the rights or the presumption of innocence that they enjoy today. In other words, if deadly force were applied, the felon received the same penalty that would have been imposed after trial (see Blumberg, 1993).

The circumstances have changed drastically; defendants now enjoy an enormous array of procedural rights, and few felons are ever executed. Further, some crimes that are considered felonies today are not life threatening or even violent. During the times of common law, if a felon escaped, he or she was rarely apprehended. Today, the technology and investigative powers of the police enable the capture and arrest of many criminals, even long after the crime was committed. Thus, the use of deadly force cannot be justified merely to apprehend suspects. In other words, the rights of the felon must be considered, and the severity of the crime must be assessed.

As Blumberg (1993:471–472) informs us:

> Despite these criticisms, the fleeing-felon doctrine remained the law in almost all jurisdictions until the 1960s. Several factors coalesced during this decade that contributed to a reevaluation of those statutes. For one thing, the Civil Rights Movement opened the door to increased political participation by blacks and other minorities in American society. Second, this was an era of heightened concern regarding the rights of criminal suspects. Third, the latter part of the 1960s was a period of racial unrest and many American cities experienced civil disorders . . ..

Perhaps the most important factor was the occurrence of racial unrest and the civil disorder which surfaced as a result of police use of deadly force (Alpert and Fridell, 1992). Many states and police departments began to restrict the use of deadly force to the apprehension of violent felons and to a defense-of-life policy. Unfortunately, it was not until 1985 and the Supreme Court decision in *Tennessee v. Garner*, that the fleeing-felon policy was legally modified.

TENNESSEE V. GARNER

At approximately 10:45 on the night of October 3, 1974, fifteen-year-old Edward Garner, unarmed and alone, broke a window and entered an unoccupied house in suburban Memphis with the intent of stealing money and property. Two police officers, Elton Hymon and Leslie Wright, responded to a call from a neighbor concerning a prowler. While Wright radioed dispatch, Hymon intercepted the youth as he ran from the back of the house to a six-foot cyclone fence. After shining a flashlight on the youth who was crouched by the fence, Hymon identified himself and yelled "Halt." He observed that the youth was unarmed. As the boy jumped to get over the fence, the officer fired his service revolver at the youth, as he was trained to do. Edward Garner was shot because the police officers had been trained under Tennessee law that it was proper to kill a fleeing felon rather than run the risk of allowing him to escape.

A divided Court held, in part, that apprehension by the use of deadly force is a seizure subject to the reasonableness requirement of the Fourth Amendment of the United States Constitution. The majority ruled that the facts did not justify the use of deadly force and that deadly force under these circumstances was unreasonable. To determine the constitutionality of a seizure, the Court detailed a balancing test: "The nature and quality of the intrusion on the individual's Fourth Amendment's interests (must be balanced) against the importance of the governmental interests alleged to justify the intrusion" (*Tennessee v. Garner*,

1985:8, quoting U.S. V Place, 1983:703). The Court held the Tennessee statute
". . . unconstitutional insofar as it authorizes the use of deadly force against . . .
unarmed, nondangerous suspect[s]" (*Tennessee v. Garner*, 1985:11). The Court
cited with approval the Model Penal Code:

> The use of deadly force is not justifiable . . . unless (i) the arrest is for a
> felony; and (ii) the person effecting the arrest is authorized to act as a police
> officer . . .; and (iii) the actor believes that the force employed creates no
> substantial risk of injury to innocent persons; and (iv) the actor believes
> that (1) the crime for which the arrest is made involved conduct including
> the use or threatened use of deadly force; or (2) there is a substantial risk
> that a person to be arrested will cause death or serious bodily harm if his
> apprehension is delayed. (cited in *Tennessee v. Garner* 1985:6–7, note 7)

In the final analysis, the Court ruled, "Where the suspect poses no
immediate threat to the officer and no threat to others, the harm resulting from
failing to apprehend him does not justify the use of deadly force to do so"
(*Tennessee v. Garner*, 1985:11). And the nature of this threat is clear, "a
significant threat of death or serious physical injury" (*Tennessee v. Garner*,
1985:11). In other words, *Garner* created a modified defense of life standard.
It is significant that this pronouncement can be reduced to a moral judgment.
This was made clear where the Court noted, "It is not better that all felony
suspects die than that they escape" (*Tennessee v. Garner*, 1985:11).

Kathryn Urbonya has summarized *Garner* as follows (1989:99–100
citations omitted):

> The *Garner* decision . . . suggests that the Fourth Amendment standard of
> liability does not question merely whether a police officer used unneces-
> sary force; it also questions whether a reasonable police officer would have
> believed that the force was necessary. Police officers are not liable for
> "every push and shove they make." The standard affords them discretion
> to act decisively. In balancing the interest of the parties under the fourth
> amendment, courts recognize the need for such discretion when they
> consider the state's interest in law enforcement.

The *Garner* Court has established a normative standard, "whether a
reasonable officer would have believed the force used was necessary" that could
be assessed by a variety of methodologies. However, in reality, the Court has
provided no more than rhetoric and ambiguity which serve as guideposts for a
post-hoc analysis. Even in *Graham v. Conner* (1986:9 citations omitted) the
Court, quoting *Bell v. Wolfish* (1979:559) acknowledged that:

> "the test of reasonableness under the Fourth Amendment is not capable of
> precise definition or mechanical application," however, its proper appli-

cation requires careful attention to the facts and circumstances of each particular case, including the severity of the crime at issue, whether the suspect poses an immediate threat to the safety of the officers or others, and whether he is actively resisting arrest or attempting to evade arrest by flight . . . The reasonableness of a particular use of force must be judged from the perspective of a reasonable officer on the scene, rather than with 20/20 vision of hindsight.

For a given fact situation, it is likely that the reasonableness of an officer's action will be addressed at several levels by analysts or experts who are asked to provide opinions. The ultimate fact finders will hear opinions tempered by the subjective interpretation of the events, hindsight, and the predetermined attitudes and values of the actors (Adams, 1995; Alpert and Smith, 1994).

The precedent established in *Garner* redefined reasonable use of deadly force and furnished law enforcement with a modified defense of life standard. In the 1990s, law enforcement officials are experiencing another modification in policies regarding deadly force. Many departments are changing their perspective and policies from defense of life to preservation of life. The subtle differences can best be illustrated by quoting from one of the most progressive policies on deadly force, the Little Rock, Arkansas police department (General Order 16, 1989: 16–2–3, emphasis added):

> The Little Rock Police Department, in establishing a philosophy for the use of deadly force, places the ultimate value on human life, while considering the legal, moral and ethical implications of its applications.
>
> The citizens of Little Rock have vested their police officers with the responsibility to protect life and property and apprehend criminal offenders. The apprehension of criminal offenders and protection of property must at all times be secondary to the protection of life. Therefore, the use of deadly force is not allowed to protect property interests. . . .
>
> Regardless of the nature of the crime or the justification for directing deadly force at a suspect, officers must remember that their basic responsibility is to protect life. Officers shall not fire their weapons under conditions that would necessarily subject bystanders or hostages to death or possible injury, except to preserve life or to prevent serious physical injury. Deadly force is an act of last resort and will be used only when other reasonable alternatives are impractical or have failed.
>
> *Officers will plan ahead and consider alternatives which will reduce the possibility of needing to use deadly force.*

This final paragraph of the Little Rock policy orders the officers to think and plan ahead. In other words, an officer who is protected by "cover," whether it is a car, tree or building must not jump out and confront a suspect. This type of action forces a shoot-don't-shoot situation and most often results in one of the participants firing a weapon. Similarly, an officer who observes a suspect who might have a weapon must not rush the suspect and force a split-second decision. The officer should seek protection and not advance. This preservation of life philosophy protects the officer as well as the suspect. It prohibits the use of deadly force in situations where the suspect does not place the officer or another citizen in a clear or imminent danger of serious bodily harm or death. In perspective, when a police officer perceives that the potential for deadly force may be an outcome of a particular circumstance, the officer must plan ahead and avoid creating a situation where deadly force must be used as self defense. Obviously, the reasonableness of the officer's actions is based upon time available, the opportunity for enacting the plan and the facts known to the officer (see Alpert and Smith, 1994 and Alpert and Fridell, 1992).

Along with writing and enforcing these new standards, many police departments will have to update and upgrade their training to go beyond firearm proficiency and to include judgmental training.

TRAINING IN THE USE OF DEADLY FORCE

Specialized training in police use of force and deadly force needs to address issues such as when force is permissible and how much force is necessary. A police officer is often required to use force to apprehend a suspect, but seldom should an officer use a firearm (see Alpert and Fridell, 1992 and Geller and Scott, 1992). Training, therefore, should provide officers with skills that will enable them to avoid deadly force and to emphasize other alternatives. Training, both at the academy and through in-service programs, must define the vague statutes and regulations on the use of force and make concrete operational suggestions. Although not every situation and circumstance can be covered, interactive training, such as role-playing or simulation, can prepare officers for policing in modern society and for street survival. The key is to link the training to the laws, procedures and philosophy of the department. The trainee must learn the amount of force and type of force that is reasonable to apply.

The discussion of police training in chapter 4 introduced the general atmosphere at the academy. Firearms training traditionally has consisted of shooting a weapon at various targets from a number of different positions and at several distances. The requirements have been that a successful cadet score a predetermined number of points within a specified time period. If an individual is unsuccessful at reaching the required score on the first attempt, he or she may practice and try again until the required score is reached and the cadet qualifies to carry and use a weapon. This training acquaints the new officer with a weapon and assures the trainers and those who certify new officers that the cadet is a relatively good shot. Until recently, that has been the extent of firearms training. It is now realized that this is insufficient training and that officers must be trained in how to avoid the use of weapons, as well as in when and how to use them. Target acquisition on a range has become a necessary but insufficient skill for a police officer.

The first generation of "new" training in police use of deadly force was oriented around the shoot-don't-shoot dichotomy. Officers were provided with different scenarios and had to choose to shoot or not to shoot. This type of training gained popularity. Consequently, some very expensive and complicated computer-driven simulators were manufactured and sold to police departments as the answer to their problems.

There was a demand for some type of magic to appease members of community groups who were screaming over the perceived increase in police shootings and the perceived dramatic increase in white officers shooting black suspects. Many individuals and businesses jumped at the opportunity to sell ideas and expensive machinery to municipalities willing to spend anything to address their problems. For example, the city of Miami experienced a rash of shootings in the early 1980s. In response, the police department purchased a very expensive shooting simulator against the advice of criminal justice experts and citizen advisory groups. The simulator had many mechanical and operational problems and failed to meet the training needs of police. It exemplifies the problems of these early machines, as it trained an officer when to shoot, not how to avoid a shooting. One of the groups that advised against the purchase of this machine was the Dade County Grand Jury. In its final report, it noted (1982:18–19):

> We find a need to re-orient our police training and philosophy so that restraint and patience are emphasized as positive attributes and possible alternatives to the use of force or weapons in many situations. Training in communication skills is at least, if not more, important than training in firearms proficiency.

The re-orientation of training recommended by the Grand Jury involves learning and practicing judgment and decision-making skills before the decision to pull the trigger is made. In other words, the officer's actions prior to the final frame should remove the need to make a split-second decision about the use of deadly force in many situations. Training must incorporate role-play exercises to simulate the judgments and decisions officers are likely to make in the field. The emphasis must be on alternatives to deadly force, with attention given to the sequence of events leading up to the final frame. The possible points in time and various strategies which might prevent the officer from placing himself in a shoot-don't-shoot situation must be taught.

The latest concept in training is commonly called violence reduction, restraint or avoidance training. This new philosophy of training also recognizes the need to reduce violence and excessive use of force but differs from its predecessor by teaching communication and restraint. Restraint training emphasizes the use of tactical knowledge and concealment strategies to avoid being placed in a situation that has a high probability of resulting in violence. For example, if a police officer responds to a call for a robbery in progress at a local convenience store with emergency lights and siren activated, he or she will possibly confront the robber and face a shootout. This scenario is likely to result in property damage, injury or death. Perhaps a more reasonable response would be to take tactical advantage of the situation, respond without confrontation, and remain concealed to avoid any unpleasant surprises. Before entering a building, firefighters will have studied the blueprints and will know where the fire escapes and stairs are located, as well as other important and potentially helpful details about the building. Police should respond to calls in a similar fashion, knowing as much as possible about a reported situation (Fyfe, 1995).

Restraint training has the potential to provide officers with techniques to resolve high-risk, potentially violent situations without violence. There are some police officers who can turn a parking ticket into a near riot, while others can arrest a violent felon and joke with the suspect all the way to jail. Unfortunately, we do not know why these differences exist or under what conditions they exist. The preliminary indicators are that interactive role playing and simulations are the best methods to expose officers to these techniques. Some police training facilities have mini-cities with store fronts, apartment houses, other buildings, and streets to simulate conditions. Combined with firearm expertise and other use-of-force alternatives, violence-reduction training may represent a new frontier in police training (see Geller and Toch, 1995). Analyzing more than just the final frame will permit a more realistic view of police use of deadly force than has been provided in the past. It can bring police use of force into line with community standards and expectations (see Alpert and Smith, 1994).

CHIEF'S CORNER
DO WE EXPECT THE IMPOSSIBLE?

While the Rodney King incident graphically illustrates indefensible police use of force, the incident also raises a flag of caution. Not all incidents are so clearly documented. There is a real danger in assuming that the police are always at fault in any future incidents.

While all decent people in law enforcement agree that what happened in Los Angeles was a travesty, there is another side of the problem that poses a challenge for both law enforcement administrators and people in the community: How do we address the problem of police officers who are daily dehumanized? How many of us, as part of the responsibilities of our jobs, chase a car at high speed through red lights and stop signs, to the point that we are on the edge of terror? After stopping the offender who caused this frightening chase, he or she steps out of the car, derisively spits in our direction and calls us every filthy name imaginable. How would we react when the adrenaline of fear changes to outrage?

How many times has the average citizen been cursed, punched and mistreated in the course of doing a job only to have the assailant bring charges of criminal and civil wrongdoing because self-defense was involved? In large metropolitan areas where drug use is pervasive, it happens as much as once or twice a month to the average police officer. In most police districts, officers are commonly called to the scene of a domestic disturbance only to be attacked by both of the adversaries if the officers try to bring the situation under control.

These are only a few of the situations in law enforcement that serve to dehumanize a police officer. The media often inflame the situation. They sometimes seem to view the police as willfully seeking to oppress citizens. Much of the coverage of the media is negative. The police officer involved is rarely looked upon as a fellow citizen carrying out the will of the people. Rather, he or she is written about in an adversarial context and must prove that decisions and conduct which took place in a matter of seconds was correct, unbiased, brave, and without malice toward any person.

While it is certainly fair to hold the police to a higher degree of behavior, it is not fair to demand that they be infallible. Drugs and an influx of automatic weapons has made the job of a police officer much different and more violent than it was for me as an officer in the early sixties. Young men and women, some without a great deal of experience, are going to make mistakes in the new, violent community they face.

Of course, we must continue to punish criminal behavior such as what occurred in Los Angeles. At the same time, it must be recognized that the continual portrayal of police officers as adversaries is having a negative effect on bringing crime under control. If the police go into the violent areas where drug dealers control the streets, they must be supported when it is necessary to use force to carry out their duties.

The police are armed so that they may protect themselves and the people they serve. The criminals are armed so that they may further their unlawful behavior. When you put these two factors together, there is going to be conflict—and yes, some mistakes by the police. As human beings police officers are likely to make a wrong call once in a while when forced to make judgments in life-threatening situations.

When errors are made, the behavior of the police is looked at with a microscope while the criminal is held to no standard whatsoever. It is accepted that criminals, by definition, act any way they want. Often, they are viewed as misguided youth acting out the dehumanizing results of their environment. We must remind ourselves that the police are also human beings who have suffered the indignities and have been dehumanized for months and sometimes years by a small segment of society they are forced to encounter every working day. Despite their best efforts, the media seems ready only to pounce on the mistakes rather than to present a balanced portrayal of police officers. Contrary to what the media tends to postulate, 99 percent of the police officers are honest, kind and caring, and interested in making the streets safe for their fellow citizens.

The real danger does not lie in the possibility of unchecked police behavior, for their behavior has and always will be monitored by the media, by the community through an assortment of review panels and groups, by the judiciary and by the police themselves. Rather, it is the unchecked behavior of criminals that has brought this nation to the point of being the most violent in the world.

Isn't it time for the media to recognize and support the sound crime-fighting activities of the police—to see them as human beings under great stress who will occasionally make a mistake? Treating all people with courtesy and dignity is a simplistic and ineffective answer to police-community relation problems. Many criminals see such behavior as weak and an area to be exploited. The media should stop using excuses such as unemployment to justify the callous killing of a convenience store clerk. Some areas of the community are economically deprived and will remain so because people rightly feel afraid to shop in areas that are controlled by a small minority of violent criminals and drug dealers.

Why doesn't the media focus on the fear in a community that forces people to seek safety behind doors with four locks on them?

In my opinion, it's time for all of us to stand up together not just in demanding exceptional police behavior but also in demanding that criminals be seen for what they are. They are not deprived citizens acting out their last hope of survival through vicious criminal acts. They are a minority of sociopaths bent on making themselves rich and powerful at the expense of the honest people of the community.

These issues we have presented are a microcosm of the problems faced by both police and the public. The next two issues, police pursuits and the legal liability of police, are not new but are resurfacing as serious problems for the administration of the police and for the safety of society.

POLICE PURSUITS

Police shootings have been discussed above as a use of deadly force. The use and abuse of weapons by the police have been scrutinized by police administrators, the public and the courts for a long time. Another use of potentially deadly force that has only recently attracted significant attention is the police pursuit (see Alpert and Fridell, 1992). The purpose of a pursuit is to apprehend a law violator. When the suspect refuses to stop and an officer engages in a chase in a high-powered motor vehicle, that vehicle becomes a potentially dangerous weapon, perhaps the most dangerous weapon (Alpert and Anderson, 1986). With all the attention given to the other uses of deadly force, it is surprising that this tactic has escaped thorough examination. In fact, the training guide for the California Peace Officer and Standards and Training, states (Learning Goal 6.1.0 [I.A.2&3]):

> We tend to think of a car as a means of transportation, which it is. But stop and think of this for a moment—a .44 magnum revolver with a 240 grain bullet develops about 1,400 foot-pounds of energy at a muzzle velocity of approximately 1,600 feet per second. Certainly a *deadly weapon.*

> Now consider an average automobile weighing about 4,000 pounds, traveling down a street at 35 m.p.h. (52.5 feet per second). It is developing *171,163* foot-pounds of energy. You had better believe it is a deadly weapon—deadly for others as well as you!

A major concern about pursuit driving is that it is a highly emotional activity that is exciting, adrenalin-driven and dangerous. Unfortunately, officers are likely to get caught up in the heat of the chase and disregard many safety considerations. The emotional aspect of pursuit coupled with the inability of a police officer to make a vehicle stop short of a deadly force application, makes pursuit driving even more dangerous. In other words, after a police officer has signaled a suspect to stop, there is no intermediate force or request the officer can make. The driver has the option to stop or continue. In fact, the driver is in control of the situation as long as the officer is in pursuit.

Granting police the permission to pursue suspected law violators poses a dilemma: On the one hand, police are to protect public safety, and pursuits are inherently dangerous to all involved. On the other hand, there is a need to immediately apprehend law violators. Determining which of these goals is most important will shape the contours of pursuit. Pursuit has three groups of participants: First, there is the suspect who has done something wrong; second, the police officer who has observed the suspect; and third, the public or innocent bystander. In a pursuit, action is necessary by the first two participants. A police officer must initiate the action and a suspect must respond to it. These actors' behavior include several options. First, a police officer may or may not initiate a traffic stop, depending on a variety of factors. Second, the suspect may not respond appropriately to the officer's request or order to stop. Third, the police officer must decide what to do if the suspect does not stop immediately. The officer's choices include continuing the effort to apprehend the suspect, which involves a pursuit, or terminating pursuit efforts. The actions of the police officer, while emotional and adrenalin-driven, can be controlled by policy, training and supervision. The initial actions of the suspect cannot be controlled as it is he or she who makes the decision to stop or flee. However, the subsequent actions of the suspect can be controlled by the action of the police. If the officer continues to chase and drives in close proximity to the suspect, it is likely that the suspect will continue to flee and even increase speed and recklessness to avoid apprehension. If the officer terminates the chase, it is likely that the suspect will slow down and try to escape without great personal risk or risk to others. It is likely that the suspect will attempt to abandon the car and flee on foot. Depending on the reason for the chase and the risk to the public, abandonment or termination may be the best choice for public safety. The critical question in pursuit is what benefit will derive from a chase compared to the risk of accident or injury to the officer, suspect or public? Deciding whether or not to pursue requires a balance of the need to enforce laws and the need to maintain the safety of the public.

Most of our information about police pursuits has come from the popular media. Classic movies and current television shows, including almost obligatory scenes of police officers involved in lengthy and dangerous high-speed chases. Life may imitate art, but it is unfortunate when our knowledge of police pursuits comes from scriptwriters' inventions and stuntmen's antics. Following the same approach taken in our brief examination of the other type of deadly force, we will look at the general information on pursuit, current pursuit standards and training.

During the 1990s, information about police pursuits has increased (Falcone, 1994; Alpert and Fridell, 1992). A working definition of pursuit includes a multi-stage process by which an officer initiates a traffic or felony stop and a suspect refuses to stop and a continued attempt to apprehend the suspect by the police officer. Once the elements of a pursuit are recognized, pre-chase, during the chase, and post-chase questions can be formulated. These include: What requirements and limits should be set on the pursuing police officer(s)? When and under what conditions should an officer terminate a pursuit?

Compared to research on police use of firearms, research on pursuit is conspicuously deficient (see Alpert and Fridell, 1992). Therefore, and unfortunately, this section summarizing pursuit driving is brief. Although some attention was given to emergency and pursuit driving in the 1960s (Fennessey et al., 1970), it took a study by the California Highway Patrol (CHP) in 1983 to generate further interest.

THE CALIFORNIA HIGHWAY PATROL STUDY

The California Highway Patrol, responding to the pleas from the decade before, conducted an exploratory study on police pursuit. Although limited to a six-month period, and substantially limited to freeways, the study provides an excellent base of information. The CHP study reports findings from an analysis of almost 700 pursuits. Two of the most important findings reported by the California Highway Patrol are that:

1. 77 percent of the suspects were apprehended; and
2. 70 percent of the pursuits ended without an accident.

The CHP study concluded that pursuits do not typically end in injury or death, contrary to the information often presented in police textbooks and by the media. The general opinion of the California Highway Patrol, based upon its data, is that pursuits are worth the inherent risks; the CHP report concluded:

> Attempted apprehension of motorists in violation of what appear to be minor traffic infractions is necessary for the preservation of order on the highways of California. If approximately 700 people will attempt to flee from the officers who participated in this six-month study, knowing full well that the officers would give chase, one can imagine what would happen if the police suddenly banned pursuits. Undoubtedly, innocent people may be injured or killed because an officer chooses to pursue a

suspect, but this risk is necessary to avoid the even greater loss that would occur if law enforcement agencies were not allowed to aggressively pursue violators (1983:21).

Not all police administrators, policymakers or politicians will agree with the conclusions drawn by the California Highway Patrol study, which uses the same argument made for the use of deadly force against non-dangerous fleeing felons. One can argue that all felons do not flee when police do not shoot! Many motorists, even knowing an aggressive pursuit will not take place, do not choose to flee when an officer signals them to stop. However, the other side of the issue is that if pursuits are not conducted aggressively, suspects may flee and avoid apprehension.

Politicians reading about the spectacular pursuits which often end in death or injury may encourage or insist that law-enforcement agencies reduce or eliminate pursuits. One excellent justification for this conclusion is a recommendation made in the California Highway Patrol, *Pursuit Study*: "[A] very effective technique in apprehending pursued violators may be simply to follow the violator until he voluntarily stops or crashes" (1983:17). Pressure brought on police administrators may influence them to restrict pursuits in one or more ways in order to avoid or reduce accidents and to meet community expectations. How these pursuits are regulated depend upon departmental policies and other control strategies.

Departmental regulations concerning pursuits vary from vague to detailed. Regulations that define many or all of the circumstances of pursuits do not allow for many decisions to be made by an individual police officer. These regulations may discourage or prohibit police from pursuing certain types of offenders. Other regulations that leave the discretion to pursue to the officer may say nothing either about who should or should not be pursued or about the conditions. Although departmental policies determine the actions which should be taken by the officers, the laws must be considered by legal advisors and policymakers when formulating guidelines for the training and supervision of pursuit driving. The overriding principle in appropriate policies is the balance of the need to immediately apprehend the suspect and the risk created by the pursuit. These terms will be discussed below following a brief look at the empirical research.

RECENT EMPIRICAL INFLUENCES

Although differences exist in the pursuit figures provided by police agencies, it is remarkable that the rates of accidents, injuries and deaths are so similar over time and location (Alpert and Fridell, 1992). Because agencies maintain different reporting procedures and levels of information, it is difficult to conduct comparative analyses, except at the most general level. Summaries of several of the readily available data sets reveal four important empirical realities. First, approximately 70 percent of all pursuits are initiated for traffic infractions. Second, approximately 35–40 percent of the pursuits result in accidents. Third, approximately 15–20 percent of pursuits result in injuries. Fourth, approximately 75 percent of the pursuits result in an apprehension but the vast majority of those offenders are apprehended for minor offenses. (Alpert, 1995; Lucadomo, 1994; Auten, 1994; State of Minnesota, 1994). It must be remembered that this figure includes all types of pursuits, both high-risk and low-risk pursuits.

As the chief mission of the police is to protect lives, it is difficult to encourage any policy or practice that has injury or death as a probable or highly possible outcome without analyzing the potential benefits which can be derived from the activity. In order to realize or accomplish the police mission in the most effective and efficient manner, restrictive policies, solid training, strong supervision and workable accountability systems must be implemented.

Most states rely exclusively on the Uniform Vehicle Code which permits officers in emergency situations certain exemptions to traffic laws. Uniform Vehicle Code (1966, Section 11–106) states that "the . . . provisions shall not relieve the driver of an authorized emergency vehicle from the duty to drive with due regard for the safety of all persons, nor shall such provisions protect the driver from the consequences of his reckless disregard for the safety of others." Although many states have adopted this language, little training is provided as to what it means or how it should be translated into behavior. In any case, the police are granted the authority to violate certain traffic laws to protect lives, not to put them at risk. Defining and understanding risk must be a critical part of any pursuit policy and training.

CREATING A PURSUIT POLICY

As mentioned in chapter 4, a policy must be built upon the laws of the state. Under that direction, some police activities should allow for officer discretion while other activities should be controlled with the unavailability of many discretionary decisions. The use of force and pursuit driving are examples of those activities which must be controlled by a strong policy and training. The development of a pursuit policy follows the same method as the development of a policy for other police activities: each has specific elements, procedures and rules.

The International Association of Chiefs of Police (IACP) has published a variety of model policies. These are excellent documents on which to design a departmental policy. Each has a set of elements which, at a minimum, are important to include. In its most recent model policy, the IACP (1990) included the following elements:

1. Purpose
2. Policy
3. Definition
4. Procedures
   a. Initiation
   b. Pursuit Officer Responsibilities
   c. Communication Center Responsibilities
   d. Supervisor's Responsibilities
   e. Traffic Regulations
   f. Pursuit Tactics
   g. Termination of Pursuit
   h. Interjurisdictional Pursuits
   i. Comprehensive Report

The IACP policy restricted pursuits to those actions for which an officer would make a full custodial arrest. The Concepts and Issues Paper discussing the model policy warns the reader (1990:3):

> The Model Policy is relatively restrictive in prohibiting pursuit where the offense in question would not warrant an arrest. Most traffic violations, therefore, would not meet these pursuit requirements. It is recognized that many law enforcement officers and administrators may find this prohibition difficult to accept and implement, particularly where a more permissive pursuit policy has been traditionally accepted. But in this critical area of pursuit driving, law enforcement administrators must be prepared to make difficult decisions based on the cost and benefits of these types of pursuit to the public they serve.

As noted by the IACP and because pursuits are potentially dangerous, an overall mission statement must be included in the policy. This statement acts as the first element of the policy and as a reminder of the danger of pursuits. Second, as the mission is to protect lives, a statement concerning the rationale of pursuit driving should follow. This analysis must include the need to apprehend a suspect immediately balanced against the danger created by the pursuit. These terms must be defined and emphasized. Third, a definition of pursuit, as suggested above, should follow the stated rationale. Fourth, there should be some statement concerning the specific tactical limitations permitted in pursuits. These limitations may be influenced by factors including the type of offense committed by the suspect, traffic, road and environmental conditions, what is known about the suspect (age and manner of driving), and the likelihood of a successful apprehension. Also, the risk to the public if the suspect is allowed to escape should be considered.

It is important that officers recognize the impact of their decisions during a pursuit and that they are not engaged merely in a contest to win. Officers must continually reevaluate the situation to determine the need of immediately apprehending a suspect balanced against the danger created by the pursuit, and they should be able to justify and explain their decisions. For example, if there is no realistic way to apprehend or capture the suspect, some reason or justification to take risks must exist.

Because officers may be caught up in the moment, it is important that the supervisor take control of the pursuit by means of radio contact. The supervisor, however, must rely upon the information provided by the lead officer in order to make proper decisions. This requires that sufficient information be provided by the pursuing officer. At a minimum, the communication must include:

1. what is known about the suspect and his or her actions,
2. the crime for which the suspect is wanted,
3. the location and direction of the pursuit,
4. the environment in which the pursuit is taking place, including vehicular or pedestrian traffic, likelihood of traffic increasing (3 P.M. on a school day),
5. the speed of both vehicles,
6. the driving behavior of the pursued, and
7. any description of vehicle and its passengers.

It is essential to stress that officers can NOT assume that an individual observed for a violation MUST be involved in something more serious because he or she is fleeing. Officers must rely on what they know, not what they think or sense. Increasing risks during a pursuit can only be justified by what is known.

The mission of the police is to protect lives. The purpose of pursuit is to apprehend a suspect. The purpose of the pursuit must always fulfill the mission of the police as well. All tactics or activities undertaken must be with both safety and apprehension in mind. It is necessary for officers and supervisors to ask themselves, if this pursuit results in an injury or a death, or even property damage, would a reasonable person understand why the pursuit occurred, why it was continued or why it was necessary? These questions will ultimately be asked and it is appropriate to have them in the guidelines. For example, the Oakdale, Minnesota, pursuit policy asks its officers, "If the pursuit should or reasonably could have resulted in injury or death to any person or significant property damage, would a reasonable person understand why the pursuit occurred or was necessary?"

One way to help officers weigh their decisions is to have them apply the same standards as firing a weapon in a situation where innocent bystanders may be endangered. Whenever the officer fires a weapon, he or she must be concerned that the bullet may accidentally hit an unintended target. In a pursuit, the officer has not only the police vehicle to worry about but also whether the pursued vehicle creates dangerous situations and whether other vehicles create danger by attempting to get out of the way. An officer would probably want to take some of these risks if chasing an individual who just robbed the convenience store and killed two clerks. If trained to do so, and in a safe environment, the officer may even choose to use a roadblock, shoot at the car or take some other drastic action which would be considered use of deadly force.

But for a traffic violator, a juvenile or a suspected property offender, what risks are reasonable? A policy should include the warning that the officer's behavior will likely be reviewed and analyzed by a "common citizen" mentality. Will the officer be able to convince a group of nonpolice that his or her behavior and the risks were reasonable under the conditions?

Again, the need to apprehend a suspect immediately must be balanced against the danger created by the pursuit. When the dangers or risks of a pursuit (the foreseeability or likelihood of a collision would be one obvious risk) outweigh the need to immediately apprehend the suspect, the lead officer or the supervisor must terminate it. This is usually dictated by the nature of the offense for which the law violator is wanted and the recklessness of the driving (see Alpert and Fridell, 1992).

There are many other questions which must be addressed by policy. Among them are the use of offensive tactics, the passing and spacing of vehicles, the use of roadblocks and ramming. Further, the specific responsibilities of the supervisor and the possibilities of an interjurisdictional pursuit must be considered and addressed in a policy. Also, once a suspect stops, the lead officer, who is most likely to be excited and influenced by adrenalin, should not be the one to make the custodial arrest. Too often, a suspect is "pulled through the vent window" by an excited and overly zealous officer. Finally, it is important to define a termination of a pursuit. In order for an officer to terminate, he or she must turn off all emergency equipment and return to the posted speed limit.

There is a strong relationship between a policy and the training necessary to support it. The more vague a policy, the more decisions an officer can make about risk. This requires significant training, supervision, control and accountability. It is unacceptable merely to hope that an offender will stop voluntarily, become involved in a collision or run out of gas. There must be some plan to take the person into custody, or the foreseeability of a collision increases as the chase takes on the characteristics of a drag race. Training must include emergency driving, decision making and risk analysis. Officers must also be trained on their departmental policy. As these are perishable skills, training must be periodic and tests must be given on all aspects of the training.

Beyond tactics, a policy includes provisions to hold accountable any officer who has been involved in a pursuit. The IACP policy refers to this as a comprehensive report. Collecting proper data and writing an analytical critique is the first step. Accountability serves several purposes: First, the information contained in a critique helps determine if the pursuit was necessary and within the prescribed guidelines; second, a critique helps determine if training needs should be considered; third, a critique will help determine if a change in policy is needed; and fourth, over a period of time, the data included from these reports will reveal trends and demonstrate specific risk factors. Many pursuits that have ended in an accident or injury result in a law suit brought against the police.

LAWSUITS AGAINST THE POLICE

When a citizen believes that he or she has been the subject of improper or illegal behavior on the part of a police officer, several methods of complaining are available. As we have seen in previous chapters, police internal affairs divisions investigate complaints against police, and some departments have civilian oversight panels to look into specific complaints brought to them. Those citizens who do not trust the police to investigate themselves, who have no access to a civilian oversight panel or who want financial remuneration can seek recourse in the courts by suing the police.

On the one hand, lawsuits against the police are often the result of frustration and the desire to censure the police. On the other hand, suing the police can result in money damages to the plaintiff who brings charges. Regardless of the desired outcome, suits against the police have increased dramatically over the past few years and have taken on a new meaning in the 1990s.

The beginning of civil litigation against the police was seen by the law enforcement community as just one more way of making their crime-fighting abilities less effective. Critics were afraid that police officers would be so cautious that they would be rendered ineffective. Proponents claimed judicial oversight of law enforcement was long overdue. The history of litigation against the police follows the same trend as litigation against prison officials, mental health facilities and other governmental entities.

Activities conducted by police officers are subject to judicial as well as administrative review. If an officer is sued for performing prescribed duties, the officer probably is not personally responsible for his or her actions. If the officer has gone beyond his or her duties and, in bad faith, violated the rights of another, he or she probably will be held responsible. This legal theory, known as *intentional tort* or *willful misconduct*, allows for compensatory and punitive damages. The logic here is that the department had no control of the officer's intentional decision to violate the plaintiff's rights and should not be held responsible.

Holding an individual officer responsible is different from holding his or her employer responsible through the theory of *respondeat superior* or *vicarious liability*. This means that supervisory personnel, along with the employing governmental agency, are held responsible for the illegal actions of employees. By challenging the actions of supervisors and a governmental agency, rather than an individual officer, a lawsuit can have more impact by forcing institutional change and/or exacting monetary damages. The issues which need to be examined include the general principles of liability, negligence for state court claims and the Civil Rights Act of 1871.

GENERAL PRINCIPLES OF LIABILITY

The legal theory underlying many lawsuits filed after an injury caused by a police officer is that of negligence. This type of litigation focuses on the reasonable care used by an officer(s), and is based on the following four elements: (1) the officer owed the injured party a duty not to engage in certain conduct; (2) the officer's actions violated that duty; (3) the officer's negligent breach of that duty was the proximate cause of the injury; and (4) the injured party suffered actual and preventable damages. It may be necessary to evaluate the status of each element to determine whether or not a lawsuit has merit. In other words, in order for an individual to file a meritorious lawsuit against an officer, that person, known as a plaintiff, must have been injured by an officer's unreasonable conduct. As noted previously, it may be instructive to ask simply: Under the given conditions, would a reasonable, prudent and well-trained police officer act in a similar manner? Unfortunately, the definition of reasonable care and proximate cause has eluded precision and accurate measurement (see Alpert and Smith, 1994; Kappeler, 1993; Urbonya, 1989).

Since the United States Supreme Court revived the Civil Rights Act of 1871 (42 U.S.C. Section 1983), it has become a predominant vehicle for civil suits alleging police misconduct filed in federal court. Although this act was originally designed as a response to the activities of the Ku Klux Klan and the apathy of southern states regarding those activities during Reconstruction, it is now an effective means of controlling government misconduct through litigation.

It is important to recognize that Section 1983 creates no substantive rights but is a vehicle for bringing suit against defendants acting under color of state law by violating another person's federal rights. This vehicle is limited to those actors who exert authority derived from the government. A plaintiff must prove that he was deprived of a federal right and was so deprived by a person who was authorized to act by a governmental agency. Further, it must be shown that harm was caused by the deprivation of that right (see Smith, 1995). In order to be shielded from liability, the person or agency being sued must show that the action was done in good faith and is immune from suit (Urbonya, 1989).

In 1961, the Supreme Court in *Monroe v. Pape* addressed the plaintiff's claim that officers of the Chicago police department had violated the constitutional guarantee against unreasonable searches and seizures. Since that time, numerous suits alleging police misconduct have been filed under Section 1983 despite the fact that the *Monroe* court held that units of local government were immune from liability. The Supreme Court's decision in *Monell v. Department of Social Services of New York City* extended activities subject to litigation to policies, regulations, practices or customs of government agencies.

The effect of *Monell* makes it easier to bring and win lawsuits against police departments and other units of government. These legal decisions, and many subsequent ones in both state and federal courts, seem to have encouraged citizens to sue individual officers and governmental units, as well as to take advantage of the "deep pockets" incentive for more money. Wrongful death awards are sometimes more than $1,000,000, and plaintiffs alleging unnecessary force have often received awards in the $500,000 to $750,000 range. There has been an increased trend to use the Federal Civil Rights Act to make claims of liability against governmental entities (see Kappeler, 1993).

Suing the police can have one or more of the following effects on police and the public. First, it can demoralize police officers and whole departments. The filing of frivolous suits that merely hassle police officers and their administrators can handcuff police efforts. Second, suing the police can result in financial awards to those whose rights were violated. Meritorious actions can serve to punish officers and departments who have conducted themselves improperly or illegally. Additionally, these actions could deter others from conducting themselves in a similar fashion. Third, suits against the police that prove inadequate administrative controls, deficient policies, or customs and practices that are improper or illegal, can force the department to correct its specific deficiencies and review all policies, practices and customs. Hopefully, this would afford the department an opportunity to bring its behavior in line with the laws and community standards.

It is unfortunate that legal actions are needed to force police departments to accept community standards and to improve themselves. Whether the issues involve the hiring of minorities, the role of women in policing, the use of force, training, police pursuits, or any other police duty or task, updating and improving performance should be an ongoing process. In our final section, we will outline one way that police departments can create an ongoing review of their practices and customs and, thus, effectively eliminate the need for lawsuits. One strategy, which was developed from research conducted in Miami, Florida, was called Neighborhood Intervention and Community Evaluation (see Alpert and Dunham, 1988). During the development of this concept, police were being encouraged to become involved with the members of the communities they serve. Intervention suggests a one-sided connection and therefore an ineffective and insufficient strategy. In today's world the relationship between the police and the community must go beyond intervention and operate on mutual involvement. Our strategy of community orientation has been modified to Neighborhood Involvement and Community Evaluation. The following section develops the duties and responsibilities of both the police and the members of the community.

POLICE AND THE COMMUNITY

The duties and expectations of the police are extremely complex, as the information in earlier chapters demonstrated. There are neither clear-cut rules for the police to follow nor are there predetermined expectations that community members can use to assist or to help orient the police (Ross, 1995; Bureau of Justice Assistance, 1994; Weisheit and Falcone, 1994; Goldstein, 1990; Skolnick and Bayley, 1986). There are, however, methods that any jurisdiction can utilize to guide planning and change.

In a society as diverse as ours, there are bound to be different priorities placed on police by different people who live in different communities. In addition, police officers are not all the same, do not have similar opinions or expectations, do not perform at the same level, and do not operate with the same style. In fact, police departments may operate under a number of separate philosophies. These differences influence the policies that allocate resources and, ultimately, determine how a police department and its officers should police the neighborhoods in which they work.

Given the mixed social character of our cities, the mosaic which makes up our social fabric, police administrators must decide how to allocate their scarce resources. In other words, administrators have to make policies concerning how well trained the officers are going to be, in what they will be trained, how they will be deployed, what their enforcement priorities will be, and what tactics they will use. This requires administrators to place priorities on police officers' use of time, choice of activities, and overall style of dealing with the public.

As we have stressed, a strategic factor in the allocation of these resources is the style of law enforcement desired by the community. Community leaders can set reasonable boundaries on police actions. These limits usually depend upon the social, economic and political characteristics of the community.

In the past, many urban police departments have adopted some sort of community policing strategy to respond to the demand for the decentralization of their police operations. In theory, community-oriented policing is an excellent way to increase the efficiency and effectiveness of police response. Police officers are expected to modify some behaviors in response to the demands of the members of the communities they serve. The pure theory of community-oriented policing, as discussed in chapter 7, includes not only administrative decentralization (which may already exist in some departments) but also appropriate training, proper interaction with members of the target neighbor-hoods, and institutionalized monitoring and rewards.

One innovative approach which is related to community policing has come to be known as problem-oriented policing (Eck and Spelman, 1989; Goldstein, 1990). Originally formulated by Herman Goldstein in the late 1970s, this approach to policing is often identified with and linked to community-ori-ented policing (see chapter 7). Goldstein argued that police traditionally fo-cused narrowly on specific incidents. He acknowledged that the strategy for most police departments has been to make a large portion of their personnel visible and available to respond to calls and observed incidents. In other words, the dominating objective for patrol has been traditionally to respond quickly, apprehend offenders, secure evidence or protect citizens, deal with any prob-lems, complete the paperwork, and return to a status enabling another response. The analogy has often been made to emergency medical technicians who do what is necessary to stabilize the injury and minimize damage but who do not treat the patient or the underlying reason for the injury.

The police have failed to engage in meaningful planning because the communication system has forced them to react to incidents. The response of patrol officers to a call is not problem solving, rather it is simply stabilizing a situation or problem. Goldstein argued that the police should group incidents around recurring problems and focus on the underlying causes. John Eck and William Spelman have explained the four-stage approach which outlines the benefits of problem solving (1989:431):

> During the Scanning stage, an officer identifies an issue and determines whether it really is a problem. In the Analysis stage, officers collect information from sources inside and outside their agency. The goal is to understand the scope, nature and causes of the problem. In the Response stage, this information is used to develop and implement solutions. Offi-cers seek the assistance of other police units, other public and private organizations, and anyone else who can help. Finally, in the Assessment stage, officers evaluate the effectiveness of the response. Officers may use the results to revise the response, collect more data, or even to redefine the problem.

Eck and Spelman continue (1989:425):

> Using this approach, police go beyond individual crimes and calls for service and take on the underlying problems that create them. To under-stand problems, police collect facts from a wide variety of sources, from outside as well as inside police agencies. To develop and implement

solutions, police enlist the support of other public and private agencies and individuals.

The problem-solving approach permits the police to direct their energy and effort toward preventing crime and solving problems, not incidents. In this way, police will be able to diagnose long-term solutions and assist in the mobilization of public and private resources to attack the problems. Incidents can be grouped into problems, and the problems can be attacked in a variety of ways.

There is a complementary relationship between community-oriented policing and problem solving. On the one hand, community-oriented policing emphasizes the importance of community members and the necessity of devel- . oping partnerships among citizens, government and the private sector. On the other hand, problem solving addresses why things are going wrong and responds with a variety of approaches, both traditional and nontraditional. As Kennedy and Moore inform us (1995:273):

> In practice, the two approaches tend to become one: Problem solving, once begun, eventually forces police to attend community concerns, and cultivate community allies, while community policing forces police to move beyond traditional tactics. *Community policing* has become the dominant label for the new policing, but most departments implementing community policing are in fact doing both . . .

The foundation of Neighborhood Involvement and Community Evaluation is also consistent with the general goals of Total Quality Management (TQM), including: (1) empowering officers through the process of setting mutual performance objectives with management; (2) mutually negotiated accountability; (3) a community orientation and concern for the enforcement priorities of the citizens; and (4) increased managerial flexibility (Manning, 1995). Many agencies have adopted or embraced these concepts but many have not internalized any specifics. That is, many agencies have developed the rhetoric but not the action. Our approach is based upon a system of police problem-solving strategies, evaluation of effectiveness and community feedback. Neighborhood Involvement and Community Evaluation underscores the need for planning, analysis and evaluation. Whether the issue is directed patrol, convenience store robberies, drinking drivers, residential burglaries, drug enforcement, etc., tactics and structure need to be adapted to the goals and objectives. Terms such as community-oriented policing and problem-oriented policing may gain and lose popularity, but the concept of applying these principles has changed permanently the structure and function of police work.

Our example of multi-agency cooperation in drug enforcement (see chapter 4) provides an excellent model of planning, and implementation. This notion of community policing "consists of a set of actors, behaviors and orientations whose purpose is to improve police-community relations, increase citizens' participation in crime control by helping them to police themselves, and reduce crime as well as fear of crime" (Ross, 1995:244).

In order for the concept of Neighborhood Involvement and Community Evaluation to be implemented effectively, several organizational elements must be added to the traditional components which exist in many community policing agencies. Most departments stress the need for police officers to return to the old meaning of "beat officer." That is, the officers should learn about the residents and business people of their neighborhoods. The officers should see citizens and be seen themselves in situations that are not always defined as negative. This is a necessary but not sufficient step. The suggested approach stresses good relations with the community and includes several key elements. First, to reduce isolation between police and citizens, officers must be assigned to target areas for an extended period. This move toward stability will increase the identification of an officer with the residents, geography, politics and other issues of a given neighborhood. Second, there must be more than the traditional police-community relations meetings or citizens' advisory groups. There must be education and action. The public must be versed in the problem-solving techniques associated with community policing and there must be activity. While different communities can benefit from different partnerships, it is necessary to identify potential partners and their problems. Then, strategies to address the problem(s) must be developed. Even when these two elements are operating, successful community policing requires proper training, feedback mechanisms, and an institutionalized reward system. The following section discusses what to do and how to do it (see Alpert and Moore, 1993).

NEIGHBORHOOD TRAINING

Appropriate neighborhood training involves two basic questions which must be answered according to an individual community's needs: what to do and how to do it. In other words, priorities regarding the utilization of police resources, whether for fighting crime or providing service, change from neighborhood to neighborhood. Police officers must recognize these needs from the consumers' perspectives, from the viewpoint of the police administration, and from their own experiences and expectations. Neighborhood training can effectively inform the officer what to expect from the residents, physical surroundings or other influences and what the community can expect from the police. This in-service training can introduce officers to community characteristics while working the streets under supervision (in a way similar to field training). An important component of this training is the education of the community members to the scope and limitations of the police. In other words, police and members of the community must have similar expectations and work toward achieving mutually agreed-upon goals. The "what-to-do" can be determined by problem-solving techniques. The problems and necessary resources can be identified. The "how-to-do-it" is the all-important style of policing that was discussed earlier. The officers must be willing to become involved in community activities and participate with community members. In addition, the police can help to organize efforts to obtain other governmental and private sector resources.

There exist clear differences among officers and citizens concerning style. Matching the style of policing to community needs and requirements will improve both the police and the community. This can be achieved through training based upon knowledge of community values and beliefs, as well as upon the attitudes and priorities of police officers. A necessary element is the constant dialogue, both formal and informal, between residents and police officers. Research on the attitudes, expectations and evaluation of services of both police officers and members of the community is a necessary element of this approach (see Furstenberg and Wellford, 1973). Specifically, measuring the effect of training and other reform efforts is critical (Alpert and Moore, 1993).

MONITORING AND REWARDING THE POLICE OFFICER

The final recommendations for this approach include institutionalized monitoring and a formal reward system. This requires an ongoing system to monitor both the community and the police. The needs of the community can be determined by periodic social surveys which, if linked to census data and local planning information, can inform officials of the changing nature of a given neighborhood. While it is relatively easy to identify what constitutes negative police behavior, it is difficult to specify exemplary behavior. The proper use of quality research, including appropriate sampling and a panel design, could provide a clear snapshot of the changing needs expressed by members of a target community. In addition, examples of exemplary police behavior reported by residents could help guide policing strategies and reward a job well done. This type of data integrated with traditional law enforcement information will permit the creation and maintenance of neighborhood profiles. These profiles can be used by the police to improve their own effectiveness and the quality of life in a community. A Blue Ribbon Committee studying the Miami Police Department after several serious civil disturbances in the early 1980s came to similar conclusions. In its final report (Overtown Blue Ribbon Committee, 1984:199), it noted:

> It is our conclusion that a minor organizational change can have a major impact on community relations and on the interrelationships between citizens and police. We believe that confidence in the police will be enhanced if the police measure and make more visible the activities they perform. Moreover, police work is usually rewarded by the gratitude an officer receives from those whom he or she helps. Status in the department, promotions, raises, commendations, etc., rest largely on his or her crime-fighting activities, the number of arrests, crimes he or she solves, etc. As a result, the patrol officer may regard service calls as a necessary evil.

The continued use of out-of-date performance measures, including arrests or tickets will perpetuate a style of policing that is not consistent with our strategy. In order to create a proper partnership, it has been suggested that

> . . . police must engage in community-based processes related to the production and maintenance of local human capital. The means by which these lofty goals are to be achieved are through the development of strong relationships with institutions and individuals in the community . . . attacking the communities' problems on a broader front . . . changes in the way the police visualize their work and their methods . . . (and) changes in internal working relationships. (Alpert and Moore, 1993:113–117)

Most police departments provide incentives for their officers. These include traditional promotions, merit increases, and "officer-of-the-month" recognition. Many departments offer several opportunities for their officers to receive or earn rewards. Traditionally, these rewards have been based upon aggressive actions which have led to an arrest(s), the capture of a dangerous felon, or some other heroic activity. These criteria for rewarding police officers are important and serve to encourage similar actions from others. Yet, there are other types of police behavior which deserve recognition but which remain lost and hidden behind the visible, aggressive activities of police officers. The activities which should receive more attention include exemplary service to the community and the reduction and diffusion of violence. Those who provide meritorious service have been recognized, but often their actions are lost behind the shooting incident or heroic rescue.

Local recognition for officers who serve their "beat" or neighborhood in an exemplary fashion is needed. A "Best Cop on the Block" recognition would be an important reward, if provided by local residents or merchants. The actions of officers who avoid shootings or take suspects into custody may not be known to supervisors. When they are, the officers may be labeled as "chickens" or ones who cannot provide needed back-up to fellow officers. It is the behavior that is consistent with neighborhood norms that must receive attention and reinforcement. Nonaggressive, violence-reduction behavior needs to be reinforced, rewarded, and established as the model for other officers to copy.

An institutional reward system should be established for officers who avoid or reduce violent situations and who avoid the use of force, especially deadly force. Once command officers, from the chief to the sergeants, support and reward violence reduction, it is possible to enlist the support of private business and service groups to provide symbolic and monetary rewards for such behavior. Institutional support for the effective policing of a neighborhood can only encourage others to consider a change in priorities and in their policing style. While this is only one aspect of the Neighborhood Involvement and Community Evaluation model, it could serve as a successful step toward meeting the joint needs of both the citizens and the police.

A worthwhile approach would be incomplete without an informational feedback loop. Both the crime-fighting and the service functions of the police need to be evaluated on the institutional and individual levels. First, an ongoing study of victimization will provide police with data on how well their system is providing services. Usually, this information is gleaned from official crime statistics, *Uniform Crime Reports* (UCR), but this process is doomed to failure because any system based on UCR data will be skewed in the direction of reported crimes. This bias will result in an incomplete and inaccurate count. A survey of crime victims can provide the whole criminal justice system with a much-needed evaluation. Second, a random survey of consumers of police services can provide administrators and planners with feedback on both their services and on the officers who provide them. This feedback can serve a dual function at the institutional and individual level.

TOWARD AN INTERACTIVE MODEL

Police departments around the country have implemented some form of community policing program and have realized some success. The few pilot projects which have incorporated several of the elements discussed above report moderate success. It is the cumulative effect of all of the information that will really improve policing (see Reiss, 1985; Goldstein, 1990). In fact, having a team or community-policing detail without proper planning, training and administration may be more harmful than not having one at all (see Skolnick and Bayley, 1986; Pate et al., 1986; and Mastrofski, 1983). The mere existence of a distinct unit to provide special services may raise the expectations of the community members. When these expectations are not met, there can be a backlash effect of disapproval and disappointment. The various aspects of this approach feed into each other and should be analyzed individually and as a total effect. They must be integrated, not added. Using data collected from the neighborhoods, a feasible plan for Neighborhood Involvement and Community Evaluation can bring police work in line with our modern world. Moore and Kelling (1983:65) have summarized these ideas quite well:

> Police strategies do not exist in a vacuum. They are shaped by important legal, political, and attitudinal factors, as well as by local resources and capabilities, all factors which now sustain the modern conception of policing. So there may be little leeway for modern police executives. But the modern conception of policing is in serious trouble, and a review of the nature of that trouble against the background of the American history of policing gives a clear direction to police forces that wish to improve their performance as crime fighters and public servants.

> The two fundamental features of a new police strategy must be these: that the role of private citizens in the control of crime and maintenance of public order be established and encouraged, not derided and thwarted, and that the police become more active, accessible participants in community affairs. The police will have to do little to encourage citizens to participate in community policing, for Americans are well practiced at undertaking private, voluntary efforts; all they need to know is that the police force welcomes and supports such activity. Being more visible and accessible is slightly more difficult, but hiring more "community relations" specialists is surely not the answer. Instead, the police must get out of their cars, and spend more time in public spaces such as parks and plazas, confronting and assisting citizens with their private troubles. This is mundane, prosaic work but it probably beats driving around in cars waiting for a radio call. Citizens would surely feel safer and, perhaps, even be safer.

Neighborhood Involvement and Community Evaluation will work most effectively in homogeneous neighborhoods and in areas where police utilize problem-solving techniques. It is important that police officers work for the community, not merely to impress their supervisors. That is why it is so important for community members to provide information to police administrators. Homogeneity can cross ethnic boundaries and, in some cases, social class distinctions. Therefore, it is an attitudinal or ideological homogeneity that is required for this approach to work. Alpert and Dunham (1988) report that this strategy can be successful in lower-class housing projects, as well as in middle-class suburbs, a conclusion debated by Pate et al. (1986).

There is no debate, however, that more research would help to identify the elements necessary to make community policing successful in different neighborhoods. Some cities will find it reasonable to split police jurisdictions, as many geographic locations attract or limit certain groups of people. Other cities may find their demographic mixture just too complex to divide into jurisdictions for this type of policing. Regardless of the administrative level of commitment, patrol officers are in the best position to understand the varied and changing needs of the community and, with help, can devise appropriate activities to control crime and to provide service. This method utilizes the officers' talents and experiences to provide expert assistance to the community. The structure of the police administration determines how much influence the police officer has in his or her patrol area. It is suggested that police departments totally commit to a system of neighborhood involvement and community evaluation.

There is a price to pay for such enhanced community involvement in policing, for this approach includes chipping away at some traditional police activities and perhaps reducing or changing administrative controls. The future of successful policing is based on ideas and the implementation of those ideas. Change is a necessary element of success, and it is time to consider certain basic changes to improve police and policing. Research shows that citizens who have confidence and trust in the police will take a more active role in reporting crime than those citizens who do not. This citizen cooperation is likely to lead to a higher reported crime rate and the corresponding need for more officers and a greater capacity to process criminals through the justice system (Dukes and Alpert, 1980).

There is an additional economic price to pay for data collection, data analysis and the social police training that has been discussed. To coin an old phrase, a jurisdiction will pay now or pay later. Policing in America must move beyond its current level and use knowledge gained from research. The knowledge and means are available, so all that is needed now is commitment. Unfortunately, there is no guarantee that this approach or any other reform will be an acceptable answer to a yet unsolved problem.

SUMMARY

In this chapter, we have focused on some issues which currently plague the police and which will be important in the near future. These issues include minority hiring and the complete integration of female police officers into the police hierarchy. Another issue is the use of force to enforce the law. There is a great need for well thought-out policies and improved training for the use of force. Two areas of policing for which problems are increasing in number and seriousness are police pursuits and lawsuits against police officers and their departments. Each of these problems and issues must be addressed with policies and training to balance the various needs of the community with the needs of law enforcement.

References

Adams, Kenneth. 1995. "Measuring the Prevalence of Police Abuse of Force." In William Geller and Hans Toch (eds.) *And Justice for All: Understanding and Controlling Police Abuse of Force*, pp. 61–97 . Washington: Police Executive Research Forum.

Adams, Thomas. 1990. *Police Field Operations*. Englewood Cliffs, NJ: Prentice-Hall.

Alpert, Geoffrey. 1985. *The American System of Criminal Justice*. Beverly Hills: Sage Publications.

Alpert, Geoffrey and Patrick Anderson. 1986. "The Most Deadly Force: Police Pursuits." *Justice Quarterly* 3:1–14.

Alpert, Geoffrey, Ben Crouch, and Ronald Huff. 1984. "Prison Reform by Judicial Decree: The Unintended Consequences of *Ruiz y Estelle*." *Justice System Journal* 9:291–305.

Alpert, Geoffrey and Roger Dunham. 1988. *Policing Multi-Ethnic Neighborhoods*. Westport, CT: Greenwood Press.

Alpert, Geoffrey and Lorie Fridell. 1992. *Police Vehicles and Firearms: Instruments of Deadly Force*. Prospect Heights, IL: Waveland Press.

Alpert, Geoffrey and Mark Moore. 1993. "Measuring Police Performance in the New Paradigm of Policing." In J. DiIulio (ed.) *Performance Measures for the Criminal Justice System*, pp. 109–42 . Washington, DC: U.S. Department of Justice.

Alpert, Geoffrey and William Smith. 1994. "How Reasonable Is the Reasonable Man?: Police and Excessive Force." *Journal of Criminal Law and Criminology* 85:481–501.

Alpert, Geoffrey, William Smith and Dan Watters. 1992. "Implications of the Rodney King Beating." *Criminal Law Bulletin* 28:469–79.

Auten, James. 1994. *An Analysis of Police Pursuit Driving Operations, Volume I & II.* Champaign, IL: Police Training Institute.

Bayley, David and Harold Mendelsohn. 1969. *Minorities and the Police.* New York: Free Press.

Belknap, Joanne and Jill Kastens Shelley. 1993. "The New Lone Ranger: Policewomen on Patrol." *American Journal of Police* XII, no. 2: 47–75.

Bizzak, John (ed.). 1991. *Issues in Policing: New Perspectives.* Lexington, KY: Autumn House Publishing.

Bloch, Peter and Deborah Anderson. 1974. *Policemen on Patrol.* Washington, DC: Police Foundation.

Blumberg, Mark. 1993. "Controlling Police Use of Deadly Force: Assessing Two Decades of Progress." In Roger Dunham and Geoffrey Alpert (eds.) *Critical Issues in Policing: Contemporary Readings*, 2nd ed., pp. 469–92. Prospect Heights, IL: Waveland Press.

Bureau of Justice Assistance. 1994. *Understanding Community Policing: A Framework for Action.* Washington, DC: U.S. Government Printing Office.

Caiden, Gerald. 1977. *Police Revitalization.* Lexington, MA: Lexington Books.

California Highway Patrol. 1983. *Pursuit Study.* Sacramento: State of California.

California Peace Officer Standards and Training Guide. n.d. Learning Goal 6.1.0 (1.A.2+3).

Dade County Grand Jury. 1982 (Spring). *Final Report.* Miami: Dade County.

Dukes, Richard and Geoffrey Alpert. 1980. "Criminal Victimization from a Police Perspective." *Journal of Police Science and Administration* 8:21–30.

Eck, John and William Spelman. 1993. "Problem-Solving: Problem-Oriented Policing in Newport News." In Roger Dunham and Geoffrey Alpert (eds.) *Critical Issues in Policing: Contemporary Readings*, 2nd ed., pp. 451–65. Prospect Heights, IL: Waveland Press.

Falcone, David. 1994. "Police Pursuits and Officer Attitudes: Myths and Realities." *American Journal of Police* 13:143–55.

Fennessy, Edmund, Thomas Hamilton, Kent Joscelyn and John Merrritt. 1970. *A Study of the Problem of Hot Pursuit by the Police.* Washington, DC: U.S. Department of Transportation.

Florida Advisory Committee to the United States Commission on Civil Rights. 1976. *Policed by the White Male Minority.* Tallahassee: State of Florida.

Furstenberg, Frank and Charles Wellford. 1973. "Calling the Police: The Evaluation of Police Service." *Law and Society Review* 7:393–406.

Fyfe, James. 1995. "Training to Reduce Police-Civilian Violence." In William Geller and Hans Toch (eds.) *And Justice for All: Understanding and Controlling Police Abuse of Force*, pp. 163–75. Washington: Police Executive Research Forum.

Geller, William and Michael Scott. 1992. *Deadly Force: What We Know*. Police Executive Research Forum.

Geller, William and Hans Toch. 1995. "Improving our Understanding and Control of Police Abuse of Force: Recommendations for Research and Action." In William Geller and Hans Toch (eds.) *And Justice for All: Understanding and Controlling Police Abuse of Force*, pp. 277–337. Washington: Police Executive Research Forum.

Goldstein, Herman. 1990. *Problem-Oriented Policing*. New York: McGraw-Hill.

Hale, Donna. 1992. "Women in Policing." In *What Works in Policing: Operations and Administration Examined*, pp. 125–42. Cincinnati: Anderson Publishing.

Hongisto, Richard. 1980. "Why Are There No Gay Choir Boys? Ask Your Friendly Chief of Police." *The Civil Rights Quarterly* (Summer): 39–42.

Independent Commission on the Los Angeles Police Department. 1991. *Report of the Independent Commission on the Los Angeles Police Department*. Los Angeles: Independent Commission on the Los Angeles Police Department.

International Association of Chiefs of Police. 1990. *Vehicular Pursuit: Model Policy and Concept Paper*. Fairfax, VA: IACP National Law Enforcement Policy Center.

Kappeler, Victor. 1993. *Critical Issues in Police Civil Liability*. Prospect Heights, IL: Waveland Press.

Kappeler, Victor, Richard Sluder, and Geoffrey Alpert. 1994. *Forces of Deviance: Understanding the Dark Side of Policing*. Prospect Heights, IL: Waveland Press.

Kennedy, David and Mark Moore. 1995. "Underwriting the Risky Investment in Community Policing: What Social Science Should be Doing to Evaluate Community Policing." *The Justice System Journal* 17:271–89.

Kizziah, Carol and Mark Morris. 1977. *Evaluation of Women in Policing Programs*. Oakland: Approach Associates.

Laws, Judith. 1975. "The Psychology of Tokenism: An Analysis." *Sex Roles* 1:51–67.

Little Rock, Arkansas Police Department. 1989. *General Order 16, Use of Force*.

Lucadamo, Thomas. 1994. "Identifying the Dimension of Police Pursuit." Master's Thesis. University of Maryland.

Manning, Peter. 1995. "TQM and the Future of Policing." *Police Forum* 5:1–5.

Maghan, Jess. 1993. "The Changing Face of the Police Officer." In R. Dunham and G. Alpert (eds.) *Critical Issues in Policing*, 2nd ed., pp. 348–60. Prospect Heights, IL: Waveland Press.

Martin, Susan. 1993. "Female Officers on the Move? A Status Report on Women in Policing." In R. Dunham and G. Alpert (eds.) *Critical Issues in Policing*, 2nd ed., pp. 327–47. Prospect Heights, IL: Waveland Press.

Mastrofski, Stephan. 1983. "Police Knowledge on the Beat Patrol: A Performance Measure." In Richard Bennett (ed.) *Police at Work: Issues and Analysis*, pp. 45–64. Beverly Hills: Sage Publications.

Milton, Catherine. 1972. *Women in Policing*. Washington, DC: Police Foundation.

Moore, Mark and George Kelling. 1983. "To Serve and Protect: Learning from Police History." *The Public Interest* 70:49–65.

National Advisory Commission on Criminal Justice Standards and Goals. 1973. *Report*. Washington, DC: United States Government Printing Office.

Overtown Blue Ribbon Committee. 1984. *Final Report*. Miami: City of Miami.

Pate, Antony, et al. 1986. *Reducing Fear of Crime in Houston and Newark*. Washington, DC: Police Foundation.

Price, Barbara and Susan Gavin. 1982. "A Century of Women in Policing." In B. Price and N. Sokoloff (eds.) *The Criminal Justice System and Women*, pp. 399–412. New York: Clark Boardman.

Reiss, Albert. 1985. *Policing a City's Central District: The Oakland Story*. Washington, DC: United States Government Printing Office.

Ross, Jeffrey Ian. 1995. "Confronting Community Policing: Minimizing Community Policing as Public Relations." In Peter Kratcoski and Duane Dukes (eds.) *Issues in Community Policing*, pp. 243–59. Cincinnati: Anderson Publishing.

Sichel, Joyce, et al. 1978. *Women on Patrol: A Pilot Study of Police Performance in New York City*. Washington, DC: United States Government Printing Office.

Skolnick, Jerome and David Bayley. 1986. *The New Blue Line*. New York: Free Press.

Smith, Michael. 1995. "Law Enforcement Liability Under Section 1983." *Criminal Law Bulletin* 31:128–50.

State of Minnesota Department of Public Safety and State Patrol. 1994. *Pursuit Reporting System*.

Sulton, Cynthia and Roi Townsey. 1980. *Women Police Officers: A Personnel Study*. Washington, DC: Police Foundation.

Sykes, Richard and Edward Brent. 1980. "The Regulation of Interaction by Police." *Criminology* 18:182–97.

Uniform Vehicle Code. 1966. Section 11–106.

United States Civil Rights Commission. 1981. *Who Is Guarding the Guardians?* Washington, DC: United States Government Printing Office.

Urbonya, Kathryn. 1989. "Problematic Standards of Reasonableness." *Temple Law Review* 62:61–116.

Weisheit, Ralph and David Falcone. 1994. "Community Policing in Small Towns and Rural America." *Crime and Delinquency* 40:549–67.

Weisheit, Ralph, David Falcone, and L. Edward Wells. 1996. *Crime and Policing in Rural and Small-Town America*. Prospect Heights, IL: Waveland Press.

William O. Douglas Institute. 1984. *The Future of Policing*. Seattle: The William O. Douglas Institute.

Cases

Bell v. Wolfish. 441 U.S. 520 (1979).

Graham v. Connor. 109 S.Ct. 1865 (1989).

Monell v. Department of Social Services of New York City. 436 U.S. 690. (1978).

Monroe v. Pape. 365 U.S. 167. (1961).

Tennessee v. Garner. 471 U.S. 1 (1985).

United States v. City of Philadelphia. 499 F. Supp 1196. (1980).

Chapter Ten

THE FUTURE OF POLICING

The future of policing is linked integrally to the future of communities. A common thread which is present throughout the history of policing and which is emphasized in this book is the role of the community in the organization, maintenance and control of law enforcement. In fact, we have come full circle from the history of policing to the future of policing. We have seen that police were created and developed in reaction to the needs of citizens. The role of the police has been modified throughout history according to what members of the community would accept. Unfortunately, we cannot always predict accurately the limits of community tolerance or anticipate the effects of change on the community (see Banerjee and Baer, 1984; Ahlbrandt, 1984). As we have noted, this complex relationship between the community and the police is worthy of analysis. Taub, Taylor, and Dunham (1984) provide us with a starting point by noting that the complicated interrelationships between police and various neighborhoods depend upon migration, economics, social policies, politics and ethnic composition, among other variables. Researchers have moved beyond the general influences and have identified some specific relationships that are important to community-oriented policing (see Goldstein, 1990; Alpert and Dunham, 1988).

The future of policing has a special and temporal meaning in that each generation's wish list for the police and law enforcement is based upon many social and economic considerations. Often, issues and suggested solutions appear and disappear in a cyclical fashion. The bottom line, however, is the community's ability to influence the roles of police and the functioning of police departments and their officers. Members of the community, assisted by police officers and administrators, can best determine the problems and analyze possible solutions for crime control, police services and order maintenance. In various cities, this problem solving can take different forms and result in different solutions, but the process remains the same.

As we enter the last few years of the decade, we are investing a large proportion of our human and financial capital and hope in community policing. Before we discuss the relationship between policing and the future, two broad categories of change need to be introduced. First, the standardization of police and second, the social influences on the structure and function of the organization.

STANDARDIZATION OF POLICE

As we have learned, many ways exist to design and administer a police agency. Similarly, a variety of styles and emphases can shape the department. One question that surfaces is whether agencies should become more standardized and follow a group of national norms. As we have mentioned, the International Association of Chiefs of Police (IACP) has created excellent model policies which are widely distributed and used by police departments. These model policies set the floor from which agencies can build their own specific policies. Another approach to the standardization of police is accreditation. Since the late 1970s, a debate has existed concerning whether or not police departments would benefit from accreditation (Bizzack, 1993).

The four largest and most influential law enforcement professional associations spearheaded this approach. These included, the International Association of Chiefs of Police (IACP), the National Organization of Black Law Enforcement Executives (NOBLE), the National Sheriffs' Association (NSA) and the Police Executive Research Forum (PERF). Representatives from these organizations worked together and formed the Commission on Accreditation for Law Enforcement Agencies (CALEA). The stated objectives were fourfold: (1) to increase the agency's abilities to prevent and control crime; (2) increase the agency's effectiveness and efficiency in the delivery of services; (3) increase cooperation among law enforcement agencies; and (4) increase citizen and employee confidence in the goals, policies and practices of the agency. The bottom line was to: "provide state and local law enforcement agencies the opportunity to show voluntarily that they could meet an established set of widely accepted law enforcement standards" (Bizzack, 1993:11).

During the past sixteen years, police agencies have made a great deal of progress in the development and acceptance of these law enforcement standards. The process of accreditation was based on the model which had been established for correctional institutions (see Bazelon, 1988). The Commission on Accreditation for Law Enforcement Agencies inherited many benefits and problems experienced by the accreditation effort in the corrections area. First, how are national standards created? Second, how are they enforced? Third, what are the benefits? These questions have been the strengths and weakness of the accreditation effort.

The development of standards was a lengthy and hotly debated process. First, what areas of law enforcement should be standardized and with what criteria? The Commission initially decided upon more than 900 standards in forty-eight areas for agencies seeking accreditation. During the 1990s, the number has been reduced significantly and may continue to be adjusted over time. The accreditation process includes a self-assessment and an outside review by a team which visits the agency to decide if the standards are in place. The benefit of accreditation is twofold: First, it is membership in an elite fraternity of accredited agencies and second, it shows that the agency has been scrutinized by outside professionals. These benefits include status and a credible benchmark for evaluating police policies and systems. The disadvantages of membership include costs and the difficulty in showing any tangible benefits (Bizzack, 1993).

There is little doubt that the standardization of selected police activities and systems will benefit the profession. Of course, many departments will maintain their own identity through a style or an emphasis on a particular approach to policing. In any case, the accreditation movement is successful and growing. In fact, many states have established their own accreditation criteria. The real problems exist in the vagueness of the standards, which is necessary so agencies with different philosophies and different perspectives can all join. The result of this problem has been an accreditation process which attempts to establish high standards for the industry by creating a floor or minimum level. The Commission's design to accept and improve on the standards has not been followed in all agencies. While many police administrators have taken the minimum standards and built upon them, others have accepted them as a ceiling and have done just enough adjusting to comply. One other concern with this accreditation process is the lack of accountability. That is, agencies may have policies in place and look good on the books but may not be following their own rules and regulations. No outside monitoring of custom and practice exists. This accountability must be an internal process conducted by an Inspections Unit, as discussed in chapter 6.

The accreditation process is built upon excellent goals and ideas. As it has become a part of American policing, agencies are feeling pressure to join. In the early stages of accreditation, Bill Tafoya commented that the accreditation movement will increase because those who are not accredited will appear unprofessional (1986). The past decade has shown his prediction to be accurate. Accreditation is one way to increase the professional standards of law enforcement. It is the development of national standards in the critical areas of policing which must be achieved. In the future, this process of developing, implementing and enforcing behaviors that meet national standards will continue to improve.

SOCIAL INFLUENCES

Related to the improvement of specific police functions and structure is the influence of society. Before we rely too heavily on the police for our safety and security, we must remember that there are problems and issues beyond the scope of the considerable powers of the police. Looking at the police or their activities without considering other aspects of society is unfair. In fact, a report on police informs us that:

> The police are not to blame for the fact that crimes are so common, neighborhoods so frightened, and civility so fragile. And more police, with more technology, will not be enough to remove crime, calm neighborhoods and promote civility . . . a police force that is better understood, better trained and better led can make critical contributions to cities in which we will still want to live and work. The police alone won't shape the life of those cities. It is enough that they make a difference. (William O. Douglas Institute, 1984:9)

Others have admitted that crime is a social problem and that the reduction of crime is beyond the limited power and control of police (see Overtown Blue Ribbon Committee, 1984). Although crime control requires more than police action, police can affect one's perception and fear of crime.

Many suggestions concerning police reform have been based upon citizen perceptions of policing and law enforcement. The President's Commission on Crime Control (1967), the National Advisory Commission on Criminal Justice Standards and Goals (1973), and the United States Civil Rights Commission (1981), among other studies, have based their recommendations and goals on research that emphasized the views of citizens, decision makers and police officers. These studies have reached similar recommendations for change. Unfortunately, police and public administrators have been searching for solutions to many of these problems without a great deal of success. In fact, policymakers are often faced with a dilemma and must choose between alternatives that are equally as bad as they are good. In other words, decisions must be made that may yield positive results for one group of citizens but may not satisfy the needs of another group.

WHAT TO EXPECT

Police in the future may resemble the police today, they may be an improvement or they may be worse. A major shift in structure or function is unlikely. Nevertheless, the question remains, change to whom and by what criteria and to what degree? In any case, it is technology, interaction with the community and a get tough approach with chronic offenders that will be modified over the next few years and will have an effect on the police function and how it is carried out. Perhaps the most likely candidate to influence policing in the future is the improvement and application of technology. There are dozens of technological advancements that can be applied to policing. For example, the use of laptop data entry terminals or voice-activated transmitters could improve traditional methods of communication and report writing. The information collected in reports filed electronically or verbally could be computer analyzed by area, defendant, type of crime or other variables for crime analysis. These aggregate data could be used as intelligence for problem solving. Offenders' finger prints could be collected and sent from mobile or satellite terminals for instant analysis. Crime-scene investigations could be fast and efficient and improve offender identification. The use of cellular telephones and facsimile machines could improve communication. Less-than-lethal weapons could be improved and used in many attempted apprehensions without endangering the officers, innocent bystanders or even the suspects. Further, the mini-transmitters could be used to record all confrontations with citizens for an after-the-fact assessment. As our military declassifies some of its technology and as we transfer some of our current technological advancements to law enforcement use, opportunities for improvement in policing will increase dramatically.

Depending on the specific technology, significant personnel training and a shift in orientation will be required. Adapting law enforcement practices to this new technology may create some changes but should prove beneficial. This issue is not significantly different from the transformation police made when they were first provided with automobiles and radios. It was not too long ago that both were new, revolutionary and controversial in law enforcement. In any case, technological advancements, at a minimum, can increase the time police officers can spend making the communities safer by preventing and solving crimes.

The improved interactions with the community fall under what we have discussed as problem solving, community-oriented policing and Neighborhood Interaction and Community Evaluation. If funds are spent on the technologies, then officers will find themselves with more time to spend on these activities than they have in the past. As officers are provided with more time and resources to interact with citizens, they may realize the positive results of community policing. Innovative approaches to community mobilization should be designed to empower citizens and build trust with government. Beyond technology, other innovations such as civilianization of the department and mobile forces assigned to areas to address problems may provide the needed manpower to identify and create a blueprint for resolving those problems.

None of these changes will make much of a difference if chronic or habitual offenders continue to roam the streets and prey on innocent citizens. The police, the courts, the prison system, and other agencies must devote more attention to the identification, removal and rehabilitation of the chronic offender. If society continues to allow violent offenders to be placed in the revolving door between the street and prison, then the police will be so busy running from one emergency to another that the improved technology and community spirit will not increase the effectiveness or efficiency of their efforts. In other words, habitual offenders will somehow have to be removed from society or habilitated to be contributing members. Similarly, society must develop and institute programs to divert members of the next generation from the same fate. We will have to find some method to identify the root causes of crime and do something about them. Beyond creating positive punishment for some, society must remove the thrill of crime and provide appropriate rewards for our youth who may not have a variety of opportunities. Without an attack from both fronts, it is likely that any change that occurs will be in small increments.

Chief Bowlin provides his insights into the future of policing in the following Chief's Corner.

CHIEF'S CORNER
THE FUTURE OF LAW ENFORCEMENT

I believe law enforcement in the late 1990s will be influenced by three distinct concepts:
1) automation;
2) a movement back to close integration with the community; and
3) specialization regarding the habitual offender.

Every day, I see things taking place which convince me of these areas of concentration. First, technology has finally been accepted in law enforcement. For example, fingerprints, methods of operations (M.O.), and descriptions, among other items, can now be compiled and computer-analyzed with little effort. The result can be a savings of hundreds of hours from manual searching. A suspect can be determined in a few seconds, rather than weeks without the assistance of automation. Line managers can update employment strategies of the uniform patrol cars hourly on the basis of reported crime data and past trends. There is a limitless future with computer-aided management.

Second, law enforcement has come full circle with the community. In the past, law enforcement has moved away from the community in its quest to provide better, more economical service. However, in the future it will be forced by a growing groundswell to move in closer contact through innovative programs such as selected park and walk areas, varieties of team policing, community advisory committees, etc. There has to be, and it has become quite apparent to me that pressure will become so great that there will be, a different service mentality of the police. For too long, many departments have envisioned themselves as knowing what is good for the community. They have delivered the service which they feel benefits both the department and the public. The fallacy in this strategy is that many of those in management positions who control service delivery do so without the benefit of input from the people they are supposed to serve. There is not a feeling that the people are our customers, and we exist to serve and protect them. Too often, there is the feeling that we are here to fight crime and the community is a necessary impediment to what we know is best for them. I see things happening, and see pressures on the police, which will force this to change in the very near future. Unfortunately, many departments will not change easily. As a result, they will suffer a great lack of positive relations with their clientele before things get better.

We are a nation of many people and cultures. Each of these groups has its special interests and conceptions of how the police should deliver services. Good administrators recognize this and will institute changes to assure that their officers understand and meet these diverse expectations. Such expectations can change from neighborhood to neighborhood, and there will be a significant training demand made on departments to deal with them. These changes must take place, whether the police like them or not.

While I see this transition period to be somewhat negative for police-community relations over the next few years, I believe that, in the long run, it will move police back into a position that they enjoyed many years ago—a position of support, respect, and positive relations which came from the delivery of the type and quality of services that the community deserved.

Finally, I see the police and the criminal justice system specializing on the career criminals and moving away from some traditional social work.

There are many studies which support the fact that there are persons who are predestined to lead a life of crime. These are the career or habitual offenders who are responsible for a disproportionate amount of crime. With the assistance of computerized technology, these individuals, identified by certain criteria, can be placed under surveillance, tracked by computer, investigated by specialists assigned to a reduced caseload, and, when arrested, followed through the system by these same officers and investigators. In short, the feeling that all who commit crimes can be rehabilitated is being replaced by more realistic views of crime and criminals. The hope for rehabilitation is being reserved for youthful offenders who show signs of wanting to change.

I believe that as this type of specialization develops, we will begin to see incidents of crime slow down. This will occur because positive police activities will be directed at real crime problems, while other problems that were handled by police in the past will be directed to other agencies which are better prepared to handle them. In such cases, I see the police stabilizing the situation and then referring the problem to social-service agencies.

The three concepts outlined at the beginning of this segment become more obvious when we realize that police can suppress crime in targeted areas, but cannot heal the problems. We must turn to automation, closer ties with the community, and specialization in the arrest and prosecution of career and habitual offenders to meet our mission more efficiently and effectively.

Law enforcement deserves more than the tinkering and small shifts in emphasis it has experienced in the past. However, major change in policing must be coupled with structural alterations in society. That is, police cannot force society to change its ways just to increase safety and decrease fear. That could result in an unwanted police state. We must reach a balance between the behaviors we are willing to change and how much fear we are willing to tolerate. Major changes in law enforcement cannot be considered in a vacuum. The collective influence of the following elements will shape the future of policing: new technology, various forms of community orientation, and protection from the violent, chronic offender.

Although many suggestions are pointing the direction for police of the future, keeping one's perspective is necessary. John Crank (1995:107) warns us: "The notion that anyone can hope to predict the future of his or her own life for even the proximate moment, let alone the future of a social institution over the next eighteen years, is pretentious." After this disclaimer, Crank, in an engaging essay, describes policing from his created perch in the year 2010! His historical look back into the 1990s is a trip through the era of community policing, its promises and its pitfalls. His final paragraph puts it all back into the perspective he warned us to keep (1995:124):

> There is one final theme in this essay. It is said that the best predictor of the future is the past. So it is here. For all the reform, for all the change in police structure, for all the education, for all the change in criminal code and in technology, line officers are doing basically what they did forty even one hundred years ago. They act like street-level bureaucrats, they cover their asses from the command hierarchy, they try to protect other officers from public and departmental oversight, and they just generally try to do what they think is right in hostile and potentially dangerous situations. They are well educated today, so they tend to do those things better than they did one hundred years ago. But they still make arrests where nothing else works or where it helps their career, they provide service if it doesn't take a lot of on-line time, and they generally maintain order as best they can. The institution of policing swirls around them in constant change and variation, yet what they do on a day-to-day basis on the street is largely unaffected.

If policing is to achieve its potential and what we hope it can achieve, professor Crank has missed the mark. However, when we discuss his keynote address to the Academy of Criminal Justice Sciences in 2010, he will probably have the last laugh and say, "see, I told you so!"

SUMMARY

Generally, the future of policing is integrally linked to the future of communities. The role of the community in the organization, maintenance and control of law enforcement will continue to increase. The future of policing, despite technological, strategic and administrative advances and improvements, remains in its personnel. Innovative approaches to the activities of police will be influenced by the criteria on which officers are rewarded. While the linkages between police and the community are critical, so is the way police will rid the community of the chronic predator—the habitual criminal. The final chapter will discuss options available for those interested in policing as a profession. Those individuals who make a commitment to law enforcement will, ultimately, shape the future of policing.

References

Ahlbrandt, Roger. 1984. *Neighborhoods, People, and Community*. New York: Plenum Publishing.

Alpert, Geoffrey and Roger Dunham. 1988. *Policing Multi-Ethnic Neighborhoods*. Westport, CT: Greenwood Press.

Banerjee, Tridib and William Baer. 1984. *Beyond the Neighborhood Unit*. New York: Plenum Publishing.

Bazelon, David. 1988. *Questioning Authority*. New York: Knopf.

Bizzack, John. 1993. *Professionalism & Law Enforcement Accreditation*. Lexington, KY: Autumn House Publishing.

Crank, John. 1995. "The Community-Policing Movement of the Early Twenty-First Century: What We Learned." In John Klofas and Stan Stojkovic (eds.) *Crime and Justice in the Year 2010*, pp. 107–25. New York: Wadsworth.

Goldstein, Herman. 1990. *Problem-Oriented Policing*. New York: McGraw-Hill.

National Advisory Commission on Criminal Justice Standards and Goals. 1973. *Report*. Washington, DC: United States Government Printing Office.

Overtown Blue Ribbon Committee. 1984. *Final Report*. Miami: City of Miami.

President's Commission on Crime Control. 1967. *Report on Police*. Washington, DC: United States Government Printing Office.

Ross, Jeffrey Ian. 1995. "Confronting Community Policing: Minimizing Community Policing as Public Relations." In Peter Kratcoski and Duane Dukes (eds.) *Issues in Community Policing*, pp. 243–59. Cincinnati: Anderson Publishing.

Tafoya, William. L. 1986. "Law Enforcement Beyond the Year 2000." *The Futurist* 20: 33–36.

Taub, Richard, Garth Taylor, and Jan Dunham. 1984. *Paths of Neighborhood Change*. Chicago: University of Chicago Press.

United States Civil Rights Commission. 1981. *Who Is Guarding the Guardians?* Washington, DC: United States Government Printing Office.

William O. Douglas Institute. 1984. *The Future of Policing*. Seattle: The William O. Douglas Institute.

Chapter Eleven

CAREERS IN LAW ENFORCEMENT

Many important issues relating to the police have been discussed through-out this book; the mission to protect lives is the central thread linking all of them. In addition, numerous responsibilities have been discussed which deal with the investigation of crime, the apprehension of criminals, and the provision of services to the community. As a result of the comprehensive nature of policing and of the limited scope of this book, we have been able to touch upon only the major aspects and issues that are a part of police work. We hope these discussions have provided valuable insights into police work and what is involved in law enforcement.

It is common to have unrealistic ideas about police and their work. Often, these unrealistic images are formed from rumors and from media representations of the police. This can be the basis of problems experienced by the public and by young officers after they enter law enforcement. These young rookies often discover that law enforcement is really quite different from what they expected.

The first month or two on the job has been characterized as a "reality shock" after undergoing intensive training at the Police Academy. Recruits assigned to the streets are often told by seasoned officers to forget what they learned at the academy. They are confronted with the realities of dealing with a sometimes antagonistic public, an unresponsive bureaucracy, and the view of higher ranking officers that "the world is against us."

As a result of this confrontation with reality, a drastic change in attitudes takes place in the short period of time between a recruit's graduation from the police academy and six or twelve months on the job. Most of the change is toward a more pessimistic view of public cooperation with the police, and realizing the importance of gaining respect by the use of force in tough neighborhoods. Recruits begin to accept the view of senior officers that it is a hostile world when it comes to police work. Poole and Regoli (1979) found a serious shift in attitudes away from professional commitment during the first six months on the police force.

It is important to understand the duties and responsibilities of the police and the variety of demands on them to get a real feel for what it is like to be an officer. This brief chapter will focus upon the variety of careers available to those interested in law enforcement.

TRENDS IN LAW ENFORCEMENT CAREERS

Our attention now turns to the procedures for beginning a career in law enforcement. Given the extremely comprehensive nature of police work and the division of labor, there are varied career choices. In most departments, one enters the profession as a recruit, graduates from the police academy, and begins his or her career as a patrol officer. The opportunities to specialize come after experience as a front-line patrol officer. Additionally, some begin as civilians. While increasing numbers of civilians are employed in police departments, they are usually restricted to clerical staff and to specialized technical positions (i.e., laboratory personnel, legal advisors, computer programmers).

A national survey of law enforcement agencies conducted in 1992 (Law Enforcement Management and Administrative Statistics, LEMAS) revealed that about 39 percent of employees working for sheriffs' departments nationwide were non-sworn civilian employees (Reaves, 1993). Twenty-two percent of employees working for general purpose local police departments were civilians. Civilian employment in both types of police departments grew nearly 28 percent from 1986 to 1992, about twice as much as that of sworn officers (13%) (Reaves, 1993). In 1992, 28 percent of full-time employees in police departments (including local police, state police, sheriffs, and special police) were civilians (Maguire and Pastore, 1994:47). While these non-sworn personnel were restricted to duties not directly involved with law enforcement, the role of civilian employees has been expanding beyond traditional clerical duties. Results from LEMAS indicate that approximately 55 percent of civilian employees work in the area of technical support. These duties include tasks related to dispatch, records, data processing, communication, fleet management, and training (Reaves and Smith, 1995). Another 12 percent are employed to assist in certain aspects of field operations, such as collecting information in nonemergency crime situations and providing follow-up contact to victims. The extended use of civilians permits sworn officers to spend more of their time patrolling and investigating crimes. The percentage of civilians in large sheriffs' agencies (31%) is higher than in local police agencies. This difference is probably due to the sheriffs' operation of jail facilities. About half of the civilian employees in sheriffs' agencies work in the jails (Reaves, 1993). Similar to sheriffs' agencies, state police agencies reported higher percentages of civilian employees (31.3%) than local police departments. Most of these civilians (72.7%) are working in the area of technical support.

CHIEF'S CORNER
CIVILIANIZATION

While many police administrators believe that civilianization is the wave of the future, I believe it is a wave that has crested and is now receding. Many factors are responsible, but the primary reason is the inability of a police organization to provide a clear career path for civilian employees. Top management of a police organization is drawn almost totally from rank-and-file personnel who have progressed through the ranks. Even if top management is recruited from some other department, they have generally progressed through the ranks. This will not change in the future, as municipal administrators will continue to require a trained professional police officer to manage their departments. As a result, civilian employees can never expect to attain management positions in any significant numbers. Because of these limitations on the access to top-management positions, career paths for civilians have been compressed to the point that, in many instances, the entry-level position is both the beginning and the end. To say that this causes burnout for civilian employees is an understatement. No matter how motivated a civilian employee is, he or she will not be able to maintain a high level of interest over a number of years. This is especially true for highly educated employees who are hired to fill the technical positions within a department.

Another factor bearing on this matter is the unwillingness of sworn officers to support or accept the leadership of those who have never been engaged in actual police work. While they will accept them in non-operational positions, a great deal of resistance arises whenever it is attempted to hire civilians as supervisors of line personnel. This same type of resistance is prevalent when employees are recruited from other departments, whether they are sworn officers or civilians. There is a general understanding in police organizations that the chief may be recruited from another department, but other promotions belong to those who came through the ranks. I know of cases where an employee has been hired at a management-level position and has been with a department for more than ten years without ever really being accepted.

I think it is critical for any police organization to provide a clear career path for its civilians if it wants to make good use of these professionals. This can be accomplished by setting aside high-level management positions for them in the support and technical areas. Even when this occurs, there will be at least moderate coordination problems between such areas and the line, but these can be mitigated through sound management practices which force them to interact on a regular basis and cross-train so that each group will have an understanding and appreciation of the other.

Police departments have been criticized for being too "incestuous" in their personnel practices. As we have noted, most departments promote from within, rather than allowing lateral entry into their more advanced positions.

SELECTION CRITERIA

Two major concerns have helped improve and standardize the selection criteria for police: the continuing desire to select applicants who are best-suited for police work and the existence of litigation challenging the criteria. Police and personnel managers are always searching for ways to determine who is suited for police work and who is not. Unsuccessful candidates often challenge these methods in court and force administrators to explain what criteria were used and why. Over the years, many police departments have settled on several similar criteria.

An ICMA survey found that nearly all departments required oral interviews (93%), background investigations (93%) and medical examinations (92%) before hiring (Fyfe, 1986). Most departments required a written (88%) and a psychological (71%) exam. Seventy-six percent of the departments in the study required a physical performance test and 30 percent had a maximum entry-level age, averaging thirty-six. Four percent of the departments surveyed indicated that they had height and weight requirements, and polygraph examinations are used in screening by 40 percent of the departments. The amount of education required by police departments is an important and somewhat controversial matter.

EDUCATION

The issue of educational requirements for entry-level police officers has put police employers in a double bind. The President's Commission on Law Enforcement and Administration of Justice concluded that "the complexity of the police task is as great as that of any other profession" and recommended that departments require a four-year college degree because "the demands on the police should preclude a lower requirement for persons confronting major crime and social problems" (1967:124). As discussed in earlier chapters, others have made similar observations and recommendations, but most police departments have not implemented them.

One reason for not following the recommendations of the President's Commission is concern for the effects of higher educational requirements on minority recruitment. The Urban League has argued:

> Education requirements should be examined with a view towards making them relevant to entry-level job requirements. A high school or General Equivalency Diploma should be the maximum requirement for most entry-level positions. A recruitment aid is to have this requirement effective only at time of appointment. This gives an interested candidate, lacking either diploma or GED, an opportunity to qualify even after taking the test. Result, more cops!

> Anything above a high school education or GED is next to validate for most jurisdictions for entry-level police officer, correction officer, deputy sheriff and court officer positions. The trend toward requiring college credits for entry into these positions has been successfully challenged in most instances. It is the entry level you are recruiting for. Education incentive and motivation after appointment should be encouraged as the route to pursue, toward further professionalization and promotion opportunity. (Reynolds, 1980:4)

There is some evidence that the educational levels of police are increasing and that many police departments are following the Urban League's recommendation to encourage in-service officers to pursue higher education. Results from LEMAS reveal that nearly all of larger agencies (100 or more officers) required recruits to have at least a high school diploma, and about 10 percent of the agencies required one to two years of college before applicants could enter the academy (Reaves and Smith, 1995). Thirty-two of the departments had a minimum requirement of a two-year college degree. In addition, about 60 percent of the large city police departments offered educational incentive pay (Reaves and Smith, 1995). Similar findings were reported in a study of state police agencies, municipal agencies serving populations greater than 50,000, and sheriffs' departments with more than 100 sworn officers (Carter and Sapp, 1990). Their results indicate that the average educational level of police officers has increased steadily over the past two decades. While only a small proportion of police departments require college for employment, the majority of agencies have educational support policies and provide incentives or benefits for recruits and officers with some college.

In sum, most departments do not require education beyond a high school diploma or a GED for entry-level positions. However, a majority of departments are paying higher salaries to those with post-high school education, and promotions are much more likely if one has some higher education. In fact, more and more departments are requiring some college or a two year degree, and many departments encourage officers to obtain college degrees after they join the force.

PROBATIONARY PERIODS

One employment practice that is nearly universal for police departments is the requirement that new officers serve a probationary period before receiving civil service tenure or becoming permanent employees. These periods range from two to forty-eight months, but the most common is a one-year probationary period. Many departments use this time to screen out substandard officers or those who, in some specific way, demonstrate that they will be problem officers. According to the ICMA survey (Fyfe, 1983), departments ranged from retaining all probationary officers to retaining only 45 percent. Probation is an important part of the screening process, because it is the first opportunity to examine the performance and potential success of the new officer in on-the-job situations. Given the extreme difficulty of validating many of the traditional pre-employment standards and tests, the probationary period takes on great importance. "It would be difficult to find a more job relevant and defensible employment criterion than actual performance in the field during the probationary period" (Fyfe, 1983:9). Still, many departments fail to make full use of this aspect of the selection process. On the one hand, few departments can afford to expend the monies to process applicants through extensive screening and training, only to terminate their employment during the probationary period. On the other hand, no department can afford to retain an inadequate police officer.

IMPORTANT CONCERNS IN CHOOSING A CAREER IN POLICE WORK

There are numerous concerns when choosing any career, especially one in law enforcement. A great deal of time and energy are invested in launching a career, and it is important to explore every possible aspect of the work, the level of remuneration, and the degree of job security. Matching these three aspects of the job with personal needs and preferences is not always easy but is essential to make an informed career decision.

We have already discussed how difficult it is to gain a realistic view of the nature of police work. However, many select police work because they are attracted to the type of work anticipated. A variety of reasons have been given for selecting a career in law enforcement. These include: the prospect of working with people; the variety in the work; that it is exciting work without a routine; that it is often outdoors; it provides the opportunity to help people; and that the work is interesting (see President's Commission on Law Enforcement and Administration of Justice, 1967; Ermer, 1978).

As with any occupation, a personal connection with others in police work is an important factor in choosing a similar career. Van Maanen (1975) found that 80 percent of recruits had a family member or close friend working in the police department when they applied. This personal connection may provide important insights into the career and the nature of the work that are difficult to obtain using survey data.

It is much easier to obtain realistic information about the remuneration for police work than about the nature of the work. Salary, benefits and job security are generally the most frequently cited reasons for choosing police work as a career (President's Commission on Law Enforcement and Administration of Justice, 1967). Female officers in one study during the 1970s listed salary most often as the reason they chose police work (Ermer, 1978). Many police officers come from working-class backgrounds and are upwardly mobile when they enter the police force (Westley, 1970; McNamara, 1967). Since the 1970s police salaries have been improving significantly, creating a larger pool of applicants for job openings. Also, job benefits are very competitive with other occupations. Generally, the larger the population served by the agency, the higher the officers' salaries.

According to the *Sourcebook of Criminal Justice Statistics–1993* (Maguire and Pastore, 1994), as of January 1993, the mean entrance level salary for police officers in cities of 10,000 persons and over was $25,128. However, there was a moderate range between the highest and lowest salaries. The first quartile averaged $20,800 while the third quartile averaged $28,461. The maximum pay for uniform officers without any promotion averaged $33,882 and ranged from a first quartile mean of $28,417 to a third quartile mean of $39,000.

Police officers are likely to have sources of income other than their regular pay. According to the LEMAS survey, most departments required overtime work from their full-time sworn personnel. While the relative amount of overtime available to officers varies among departments (especially between large and small departments) the average overtime for officers in 1993 ranged from $1,278 for sheriffs to $2,334 per year for municipal police. In addition to working overtime hours, many officers earn extra pay for performing duties classified as hazardous, for working less desirable shifts, and for obtaining additional education. For example, in municipal police departments with over 100 employees, 70 percent authorized educational incentive pay, 25 percent offered hazardous duty pay, 43 percent offered shift differential pay, and 30 percent offered merit pay (Reaves and Smith, 1995). In another study (Reiss, 1988), it was found that about half of the officers surveyed worked off-duty in uniformed security jobs, as motorcycle escorts, and in other related employment.

Job security is another positive aspect of police work. Civil Service rules apply to most police departments and guarantee a high level of job security. After a relatively short probationary period, specific reasons must be given for firing officers. Officers have the right to appeal any decision affecting their employment.

The working conditions for police are sometimes less attractive than for other occupations. Police officers, detectives and special agents usually work a forty-hour work week. However, because police protection must be provided twenty-four hours a day, officers must work nights, weekends and holidays. Some work split shifts or four ten-hour days. Most officers are subject to call at any time their services are needed, and many work overtime when circumstances warrant. Some of the working conditions for police are similar to those of nurses. However, police officers and detectives may have to work outdoors for long periods and endure adverse weather conditions. The injury rate among police officers, detectives, and special agents is higher than for most occupations because of the risks in pursuing speeding motorists, apprehending criminals, and dealing with public disorders.

TYPES OF LAW ENFORCEMENT CAREERS

There are approximately 17,358 state and local law enforcement agencies in the United States (Maguire and Pastore, 1994:48). The majority (12,502) are local agencies with jurisdiction over towns and cities. Another 3,086 are local sheriffs' agencies which have jurisdiction over unincorporated county areas. Additionally, there are forty-nine state police agencies (Hawaii is the exception). There are about 1,721 special police agencies. A tremendous amount of variation in size and function exists among these agencies. Some have fewer than five employees, while others employ thousands; some agencies have specialized functions such as enforcing violations of tax laws, while others are given a more general mandate. In the next section, the organization and duties of some representative examples of these diverse police agencies are outlined.

URBAN POLICE

Metropolitan police comprise the majority of the nation's law enforcement personnel. Regardless of the size of the city or urban county police department, nearly all are called upon to perform the same standard functions, tasks and services. The larger departments have more specialized personnel and divisions, while the smaller departments call upon the same officers to perform a wide variety of functions and services. In a small department, the same officer might be involved in such diverse tasks as apprehending and arresting a law violator, giving directions and tourist information, providing crowd control at public events, and issuing licenses and permits. An officer in a large department may specialize in one function or service, such as vehicular homicide, and spend most of his or her time on that one task or function.

Municipal police departments in cities of 250,000 or more employed nearly 127,000 full-time sworn officers and served 46 million citizens in 1992 (Maguire and Pastore, 1994:60). These departments confront America's most difficult and troubling social problems.

The large departments surveyed in LEMAS had motorized patrol units scheduled around the clock. Further, approximately 90 percent of these motorized patrol hours were represented by one-officer units. Officers on foot patrol represented an average of 2 percent of all regularly scheduled patrol hours. Most foot patrols took place in the largest cities with populations of one million or more, in which foot patrols represented about 10 percent of all regularly scheduled patrol hours (Reaves and Smith, 1995). Police officers spend considerable time patrolling, and most of their time is spent in motor vehicles.

Another finding from LEMAS demonstrates the need for police officers to be trained in the use of computers. Approximately 85 percent of these large departments used mainframe computers, 95 percent used personal computers, and 60 percent used laptop computers (Reaves and Smith, 1995). An increasing number of police functions are assisted by computers, including record keeping (94% of the surveyed departments), budgeting (85%), manpower allocation (62%), crime analysis (85%), criminal investigation (85%), and dispatching (78%). In addition, much of the information important to departments is stored on computer files. This includes information on arrests, service calls, stolen property, warrants, criminal histories, payroll, personnel, and crime statistics (Reaves and Smith, 1995). Certainly, criminal history information will have to be stored on computer file for immediate retrieval for crime checks when citizens purchase weapons and for other services. These data include offender-based information (including arrest and conviction data) and offense-based information identifying common patterns in crimes (modus operandi) or individuals who are under investigation in different jurisdictions. Further, it is hoped that these data will be linked to the new National Incident-Based Reporting System and may be used in network expert systems.

The LEMAS found that special units are common in large police departments. As discussed earlier, these units or divisions are created as a response to the needs of the agency and the community. For example, nearly all of the large departments surveyed in the LEMAS survey operated a special unit for community crime prevention. A majority of these departments also had special units for child abuse (83%), drug education in schools (95%), missing children (80%), drunk driving (73%), prosecutor relations (55%), and repeat offenders (50%) (Reaves and Smith, 1995). Many large departments also had special units for victim assistance (42%), domestic violence (54%), and bias-related crime (56%) (Reaves and Smith, 1995).

This high degree of specialization necessitates a considerable amount of training. LEMAS found that a newly recruited police officer receives training that includes classroom as well as field training (Reaves and Smith, 1995). Municipal departments required an average of 640 hours of classroom training and 480 hours of field training.

It was also reported in LEMAS that it is common for a municipal department to require recruits to live within the city's boundaries, or at least within a specified distance from those boundaries. Fifty percent of the departments surveyed had some type of residency requirement with 26 percent of those requiring residence within the city limits (Reaves and Smith, 1995).

RURAL LAW ENFORCEMENT

Most rural law enforcement agencies are county police departments whose senior officer is an elected sheriff. The duties of a county sheriff's department vary according to the size and characteristics of the county. In most rural counties, the sheriff's department provides many varied functions and services. Officials within the department may serve as coroners, tax assessors, tax collectors, overseers of highways and bridges, custodians of the county treasury, keepers of the county jail, court attendants, and executors of criminal and civil processes. In fact, some county sheriffs' departments (especially in the eastern United States) have been divested of law enforcement authority and function fully in nonpolice functions (Bartollas et al., 1983). In these areas, law enforcement is the responsibility of city police departments.

STATE POLICE

Most state police agencies were created in response to the advent of the automobile, which resulted in highly mobile law breakers. Most local police agencies were unable to apprehend effectively the highly mobile criminal who committed crimes randomly throughout a state. As a result, most state police agencies today specialize in protecting the motorist and direct most of their attention to the enforcement of traffic laws on state highways. However, about half of the state agencies have the same general police powers as municipal police departments and can operate within the entire state. Many are involved in highly sophisticated traffic and highway safety programs, which include the use of helicopters for patrol and rescue and conducting examinations to determine the causes of fatal accidents.

FEDERAL LAW ENFORCEMENT AGENCIES

The federal government has within its jurisdiction a number of law enforcement agencies with the mandate to protect the rights and privileges of United States citizens. Many of these agencies have been created to enforce specific laws concerning specific types of situations. Federal police agencies have no particular rank order or hierarchy of command or responsibility, and each reports to a specific department or bureau. Information about some of the most important of these agencies follows.

The United States Department of Justice is the legal arm of the United States government. It is headed by the attorney general and is empowered to enforce all federal laws, to represent the United States when it is party to a court action and to conduct independent investigation through its law enforcement services. There are a number of divisions within the United States Department of Justice. The legal divisions are responsible for enforcing federal laws and protecting citizens. For example, the Civil Rights Division acts against violations of federal civil rights laws that protect citizens from discrimination on the basis of their race, creed, ethnic background, or gender. The Tax Division brings legal actions against tax violators. The Criminal Division prosecutes violators of the Federal Criminal Code. Its responsibility includes enforcing statutes relating to bank robbery, kidnapping, mail fraud, interstate transportation of stolen vehicles, and drug trafficking, among others.

In addition to the legal divisions, there are a number of investigative divisions that come under the administrative control of the Department of Justice. The Federal Bureau of Investigation (FBI) is one of these investigative agencies. The FBI is not a police agency; rather, it investigates all matters in which the United States is, or may be, an interested party. Its jurisdiction is limited to federal laws including all federal statutes not specifically assigned to other agencies. These include espionage, sabotage, treason, murder and assault on federal officers, mail fraud, robbery and burglary of federally insured banks, kidnapping, and interstate transportation of stolen vehicles and property.

Perhaps the most important division to criminologists is the Office of Justice Programs. This office includes the National Institute of Justice (NIJ), Bureau of Justice Statistics (BJS), Bureau of Justice Assistance (BJA), Office of Juvenile Justice and Delinquency Prevention (OJJDP) and Office of Victims of Crime (OVC). The National Institute of Justice was created in 1968. The Institute sponsors research and development projects to improve and strengthen the components of the criminal justice system. In addition, projects are funded to evaluate the effectiveness of law enforcement programs and to test new approaches to policing. The Bureau of Justice Statistics is the primary source for criminal justice statistics. The Bureau collects, analyzes and publishes information on crime, criminal offenders, victims and the operations of criminal justice agencies. The Law Enforcement Management and Administrative Statistics (LEMAS) program is part of BJS. The Bureau of Justice Assistance focuses primarily on national scope demonstration projects designed to help local and state governments reduce crime and violence. The Office of Juvenile Justice and Delinquency Prevention was established to provide a comprehensive, coordinated approach to prevent and control juvenile crime and to improve the juvenile justice system. The Office of Victims of Crime provides funds for the identification and promotion of promising practices to serve crime victims.

The Drug Enforcement Administration assists local and state authorities in their investigation of illegal drug use. These agents also complete independent surveillance and enforcement activities to control the importation of illegal drugs. The DEA also has an Office of Intelligence which coordinates information and enforcement activities with local, state and foreign authorities.

The Office of the United States Marshal, another Department of Justice agency, consists of court officers who help implement federal court rulings, protect witnesses, transport prisoners, and enforce court orders.

The Immigration and Naturalization Service is responsible for the administration, exclusion and deportation of illegal aliens and the naturalization of aliens lawfully present in the United States. This service also maintains border patrols to prevent illegal aliens from entering the United States.

The Organized Crime and Racketeering Unit falls under the direction of the United States Attorney General and coordinates federal efforts to curtail organized crime.

The United States Treasury Department has several enforcement branches, each of which focuses on the enforcement of specific laws. The Bureau of Alcohol, Tobacco, and Firearms helps control sales of untaxed liquor and cigarettes. Also, this bureau has jurisdiction over the illegal sale, importation and criminal use of firearms and explosives. The Internal Revenue Service enforces violations of income, excise, stamp and other tax laws. Its Intelligence Division actively pursues gamblers, narcotics dealers, and other violators who do not report their illegal financial gains as taxable income. The Customs Bureau guards points of entry into the United States and prevents smuggling of contraband into or out of the country. In addition, it insures that taxes and tariffs are paid on imported goods. The Secret Service was originally charged with enforcing laws against counterfeiting. Today, the Secret Service also is responsible for protecting the president and the vice president, as well as their families, presidential candidates, and former presidents. The White House Force protects the executive mansion, and the Treasury Guard protects the United States Bureau of the Mint.

EMPLOYMENT OUTLOOK

According to the Bureau of Labor Statistics of the United States Department of Labor, the employment outlook for police related work is optimistic (Bureau of Labor Statistics, 1992). The employment of police officers, detectives and special agents is projected to increase more rapidly than most occupations through the year 2000 due to increases in the nation's population, increasing concern about crime, and legislative initiatives to control crime. The projections of growth may be tempered by continuing budgetary constraints of the different levels of government. This may result in the increased use of lower paid civilian employees in traffic enforcement and in various clerical, administrative, and technical support positions. In addition, private security firms may increasingly assume some routine police duties, such as crowd surveillance at airports and other public places.

Actual figures support these projections. Comparisons between 1988 and 1992 indicate that there was a 17 percent increase in the number of full-time employees in state and local law enforcement agencies (Maguire and Pastore, 1994:49). The largest increases were in sheriffs' departments (35%) and the state police had the lowest rates of increase (9%). It is of interest to note that civilian employees increased by nearly 28 percent while sworn officers increased only 13 percent.

According to these projections, competition will remain keen for job openings, especially for positions in large police departments. Because of the attractive salaries and benefits, the number of qualified candidates exceeds the number of job openings in many federal agencies and in state and local police departments. This results in increased hiring standards and selectivity by employers. The outlook should be best for persons having college training in law enforcement (Bureau of Labor Statistics, 1992).

Competition is expected to be extremely keen for specialized positions such as special agents with the FBI and U.S. Treasury Department. These positions attract a far greater number of applicants than the number of job openings resulting in only the most highly qualified candidates obtaining jobs.

SUMMARY

There are numerous law enforcement agencies, each having employment potential for those interested in different aspects of police work. In addition, there are numerous private security agencies which provide job opportunities. The purpose of this chapter has been to review some of the opportunities available within a wide range of agencies and organizations.

References

Bartollas, Clemens, Stuart J. Miller, and Paul B. Wice. 1983. *Participants in American Criminal Justice: The Promise and the Performance.* Englewood Cliffs, NJ: Prentice-Hall.

Bureau of Labor Statistics, United States Department of Labor. 1992. *Outlook: 1990–2005.* Bulletin 2402 (May). Washington, DC: United States Government Printing Office.

Carter, D. and A. Sapp, 1990. "The Evolution of Higher Education in Law Enforcement: Preliminary Findings from a National Study." *Journal of Criminal Justice Education* 1:59–85.

Ermer, Virginia B. 1978. "Recruitment of Female Police Officers in New York City." *Journal of Criminal Justice* 6 (Fall): 233–46.

Federal Bureau of Investigation. 1990. *Crime in the United States, 1989.* Washington, DC: United States Government Printing Office.

Fyfe, James F. 1986. *Police Personnel Practices, Baseline Data Reports.* Vol. 18, no. 6 (November/December). Washington, DC: International City Management Association.

———. 1983. *Police Personnel Practices, Baseline Data Reports.* Vol. 15, no. 1 (January). Washington, DC: International City Management Association.

Maguire, Kathleen and Ann Pastore. 1994. *Bureau of Justice Statistics Sourcebook of Criminal Justice Statistics—1993.* Washington, DC: U.S. Government Printing Office.

McNamara, John H. 1967. "Uncertainties in Police Work: The Relevance of Police Recruits' Backgrounds and Training." In David Bordua (ed.) *The Police: Six Sociological Essays*, pp. 223–52. New York: John Wiley and Sons.

Police Executive Research Forum and Police Foundation. 1981. *Survey of Police Operational and Administrative Practices—1981.* Washington, DC: Police Foundation.

Poole, Eric and Robert Regoli. 1979. "Changes in the Professional Commitment of Police Recruits: An Exploratory Study." *Journal of Criminal Justice*, 7 (Fall): 243–47.

President's Commission on Law Enforcement and Administration of Justice. 1967. *Task Force Report: The Police.* Washington, DC: United States Government Printing Office.

———. 1967. *Field Surveys, III, Studies in Crime and Law Enforcement in Major Metropolitan Areas*, vol. 2. Washington, DC: United States Government Printing Office.

Reaves, Brian. 1993. *Census of State and Local Law Enforcement Agencies, 1992.* Bureau of Justice Statistics. Washington, DC: Bureau of Justice Statistics.

Reaves, Brian and Pheny Smith. 1995. *Law Enforcement Management and Administrative Statistics, 1993: Data for Individual State and Local Agencies with 100 or More Officers*. Bureau of Justice Statistics. Washington, DC: Bureau of Justice Statistics.

Reiss, Albert J. 1988. *Private Employment of Public Police*. Washington, DC: United States Government Printing Office.

Reynolds, Lee H. 1980. *Eliminators or Obsolete Irrelevant Selection Criteria*. New York: National Urban League.

Van Maanen, John. 1975. "Police Socialization: A Longitudinal Examination of Job Attitudes in an Urban Police Department." *Administrative Science Quarterly*, 20 (June).

Weisheit, Ralph, David Falcone, and L. Edward Wells. 1996. *Crime and Policing in Rural and Small-town America*. Prospect Heights, IL: Waveland Press.

Westley, William A. 1970. *Violence and the Police*. Cambridge, MA: MIT Press.

INDEX

Academy, 58, 61-63
  curricula and, 61-62, 64-66
Accreditation process, 100
  and police standardization, 261-62
Action orientation, among police officers, 117-19
Administration, of police organization, 76-77, 94
Administrative theories, 95-96
Affirmative action, 46, 217
Alcohol abuse, among police officers, 201-203
Alpert, Geoffrey, 145, 173, 180, 253
Americans with Disabilities Act (ADA, 1990), 49-50
Assessment center, 56-57
Auten, James, 88
Authoritarianism, in police personality, 109, 111-12

Bayley, David, 169, 181
Bell v. Wolfish, 226
Benevolent associations, 116
Bittner, Egon, 87
Bizzack, John, 214
Black, Roy, 5
"Blue code of silence," 107
Blumberg, Mark, 225
Boston, first police force in, 25-26
Bowlin, Dale, 6-8, 14, 43, 59, 106, 137, 139, 155, 192-93, 205–6, 221, 231-32, 265-67, 274
Brenner, Allen, 54
Broderick, John, 153
  typologies and policing styles of, 153-54
Brooks, Laure, 164-65
Brown, Michael, 108, 113, 152
Brown, Richard, 21
Buckley, Joseph, 158-59

Burbeck, Elizabeth, 54, 111
Bureaucracy
  administration and administrative theories of, 94-96
  leadership in, 96-98
  of police, 77-81
  politics in, 93-94

Caiden, Gerald, 218
California Highway Patrol, study of pursuit driving, 235-36
California Peace Officer and Standards and Training guide, 233
California Peace Officers' Association, 33
Careers, 272-87
  concerns in choosing, 277-79
  educational requirements for, 275-77
  employment outlook for, 284-85
  in federal law enforcement agencies, 282-84
  hiring requirements for, 275
  probationary period for, 277
  in rural law enforcement, 281-82
  in state police, 282
  trends in, 273-75
  urban police and, 280-81
Carter, David, 49, 195-96
Chaiken, Jan, 84
Chain of command, 89-90
Change, organizational, 98-101
Christopher Commission. *See* Los Angeles Police Department, Independent Commission of
City of Canton, Ohio v. Harris, 88
Civilian employment, in police agencies, 273
Civilian oversight board, 116, 142-43
Civil Rights Act (1871), 243
Civil Rights Act (1964), Title VII of, 44-45
Civil Service, and police job security, 279

Clark, Marcia, 5
Code of Secrecy, 92-93
  and police deviance, 127
Coercive force, 4
College students, recruitment of, 48-49
Commission on Accreditation for Law En-
    forcement Agencies (CALEA), 261-62
Communication
  formal procedures of, 90-92
  history of police, 29-34
  in pursuit driving, 239
  system of, 78
Community. *See also* Community relations
  community-oriented policing and, 245-46
  evaluation of police services and, 170-74
  formal police reward system and, 250-51
  and hiring minority police, 216-17
  monitoring and, 249-50
  Neighborhood Involvement and Commu-
    nity Evaluation and, 247-48
  neighborhood training and, 248-49
  police and, 2-8, 156, 165-70, 245-53
  politics in, 94
  problem-oriented policing and, 247
Community-based policing, 174-80, 181
Community-oriented policing, 245-46
  interactive models and, 251-53
  and problem-oriented policing, 246
Community relations
  effect of patrol car on, 31
  race-related problems and, 34, 35
Computers, and police usage, 280-81
Coordinating specialized units, 85-86
Cordner, Gary, 58, 177-79
Corruption, police, 37, 124-47. *See also*
    Deviance
  Barker and Roebuck's empirical typo-
    logy of, 133-36
  controlling, 138-44
  defining, 129-31
Courts, 13-17. *See also* Supreme Court
  plea negotiation (plea bargain), 16
  preliminary hearing (arraignment), 15
  ROR, 15
Coyle, Kenneth, 162
Crank, John, 267-68
Crime prevention, 178
Crime statistics
  effect on police policies, 160-63
  history of, 33
  politics of policing effect on, 162-63
Criminal justice system, police in, 10-17

Dade County Grand Jury, 229
Dahmer, Jeffery, 126

Danger, in police work, 108-9
Davis, Kenneth Culp, 164
Deadly force. *See* Force
Decker, Scott, 140
"Deliberate Indifference," 88
DeLuca, Stuart, 51-52, 90
Dempsey, John S., 194
Departments, police. *See* Organization, po-
    lice
Deviance. *See also* Corruption, police
  defining, 129-31
  external controls on, 141-44
  internal controls on, 138-41
  opportunity structure for, 125-28
  research and, 129
  socialization and, 128-29
  types of, 131-33
Discretion, in police work, 126, 164-65
Discrimination, in police recruitment, 44-45
Divorce, police work, and stress, 199-200
Donovan, Edwin, 98
Drug Enforcement Administration (DEA),
    283-84
Drug enforcement division, 84-85
Dunham, Jan, 260
Dunham, Roger, 173, 253

Early Warning System (EWS), 140-41
Eck, John, 246-47
Education
  and police professionalization, 114-15
  requirements for employment, 275-77
Employment
  outlook for police, 284-85
  police agencies and civilian, 273
Enforcement, 83
English law enforcement, history of, 21-25
Esprit de corps, 92-93
Ethics, 124
Evaluation, of police performance and serv-
    ices, 170-74, 249-51
Excessive force, 223-24
External stressors, 194-95

Family life, effect of police work on, 198-
    200
Farley, Jennie, 44, 46
Federal Bureau of Investigation (FBI), 283
  crime statistics and, 33-34
Federal law enforcement agency careers,
    282-84
Fielding, Henry, 23
Fielding, John, 23
Field training, 66-68
Fleeing-felon doctrine, 224

Force
    excessive and deadly, 223-25
    police use of, 220-33
    Tennessee v. Garner and use of, 225-28
    training in, 228-30
    violence reduction and, 230
Fuhrman, Mark, 107, 127-28
Furnham, Adrian, 54, 111
Future, policing in, 260-69

Garner, Edward, 225
Gender bias, in policing, 218. *See also*
    Women
Goldstein, Herman, 129, 176, 246
Graham v. Conner, 226
Grant, J. Douglas, 55
Grant, Joan, 55
*Guardian Association of the New York Po-
    lice Department, Inc. v. Civil Service
    Commission of the City of New York*
    (1980), 53

Harrington, Penny, 219
Hazards, of police work, 188-211
    and effect on family life, 198-200
    occupational stress and, 194-98, 200-7
    personal assault, 189-94
Health problems, as stress consequence,
    201
Hepburn, John, 163
Hierarchy, in police organization, 77-79
Hiring, of minorities, 215-17. *See also* Re-
    cruitment
History, of police, 20-37
Holden, Richard, 57
Hoover, Herbert, 34
Human relations skills, 97
Hymon, Elton, 225

Inbau, Fred, 158-59
Independent Commission on the Los Ange-
    les Police Department, report of, 223
Indicators of unrest (IOU), 176
Individual stressors, 195
Individual styles, of policing, 152-54
In-service training, 68-70
Institutional style, of policing, 150-52
Internal stressors, 195
International Association of Chiefs of Po-
    lice (IACP), 33, 57, 70, 100, 117, 138-
    39, 261
    pursuit driving model policies of, 238
Interrogations, tactics and techniques for,
    158-59
Isolation, in police work, 109

Jayne, Brian C., 159
Job security, of police work, 279
Justice Department, divisions of, 282-84

Kansas City Preventive Patrol Study, 167-68
Kappeler, Victor, 16, 140, 145
Kelling, George, 65, 168, 176, 252
Kennedy, David, 247
King, Rodney, 4, 5, 55, 221, 223
Kraska, Peter, 140

Lateral entry, 50-51
Law
    police and, 11-13
    procedural, 11-12
    substantive, 11
Law Enforcement Assistance Administra-
    tion (L.E.A.A.), 36
Law Enforcement Education Program
    (LEEP), 114-15
Law Enforcement Television Network
    (LETN), 68-69
Laws, Judith, 220
Lawsuits, against police, 241-44
Leadership, in police bureaucracy, 96-98
Legalistic style, of policing, 151
Legal liability
    effects on police and public, 244
    general principles of, 242-44
    of police work, 188-89, 241-44
Legal system, effect on policing styles, 157-
    60
LEMAS, 280-81
Little Rock, Arkansas, police department,
    227-228
Los Angeles Police Department, 4
    Independent Commission of, 55
Low visibility, and police deviance, 126-27
Lundman, Richard, 130-31

Maghan, Jess, 216
Manning, Peter, 64
Martin, Susan, 219-20
McDuffie, Arthur, 5
McMullan, M., 129
Media, police image and, 2-3
Metro-Dade Police Department, 5, 68, 88,
    176
Miami Overtown Blue Ribbon Committee,
    47
Miami Police Department, 250
    minority recruitment and hiring in, 47,
    215-16
    recruiting and selection processes of, 55

Minorities
   educational requirements and recruit-
      ment of, 276
   hiring and promoting in police agencies,
      215-17
   recruitment of, 46-48
*Monell v. Department of Social Services of
   New York City*, 243
Monitoring, police and community, 249-51
Monroe v. Pape, 243
Moore, Mark, 180, 247, 252
Muir, William Ker, 152, 154
Murders, of law enforcement officers, 189-
   91
   and stress caused by fear of, 191-94
Murphy, Patrick, 65

National Advisory Commission on Civil
   Disorders (1967), 35-36
National Advisory Commission on Crimi-
   nal Justice Standards and Goals, 36, 52-
   53, 115, 156, 165-66, 263
National Commission on Law Observance
   and Enforcement (Wickersham Commission), 34
National Crime Victims Survey (NCVS),
   163
National Fraternal Order of Police, 203
   suicide prevention program of, 207, 208
National Incident-Based Reporting System
   (NIBRS), 161-62
National Organization of Black Law En-
   forcement Executives (NOBLE), 100,
   261
National Sheriffs' Association (NSA), 100,
   117, 261
Neighborhood Intervention and Community Evaluation, 244
Neighborhood Involvement and Community Evaluation
   and community policing, 244, 252-53
   Total Quality Management (TQM)
      goals, and 247-248
Newark Foot Patrol Experiment, 168-69
New York City, development of police
   force in, 26-27

Oklahoma City bombing, 4, 5-6
Open-systems theory, 95-96
Operations, police, 81-86, 96
   coordinating specialized units, 85-86
   drug enforcement, 84-85
   investigation, 84
   patrol, 81-82
   traffic, 83

Opportunity, and deviance, 125-28
Organization, police, 76-77. *See also* Bureaucracy, police; Operations, police
   bureaucratic form of, 77-81
   chain of command, 89-90
   esprit de corps and code of secrecy in, 92-
      93
   formality of communication in, 90-92
   organizational change and, 98-101
   policies and procedures in, 87-89
Organizational change, 98-101

Pate, Antony, 253
Patrol division, 81-82, 165-70
   Kansas City Preventive Patrol Study and,
      167-68
Peel, Robert, 24-25
Pendleton Act (1883), 40-41
Personal assault, on police officers, 189-94
Personality, police, 105, 108-12
Police. *See also* Policing
   assault on and killing of, 189-91
   community and, 2-8
   in criminal justice system, 10-17
   history of, 20-37
   media and image of, 2-3
   personality characteristics of, 108-12
   problems in 1990s of, 37
   qualifications for, 41-43
   training of, 57-70
   trickery of, 158
   unity of, 112-13
   use of force and, 220-33
   women as, 217-20
Police agencies
   federal, 10, 282-84
   state and local, 11, 282
Police brutality, 221. *See also* Force
Police Executive Research Forum (PERF),
   100, 261
Police Foundation, 170
Police report, 13
Police Services Study, 171
Policies and procedures, departmental, 87-89
Policing
   functions of, 10
   future of, 260-69
   styles of, 150-85
   technology and, 264
Politics, police
   effect on crime statistics, 162-63
   in police organization, 93-94
Poole, Eric, 272
Pregnancy, and police work, 219-20
Prejudice, in police personality, 112

President's Commission on Law Enforcement and Administration of Justice, 35, 52, 114, 263, 275
Probationary periods, in police employment, 277
Problem-oriented policing, 246-47
Problem-solving policing, 179
Professionalism, history of, 32-34
Professionalization, 105, 113-15
Programmatic dimension, 178-79
Psychological screening, 52-55
Pursuit driving, 88-89, 233-41
    California Highway Patrol study of, 235-36

Qualifications, for police officers, 41-43

"Reality shock," 272
Recruitment, 43, 44-51
    Americans with Disabilities Act (ADA, 1990) and, 49-50
    of college students, 48-49
    discrimination and, 44-45
    in early America, 27, 28
    educational requirements and minority, 276
    lateral entry and, 50-51
    of minorities, 46-48
    qualifications for police officers, 41-43
    recruiting officers and, 45-46, 48
    selection process in, 43, 51-57
    of women, 46
Reform, history of, 32-34
Regoli, Robert, 272
Reid, John, 158-59
Remuneration, for police work, 278-79
Restraint training, 230
Reward system, for police officers, 249-51
Roosevelt, Theodore, 27
"Rotten apples" theory, of deviance, 131-32
Rubenstein, Jonathan, 24, 30
Rural law enforcement careers, 281-82

St. Louis Metropolitan Police Department, 174
Sapp, Allen, 49
Screening methods, in selection process, 52-57
    assessment center, 56-57
    psychological tests, 52-55
    for recruits, 42
Search and seizure law, 12, 159-60
Selection process, 43, 51-57
    criteria for, 275-77
    educational requirements and, 275-77

probationary periods and, 277
    screening methods in, 52-57
    tests in, 51-52
Service-oriented style, of policing, 151-52
Sheehan, R., 58
Sheriff
    county, 281
    in early America, 25
Sherman, Lawrence, 126, 131, 132-33, 172-73
Sherman Report, 48-49
Simpson, O. J., 5, 107
Skogan, Wesley, 176
Skolnick, Jerome, 157, 169, 181
Sluder, Richard, 145
Smith, Phillip, 23
Smith, William Kennedy, 5
Social influences, on future policing, 263
Socialization, of police, 104-6
    and police deviance, 128-29
Sourcebook of Criminal Justice Statistics-1993, 278
Spelman, William, 246-47
Standardization, of police, 261-62
Stephens, Darrel, 49, 143-44
Stone, Alfred, 51-52, 90
Stress, 189-94
    and alcohol abuse, 201-3
    effect on marriage, 198-200
    health effect of, 201
    legal liability and, 188-89
    occupational, 194-98
    personal assault and, 188, 189-94
    solutions and programs for, 207-8
    suicide and, 203-7
    vulnerability to, 196-98
Styles, of policing, 150-85
    community-based, 174-80
    individual, 152-56
    institutional, 150-52
    patrol, 165-70
    variation sources in, 157-63
Subculture, of police, 107-13
    and deviance, 127
    police personality of, 108-12
    unity of, 112-13
Suicide, police occupational stress and, 203-7
Supreme Court
    deadly force usage and, 225-28
    police legal liability and, 243-44
    promoting (and hiring) police and, 45
Sylvester, Richard, 32

Tafoya, Bill, 262
Taub, Richard, 260

Taylor, Garth, 260
Technical skills, 97
Technology
    and future policing, 264
    and police communication, 30, 91-92
Tennessee v. Garner, and use of deadly
    force, 225-28
Thomas, Charles, 162-63
Total Quality Management (TQM), and
    Neighborhood Involvement and Commu-
    nity Evaluation, 247-48
Traditional organization theory, 95
Training, 57-70
    academy, 61-66
    in deadly force usage, 228-30
    in-service, 57, 68-70
    in field, 66-68
    initial, 57
    neighborhood, 248-49
    restraint, 230

Uchida, Craig, 22
Uniform Crime Reports (UCR), 33, 160-63
    National Incident-Based Reporting Sys-
        tem of, 161-62
Uniform Vehicle Code, 237
Unions and unionization, 34, 115-17
United States, history of police in, 25-29
United States Commission on Civil Rights,
    215, 263
United States v. City of Miami, 47

"Unity-of-command principle," 90
Urban League, 376
Urbonya, Kathryn, 226
Use-of-force policies, 222-23

Van Maanen, John, 63, 66, 109, 278
Violanti, John, 204
Violence reduction concept, 230
Vollmer, August, 31, 32-33, 114

Wagner, Allen, 140
Walker, Samuel, 20, 26, 28, 141
Walsh, William, 98
Wambaugh, Joseph, 2, 118
Washington, D. C., police, 41
Watch style, of policing, 151
Westley, William, 150
White, Susan, 154
Whitman, Charles, 85
Who Is Guarding the Guardians, 215
Wilson, James Q., 150-51, 168, 176
Wilson, O. W., 32, 33, 165
Women
    as police administrators, 219
    police career choice, salary, and, 278
    in police work, 217-20
    recruitment of, 46
Worden, Robert, 154
Wright, Leslie, 225